FANTASTIC VICTORY

*Israel's Rendezvous
with Destiny*

To My Good Friend
"Mike" Bard

FANTASTIC VICTORY

*Israel's Rendezvous
With Destiny*

by
W. Cleon Skousen

From a Mormon

Ernie

BOOKCRAFT
Salt Lake City, Utah

First Printing, 1967

Lithographed by
Publishers Press

Salt Lake City, Utah
United States of America

Dedicated to
Franklin and Clara Murdock
My good friends and wonderful traveling companions
with whom I first enjoyed the fascinating marvels of
the ancient Holy Land.

Contents

PART III—THE SWEEPING VISTA OF JEWISH HISTORY

PART IV—PROPHECIES CONCERNING THE FUTURE

APPENDIX

It would seem to me that after 3,000 years the time has arrived to accept Israel's nationhood as a fact. Here is the only state in the international community which has the same territory, speaks the same language and upholds the same faith as it did 3,000 years ago.

Abba Eban—Israel's Foreign Minister speaking before the U.N. Security Council, June 6, 1967

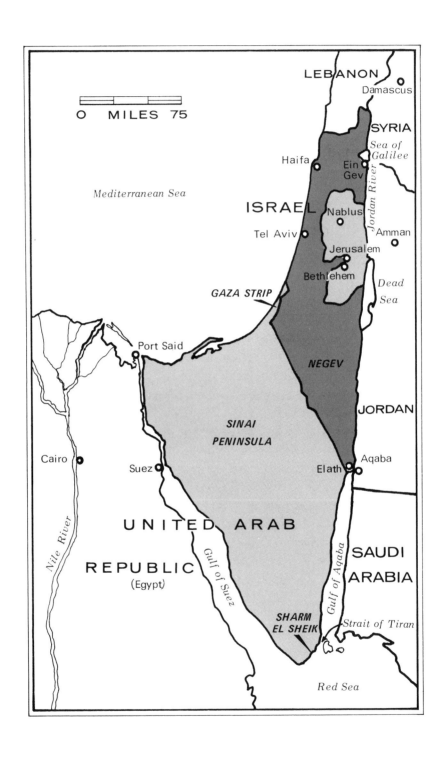

Introduction

A VISIT TO THE HOLY LAND JUST BEFORE THE WAR

I left the Holy Land area just three weeks before the 1967 crisis began to boil. It was my fifth trip in four years. Only here and there was the visitor able to detect the slightest hint that war was imminent.

Nevertheless, on every trip there had been signs of tension if one looked for them. Always there had been "incidents" of recent date involving guerilla raids. On every trip there had been some kind of "new rules" to accommodate the latest political power shift. Nevertheless, our official hosts would continually assure us that "things seem to be settling down now."

But instinctively one sensed that there *was* something different about the trip in 1967. For example, in April there was the sudden seizure of power by the military in Greece. The new government arrested 5,000 Communist Party activists and declared that the military junta had barely averted a Soviet-inspired *coup d' etat* in that country. As we entered Athens after a one-hour delay at the airport, we found tanks fixed at strategic intersections. Government buildings were patrolled by soldiers packing heavy automatic weapons. Military leaders warned that the Soviet Union was out to make a great show of strength in the Mediterranean this year.

Then there were the extremely inquisitive border officers as we entered Syria. They were more brittle and prickly than usual. Two of our party were turned back by the Syrian guards and forced to take a taxi all the way back to Beirut in Lebanon. The guards said their passports showed that they had been in Israel three years earlier. There was no doubt about the feelings which these Syrian officials felt toward the Israelis and anyone who would have any contact with them. I had been in Israel only six months before, but my passport had expired and the new one showed no Israeli visa posted in it so I was allowed to pass.

As we came into Damascus I asked our host about the numerous tank traps flanking the highway. "Oh, they're left over from World War II," he replied casually. From all appearances the concrete was barely dry.

Damascus, the capital city of Syria has much to interest the visitor. We enjoyed the delicious Syrian food and were thoroughly entertained by the Arab guides who enthusiastically showed us the sights of this extremely ancient historical metropolis. We had been warned by Arab friends in Lebanon not to ask the Syrians about any political matters because a left-wing cadre of military officers had seized power and the Syrian Government was not at all adverse to picking up Americans as suspected "Israeli spies."

However, we found that this did not reflect the spirit of the people below the official government level. The Arabs in Syria were friendly, vivacious and their admiration for Americans showed in a dozen different ways. We gained the impression that as loyal Syrians they were expected to fume ferociously against Israel but that as ordinary members of the human family they really wished things would settle down so they could get on with the business of earning a living and building up their country.

We gained the same impression from the Arab people in Egypt. There seemed to be a wide gap between official Egyptian policy and the feelings of the populace generally. We could not have received kinder or more considerate treatment. There was no evidence whatever of the resentment and insulting contempt which Egyptian officials suddenly poured down on the heads of all resident Americans just a few weeks later when the war broke out.

While we were at Luxor an Egyptian workman from the Aswan Dam project said, "When the Russians have finished building the Dam we should tell them goodbye. They are not good for Egypt. The workers at the Dam don't like them. We should make friends with the United States."

One could not help but wonder how Nasser would react to such a statement after all of his anti-American propaganda and his avowed friendship for the USSR. Historically, there is really no valid basis for Nasser's expressed hatred of the United States, particularly in view of the hundreds of million of dollars in U.S. aid which has been given him. I personally felt that many Egyptians seemed to sense the incongruity of Nasser's position.

Because an American finds it easy to like the Arab people he instinctively wants them to succeed. He feels good about the gigantic model city of high-rise apartments which is being constructed (with American help) on the outskirts of Cairo. He likes the development of electric power and the budding industrial projects which have begun to show up here and there. By the same token, an American recoils instinctively against the political harangue on the Cairo radio and the feverish beating of fanatical war drums which can mean nothing but economic hardship and political deterioration for the Arab League peoples.

As we flew into Cairo we expected the usual delay at customs while the Egyptian officials went through the volumes of paper work for which they are famous. However, the delay was even longer this time. Coming into Cairo we could see one air field covered with military planes which were parked wingtip to wingtip. I had recalled that on an earlier trip our bus had driven from

the Cairo airport past a large military camp which was
being set up. On the 1967 trip I specifically asked our
guide to take us down that same highway but he made
some kind of excuse and drove us another way so as to
miss this encampment.

Flying over the desert we noted a number of circular
installations. We didn't know it then, but these were later
disclosed to be missile pads and rocket-launching sites
built by Soviet technicians.

Over in Jordan our good Arab friend, Fareed, welcomed
us warmly at Amman, the capital of Jordan. Several local
officials turned out to greet us and have their picture taken
with us. All seemed perfectly normal. However, as our
visit continued we noted that our host (who is fairly close
to King Hussein and the government administration)
seemed extremely preoccupied and studiously introspective.
I had learned that in spite of the Arab embargo against
the Jews there had been some secret trading going on
between Jordan and Israel and a more cordial relationship
seemed to be developing between the two countries. I
commented to Fareed that we Americans hoped this was
a sign of greater stability and the foundations for a continuing peace. He remained non-committal but said—
almost sadly— "We can only pray God it may be so."

Fareed is the kind of devout Moslem who impresses
the visitor with the inherent greatness of the Arabian
people. Well-educated, refined, gracious and scholarly,
he leads visitors to the holy shrines of Jerusalem with a
dignity and sensitive respect for all religions that reflects
the most exceptional kind of mature and well-balanced
human personality. His rich sense of humor sends a guest
into gales of laughter as he turns mimic and does a superb
job of impersonating one of his former English professors
at Oxford.

In his home are the essential comforts as well as the
frugally gathered refinements of a man with superior tastes.

In his wife will be found all the modest sweetness and traditional mistique of Arabian femininity. With an energetic but quiet charm, she runs a disciplined home. This is reflected in her children who speak three languages and are as bright and well-behaved as those of any household one is likely to find. It is always a highlight when this whole family joins us at Jerusalem for our bus tour up to Nablus or down to Jericho.

Fareed is part of a rich heritage which belongs to the Arabian people. Descendants of Abraham through Ishmael and Esau, they take great pride in being identified among the people of God's book—meaning the Bible. They accept Jews and Christians as also being "people of The Book." The religious basis for Arab friction with the Jews is something we will discuss later.

The Arabs were the custodians of western civilization during the Christian Dark Ages. They spread all across North Africa, moved up into Spain and Portugal, swept around the eastern Mediterranean to occupy Palestine, the Levant and the whole Mesopotamian basin lying between the great Tigris and Euphrates rivers. And they occupy much of these same territories today. Over a hundred million of them. From Morrocco in northwest Africa right across through Algeria, Tunisia, Lybia and Egypt, the people of these countries are almost exclusively Arabs. The people of old Carthage are gone. The people of the ancient Roman colonies are gone. In their places are Arabs who either conquered or assimilated those who preceded them. The same thing is true of the great Arabian peninsula and the great Fertile Crescent just above it. All of this territory is Arab today except the tiny enclave of Israel.

It was the famous Queen Isabella and King Ferdinand of Columbus' day who drove the Arabs out of Spain. They also drove out the Jews. The Arabs of Spain and Portugal had been known as the Moors and they had built cities such as Cardova, Toledo and Seville into some of the greatest centers of learning and culture then in existence. Jews and Arabs had lived harmoniously together in those Moorish centers enjoying mutual respect and unprecedented prosperity for both. But when Columbus prepared to make his famous voyage in 1492 he couldn't use the port of Cadiz because that city was jammed with thousands of Jewish refugees who were being driven out by the new Christian conquerors after centuries of peace and progress under the Arabs. Such are the incongruities of history!

In fact, it is interesting that many of the Jews of that day could only find refuge in Arab-controlled territories such as the Levant.

Before it was over, Christian civilization found itself deeply indebted to both the Arabs and the Jews. The Arabs are specifically credited with giving us our system of numerals, preserving many of the Greek classics, advancing the sciences of mathematics, physics, chemistry, and medicine as well as making major contributions in the fields of architecture, literature and art.

At the famous Garden Tomb on the Jordan side of Jerusalem we visited our friend, the reverend Dr. Matter, faithful custodian of the site which many believe to be the Golgotha of Christ's time and the area where the Savior was entombed. Little did we know that in a few brief weeks Dr. Matter would be shot dead and remain unburied for four days on the very spot where we were then talking with him.

Eventually, we passed through the Mandelbaum Gate near the U.S. Embassy and walked over to the Israeli side. People were friendly but there seemed to be more tenseness than when I had been there six months earlier. Waiters, clerks, bellhops, all seemed a little slow to smile. There was talk of a new rash of border raids by the Syrians up near the Sea of Galilee and we were told that the Cairo radio was blasting the air waves with demands that the Israeli Jews be driven into the Mediterranean.

We noted that Israel was doing a booming building business and that the hundred million trees they have planted since 1949 made the mountains, hills and plains look like an aboreal paradise compared to the sterile, barren and rocky outcroppings just across the border.

The Israelis proudly took us to see their impressive new memorial built to the memory of President John F. Kennedy.

As on other visits we were impressed with the burgeoning, modern metropolis of Tel Aviv. We were equally impressed with the orange, lemon, grapefruit and banana belt extending all along the coast which the Jewish settlers had created with virtually bare hands from the swamps of Sharon. Another swampy area, the famous Jezreel valley, has also been rehabilitated into one of the most prosperous agricultural districts in the Middle East.

Up around Nazareth we noted that the 100,000 Arabs who had not fled during the war of 1948 but had accepted the promise of the Israeli leaders that they would be treated fairly, were prospering. Gradually, these Arabs were giving up their traditional mud-brick villages to build better homes and participate in the remarkable wave of prosperity which has become practically universal throughout Israel.

In fact, with good leadership, the Arab people can make far faster progress than those of most so-called underprivileged nations. This is dramatically demonstrated in Lebanon where the most advanced democratic nation in the Arab world has been built. It is also the most prosperous. Its capital, Beirut, has changed almost overnight from a drab, rambling, Turkish Empire village to a beautiful modern city with affluent homes, apartments and office buildings, and an excellent seaport with attractive bathing beaches. Across the Lebanon mountains one discovers the luxurious Bekka Valley with its modern farms and rising prosperity everywhere evident.

Even little Jordan with its rather barren, desolate hills and desert wastes has suddenly come alive. On the 1967 trip we noticed that Jordan had made tremendous strides in duplicating the Israeli technique of terracing the hills and clearing off the rocks for the planting of olive trees, grapes and other growth to prevent erosion. We were told that this was being done largely by labor from the refugee camps—something long overdue. The Arabs in Jordan were particularly proud of the great difference this new program had made in the appearance of the terrain between Bethlehem and Hebron as well as in the region up around Nablus—site of the former capital of ancient Israel after the northern ten tribes broke away from Judah.

I felt convinced that if conditions could continue to favor this growing cordiality between Jordan and Israel, it would not be long before the Arabs and Jews could be working together for the broad development of this entire territory. But, for the moment, this was not to be.

By the time we reached Rome enroute to the U.S.A. I had the uncomfortable feeling that it might be some time before we could visit the Holy Land again. I told those who were with us that we might look back and consider ourselves especially fortunate to have been on this particular tour because great changes could take place any moment. This tour proved to be one of the last groups from our part of the world to visit the Holy Land prior to the war. Only two weeks later, a large university-sponsored tour was turned back. By that time the hostile political forces had surfaced sufficiently to clearly portend what was about to break. A terrible bloodbath had been prepared for Israel by the political hotheads of the Arab League.

As it turned out, one of the monumental milestones of prophetic history had finally been reached.

PART I

ISRAEL'S AGONY ON THE EVE OF THE WAR

A NATION THREATENED
WITH ANNIHILATION

It was Sunday, June 4, 1967. All the newspapers carried the doleful account describing the terrible predicament in which the diminutive country of Israel had suddenly found herself. A country no larger than the state of Massachusetts with a population of only $2\frac{3}{4}$ million was being completely encircled by the League of Arab States. These states represented a population of 50 million and they were allied with other Arab States representing 60 million more. A military massacre appeared inevitable.

During recent years the Soviet Union had been lavishing approximately two billion dollars on these various Arab States to give them the latest Soviet fighting planes, Soviet tanks, heavy artillery and ground-to-air missiles. As a result, the Arabs stood poised on the borders of Israel with a combined strength of 631,000 fighting men, 2,382 tanks, and 862 warplanes. This gave Egypt and her Arab League more than twice as many ground forces as Israel, three times as many tanks and over twice as many fighter and bomber planes.[1]

For several weeks Egyptian Arabs had been demonstrating in the streets of Cairo, many of them crying in unison, "We want war! We want war!"[2]

Every two hours news bulletins from Cairo called for a Jehad—a massive holy war against Israel.[3]

1. *U.S. News and World Report*, June 12, 1967, pp. 32-33.
2. *Israel's Swift Victory*, a special edition of *Life*, June 23, 1967, p. 4.
3. *Israel's Finest Day*, a day-by-day report, West Pittston, Pa.: Marx Publishing Co., p. 7.

On May 28th, Egypt's President Gamal Abdel Nasser told the Arab world, "We intend to open a general assault against Israel. This will be total war. Our basic aim is the destruction of Israel!"[4]

It was obvious that unless something almost miraculous happened, Egypt and her Arab League were perfectly capable of fulfilling their own prophecy.

Israel's Point of View

Although the world was not generally aware of it, the Israelis had been wailing against the massive walls of the United Nations for nineteen years claiming that a continuous campaign of sabotage and guerilla warfare had been waged against Israel's border settlements by her Arab neighbors, especially Syria.[5] If this were true, of course, it would constitute an aggravated and continuing violation of the 1949 armistice agreement.

For some reason, however, the United Nations peace-keeping agency assigned to Palestine had never taken these complaints seriously. Its officers consistently refused to intercede or make a critical issue out of these attacks. As a result, the Israeli government would come under biting criticism from its own people and there would be bristling demands from the border settlements that the government take direct, defensive action. However, whenever this was done, the Israelis found that *their* action would always attract world headlines and there would be widespread charges in the United Nations that Israel was an aggressor.

An incident of this kind occurred during my trip to the Holy Land in 1963. At that time the Israeli officials told us they could not allow us to go out on the Sea of

4. *Ibid.*
5. Robert J. Donovan, *Israel's Fight for Survival,* New York: The New American Library, 1967, p. 47.

Galilee because the Syrians were firing cannon from the high ridges on the east side of Galilee. They said the Syrians had been sinking fishing ships and killing people who were living in the Jewish settlements just below Tiberias on the western shore.

At the time, I was astonished that the United Nations refused to consider this a breach of the peace. The officials merely said there would be an investigation. Such an investigation would not be difficult because the UN had squads of observers on both the Syrian and Israeli side who could certainly see as well as we could that overt acts of unlawful aggression were taking place.

Nevertheless, nothing was done.

After giving the UN written notice of a specific time limit of one week in which to stop the shooting, the exasperated Israelis finally crossed the Syrian border with tanks, planes and infantry in order to wipe out the Syrian artillery nests overlooking Galilee.

There was nothing gentle about this retaliatory attack. It hit hard and fast. There were heavy casualties on both sides. But immediately a great hue and cry was raised by the UN peace-keeping agency. Its officers charged that Israel had violated the armistice agreement and should be branded as an aggressor. Practically no consideration seemed to be given to the Syrian breach of the peace which had provoked the attack.

This exchange took place right while we were staying at Tiberias on the shores of Galilee so we had an excellent opportunity to judge for ourselves what had really happened. The ineptness and indifference of the UN peace-keeping agency seemed to be characterized by a visitation of functional paralysis whenever the Syrians were conducting raids, but just the moment the Israelis retaliated it became an instrument of howling protest. It provoked many of us to comment that if we Americans were receiving this same kind of treatment it would require the most disciplined restraint to keep our people from taking up arms and initiating direct military action on a massive scale.

Since they became a nation, the Israelis have claimed that there is no reason why there should not be peace in the Middle East. They have asked only that they be left alone. They were created as an independent nation by formal declaration of the United Nations in 1948 and they feel they are entitled to be recognized by all other nations including the Arab States.

For reasons which we shall discuss in a moment, the Arab political leaders have consistently refused to recognize Israel as a legal entity. They have refused to have any diplomatic relations with her whatever. And they have refused to leave Israel alone. "Death to the Jews" is a slogan which is heard more often on the airwaves of Cairo and Damascus than any other single theme. Guerilla raids and acts of harassment have therefore increased rather than diminished over the years, and a crisis such as that of June, 1967, was practically inevitable.

Why have the Arab leaders done this?

The Arab Point of View

Politically, the Arab leaders look upon the Jews as usurpers, squatters, intruders. They feel the Jews have no legitimate rights in the area either as a nation or as a people. That is why the more radical Arab leaders such as Nasser declare their goal to be total extermination of Israel—a genocidal proclamation as real as any coming from Hitler.

Historically, however, the Arabs seem to have difficulty supporting their position. I have tried to discuss the problem with many of them but just the moment they realize you are questioning their "official" line on the Arab-Israel dispute they quickly close the subject with a shrug, saying, "I'm afraid you would never understand."

Actually, the visitor *wants* to understand.

On my first trip I just listened to their story. It was a heartrending account of Israeli brutality, Israeli aggressions and Israeli atrocities. They described how a million Arabs, living in Israel, had been ruthlessly driven from their homes and from their land during the war of 1948. They pointed to the pitiful conditions in the refugee camps where hundreds of thousands of Arabs are barely subsisting on frugal rations administered to them by an agency of the UN. The camps which I saw were indeed a sight to touch the most calloused conscience. Dirt, rags and abject poverty seemed to be the permanent lot of all these people. The condition of the children was especially pitiful. It seemed a certainty that someone surely should be held responsible for this terrible injustice.

The Arabs assured us that this was entirely the result of Israeli aggression and cruelty. They said this was why the Jews must be completely driven out of Palestine so that these refugees could be returned to their rightful possessions.

The whole situation was not only extremely impressive but emotionally stirring and downright shocking.

It was not until considerably later that I began to pick up hints of first one sort and then another that some elements of this story did not quite fit together. Common logic raised the first doubts. For example, assuming that these multitudes had been unjustly driven from their homes by Israeli terrorists, *why were they still being held virtual prisoners in these slum camps fifteen years later?* And after several hundred millions in direct assistance had been furnished by the UN? Why weren't the wealthy Arabs who had made fantastic riches in oil doing something to help their own people?[6] Why weren't the refugees themselves

---

6. In fairness to the Arabs in Lebanon, half of whom are Christian, it should be mentioned that these people did more to help the refugees assigned to them than any

doing more to help? At least they could dig trenches and build decent latrines. The sanitation conditions in these camps were abominable!

An Arab With a Different Point of View

One evening an Arab who was assigned to us as one of our drivers came to me privately and said in rather good English, "You are not being told the whole truth. I am one of the Arab refugees from Israel. I will tell you what really happened."

A conversation then took place which I later attempted to recapture and reconstruct for my diary notes. Essentially, this is what the Arab said:

"When Israel was made an independent nation by the UN, the Palestine Arabs were also given territory for an independent nation. But instead of accepting this plan which was supposed to go into effect in 1948, the Palestine Arabs decided to get six other Arab nations to join them in declaring war on Israel so they could drive them out. That way they would get all the land.

"The leaders of these Arab nations sent word to us Arabs living in Israel that we should move over into Jordan territory so we wouldn't get hurt during the war against the Jews. The Arab leaders promised us that we would be away from our homes only a short time, not more than three weeks at the longest. Then they said we could return and possess not only our own property but the land and buildings of the Jews as well.

"Most of the Arabs in Israel moved over into Jordan just as soon as they could although some stayed because the Israeli government promised them good treatment if they would remain."

---

of the other Arab nations. They did allow the refugees a little more freedom to obtain jobs and gradually assimilate. Lebanon, however, had only a small contingent of the refugees compared to Jordan, Egypt and Syria.

"How many stayed?"

"About a hundred thousand, mostly those up around Nazareth."

"Then what happened to the million who came out?"

"We had a holiday at first. Everyone expected the Jews to be defeated quickly. But they fought hard. They were stronger and better fighters than the Arab leaders had expected. After awhile the Arabs had to give up because the Jews were beginning to win more territory than they had in the first place. In a few months an armistice was signed. This left all of us Arabs from Israel without any homes. The Jews said they would hold our land in trust for us but they said that since we had joined the enemy we could not return until the Arab nations had agreed to recognize Israel and sign a permanent peace treaty. This never happened so the next thing we knew all of us Arabs from Israel were confined to special camps set up by the Arab governments. Most of us were confined in Jordan but some were located in Egypt and Lebanon. A lot were held by Egypt in the Gaza strip.

"We were not allowed to seek jobs, farm the land or become citizens of these countries. The refugee camps became prison camps with our Arab brothers standing over us as guards."

"How did you happen to get this job as a driver?"

"For fifteen years my wife and I and our children lived like animals in the camp. Our lives were wasting away. I pleaded with the officials to let me go out and get a job but they would not. They said we must wait until we could be sent back to Israel. But as the years went by the tourist business began to get very good. Last year the officials said they badly needed any Arabs who could speak English, French or German to serve as guides and drivers. I could speak English so they let me out to have one of these jobs which no other available Arab could fill."

"What happened to the Arabs who remained in Israel?"

"They say they are doing very well. They elect their own representatives. They use their own language in the schools. They are allowed to study the Moslem Koran instead of the Jewish Bible. Some of them come to Jordan on business or to visit so we get to talk to them. They sometimes complain that the Jews compete for their business. Still, they tell me about their new houses and about buying new cars so I guess they are doing all right."

"What about the story that the Israelis drove thousands of the Arabs from their homes?"

"Yes, I think this happened to some, especially around Jaffa and Haifa and later along the border of Jerusalem. But what your guide told you was not the whole story. During the winter of 1947 and 1948 the British were angry at the Jews, and the Arabs in Israel found that they could make raids on the Jews without any interference from the British. I was against it because the Jews had been storing up weapons and I knew they are mean fighters when they get mad. Eventually they did get mad and they attacked Jaffa and Haifa. A lot of Arabs fled from these main centers but they did not have to leave Israel unless they wanted to.

"Later, when the Arab leaders ordered us to leave Israel the Jews had sound trucks go up and down the streets for several days asking us not to leave. They told us that if we stayed we would not have to fight to help the Jews and that we would be treated well as long as we were neutral and didn't help their enemies."

"But most of them left?"

"Yes."

"Did you go at that time?"

"No. I moved over near the Jerusalem border so I could cross if things became hot. And that's what happened. During the war there was a lot of bombing along the border between Old Jerusalem and the Israeli

Jerusalem. I decided to move my family into Jordan where I thought we would be safe until the war was over. I wouldn't have come if I had thought the Jordanians would put us in a prison camp for fifteen years."

"Why do you think they did that?"

"They were afraid we would get their jobs or take away their business. Some of us had good educations and had been very successful in Israel before we became refugees."

"But couldn't they put you to work? The Jews have absorbed a million refugees and used them to make their country productive and prosperous."

"Of course, and the Arabs could have done the same."

The Beginning of Arab-Jewish Friction

I was anxious to get the point of view of this Israeli Arab on the earlier history of the Arab-Jewish conflict, so I asked him, "When the Jews first came to Palestine, did the Arabs resent them?"

"No," he replied, "They welcomed them. The Jews had money to buy land and there were only a few at first."

"When did the Arabs start resisting the Jewish migration?"

"When World War I was over and the Jews began talking about setting up a national home in Palestine."

"Who did this territory belong to before World War I?"

"It was part of the Turkish Empire, but Arabs were living on most of the land."

"And the Palestine Arabs wanted to become an independent nation in the same territory the British had promised to the Jews for their national home?"

"Yes, the British had promised the Arabs independence if they would fight against Turkey and the Germans."

"And the British had promised the Jews a national home in Palestine also?"

"Yes."

"Didn't the Jews later offer to organize the new government of Palestine on a bi-racial basis with representation based on the respective populations of both Arabs and Jews?"

"Yes, providing the Arabs would agree to let additional Jews migrate as fast as the Jewish agency could afford to buy land for them."

"Didn't the Arabs want this?"

"No. The Jews were organized. At the time there were several Arabs for every Jew but in time they would probably outnumber us. You know how the Jews are."

"But the Arabs wouldn't have to sell land to the Jews unless they wanted to. Couldn't you control the territory and the population by continuing to retain most of the land?"

"No. The Arabs are not that united. Always some Arabs will sell if the price is right. Especially the Arabs from Lebanon who owned a lot of the swampland along the coast and up around Megiddo (Jezreel Valley). No Arabs dared to try to farm any of this region because they got sick (malaria, etc.) So the Jews were able to buy this land very cheap. They worked for many years and finally they learned how to drain off the water and it became some of the best farming land in the country."

"What are the Jews doing with all the property that was abandoned by you Israeli Arabs after you left and came over to Jordan?"

"The Jews are using it."

"Have they offered to pay for it?"

"We heard that they did but none of us have ever received anything."

(I subsequently learned that since no permanent peace agreement could be worked out with the Arabs, the UN

Conciliation Commission for Palestine put a value of $336 million on the former Arab holdings in Israel and asked the Israeli government to pay that amount.[7] The Israeli government accepted the principle of giving the Arabs compensation but nothing else came of it because the Arab nations began quarreling among themselves as to just what the compensation should be and they never could agree on a specific amount. In fact, they later refused to consider any settlement short of complete restoration of all properties to the original owners themselves. The Israelis said this would be possible only when the Arab nations agreed to officially recognize Israel as a legal entity and sign a permanent peace treaty. The Arabs refused to do this so the compensation issue was stalemated.[8])

Moslem Resentment of the Jews as a "Chosen People"

Watching from the sidelines, it is often impossible to discover the rational basis for many policies adopted by the Arab leaders. They often seem to be doing the very thing which is most likely to hurt them. However, in order to catch their point of view and grasp some semblance of understanding of how the Moslem-Arab mentality functions; it is essential to talk to them about their religion. It is amazing how much Arab policy is rooted in religious convictions. This is particularly true when it comes to the Moslem Arab's attitude toward the Jews.

The Moslems have their own version of Bible history but they accept the Bible in general terms as the inspired scripture antedating the Koran. Mohammed had frequent occasion to be with Jewish Rabbis and Catholic fathers

---

7. Robert J. Donovan, *Israel's Fight for Survival*, pp. 43-44.
8. *Ibid.*

and was extensively tutored by a monk named Bahira.[9]
Mohammed's writings therefore include teachings from
both the Old and New Testaments. Theoretically, the
followers of Mohammed (usually called Moslems or the
people of Islam) look upon the Jews as fellow Semites
(descendants of Shem) and "the people of the Book"—the
Bible. But I noted that the Moslems in Jerusalem present
the Arabs as the "chosen people" rather than the Jews.
They told us it all goes back to the time when Abraham
offered up his son, Isaac, as a sacrifice.

According to the Moslem Arabs in Jerusalem, it was
Ishmael, son of Hagar, and not Isaac who was offered up
as a sacrifice. The Arabs say God intervened to save Ishmael's life because He intended to make a great people of
Ishmael. They believe that since God saved Ishmael from
being sacrificed it showed that he was preferred of the
Lord and that his descendants, the Arabs, would be a preferred people.[10]

The sacrifice or offering of Abraham's son took place
on Mount Moriah in Jerusalem. Both Jews and Arabs
agree as to that. It is supposed to have taken place on
the white outcropping of limestone which is beneath the
famous and beautiful Moslem mosque called "The Dome of
the Rock." This is located in the midst of the temple
block in Old Jerusalem. It was the former crest of Mount
Moriah and the walls of the square had to be built around
the area to shore it up and make it possible for Solomon
to build a temple on this sacred spot. Jewish tradition
has it that this spot was once covered by the magnificent
temple of Solomon and that this rock was actually in the
Holy of Holies where the Ark of the Covenant rested.

It immediately can be seen what an explosive issue

---

9. Anthony Nutting, *The Arabs*, New York, Mentor Books, 1964, pp. 26-27.

10. Ishmael consistently appears before Isaac in the Koran and is presented as the
confidant of Abraham in establishing Mecca, building the Kaaba or temple and
setting up this center as a place of worship for all true believers. See the Koran II:
133, 136, 140; IV: 163; VI:87; XIV:39; XIX:54ff; XXI:85; XXXVIII:49.

the possession of this site has become insofar as these two great tribal peoples are concerned.

The Moslems say this spot was further sanctified to them in the seventh century A.D. when Mohammed told his followers that during a dream his soul was brought from Arabia to this place and that from here he ascended to heaven on a white horse.[11] Mohammed said he met all of the major prophets mentioned in the Bible (including Jesus whom Mohammed said was a great prophet) and that afterwards God personally instructed him as to the manner in which Moslems were to live and worship. Mohammed said the white horse then brought him back to Jerusalem This is an additional reason why Jerusalem thereupon became, and has ever since remained, one of the most sacred shrines of devout Moslems.

During one of the United Nations sessions on Palestine, the Israeli representative pointed out that the Jews must have access to Jerusalem since otherwise they cannot fulfill their mandate from God to rebuild the temple. The Arab representative promptly replied with great vehemence that before Moslems permitted the Jews to disturb that sacred spot where the Dome of the Rock is located, there would be Jehad—Holy War!

Because Ishmael is looked upon by the Arabs as their great patriarchal ancestor, they memorialize the important events of his life. For example, at Mecca the second most sacred shrine to all Moslems, is the famous well, the Zam-zam, where they believe the angel of the Lord miraculously provided water to save the life of Ishmael and his mother, Hagar.

Another incident in the Bible which is a bone of contention between Arabs and Jews is the occasion when Jacob took away Esau's birthright.

It will be recalled that Isaac had twin sons, Jacob and Esau. Esau was the elder but he sold his birthright to

---

11. Anthony Nutting, *The Arabs,* p. 29.

Jacob for a mess of pottage.[12] By subterfuge Jacob sub-
sequently obtained the birthright blessing from his father.[13]
Eventually, the disinherited Esau married a daughter of
Ishmael[14] and his descendants thereafter mingled with the
seed of Ishmael to create the princely kingdom of the
Edomites, the first Arab nation. Jacob went on to have
twelve sons, one of whom was Judah, ancestor of the Jews.
Modern Arabs say that just as Jacob cheated Esau, so today
Jacob's descendants are trying to cheat Esau's descen-
dants out of their birthright.

From these examples it is easy to appreciate why some
Arab antagonisms toward the Jews are not a superficial
or recent development but go back to their interpretation
of events which occurred almost 4,000 years ago.

The Moslem Rejection of Jewish Prophecy

Of course, in the Bible (which Moslems accept as a
sacred book) it is very clear that the Jews, after their long
dispersion, must return to Jerusalem and rebuild their temple. How will the Arabs deal with that? They have an
answer. They say those are true prophecies but they were
all fulfilled 1,400 years ago!

They point out that when the Jews were captured by
the Babylonians in a series of attacks which culminated
in the destruction of Solomon's temple and the sacking
of Jerusalem (587 B.C.), *that* was the dispersion of the
Jews the Bible was talking about. All the survivors of
that great destruction were hauled off to Babylon and
assigned to a number of colonies. However, when Persia
conquered Babylon, the great Persian ruler, Cyrus, allowed

---

12. Genesis 25:29-34.
13. Genesis, Chapter 27. For a commentary on this incident see W. Cleon Skousen,
    The Third Thousand Years, pp. 39-44.
14. Genesis 28:8-9.

the Jews to gather again and return to Jerusalem. In due time they rebuilt their temple (admittedly not as fine as Solomon's but they did rebuild it) and it was finished in 516 B.C. This, the Arabs say, put the Jews back in Palestine as God had promised them. However, according to the Moslems, the Jews did not remain true to God's commandments. Therefore they were conquered—first by the Greeks, then by the Syrians, finally by the Romans. In 70 A.D. the Romans besieged Jerusalem and eventually drove the Jews forever from that place. The Arabs say this was God's punishment. Because of their wickedness He disinherited the Jews and left all their lands to be taken over and cared for by the Arabs.

They further point out that in the days of the Crusades the Christians tried to take Palestine away from the Arabs but God blessed Saladin and his Arab warriors with victory. They say that now the Jews are trying to take Palestine again, but God will utterly desolate them through the vengeance of Arab arms. In the eyes of the believer, eventual destruction of Israel is inevitable.

This will explain why the Arab leaders call their war to exterminate Israel a *Jehad*. It is a holy war to fulfill the will of Allah. Consequently, Nasser and his associates in the Arab League reason that no Arab nation should give diplomatic recognition of Israel or give her the least excuse for thinking she will enjoy a permanent peace. There has been some heated discussion among the Arabs as to just how the Jews should be exterminated. Nasser has insisted that there should be a massive buildup of arms and devastating modern weapons so that Israel can be wiped out in one mighty blow of total destruction. The Syrians, on the other hand, have contended that Israel should be worn down with terrorism and guerilla warfare along her borders. Actually, the Arab leaders have tried both.

Nasser's 1956 Campaign Against Israel

The last time the Arabs waged a holy war against Israel was in 1956. That campaign, like the one in 1967, was fought under the supreme command of Gamal Abdel Nasser. That war came at a time when Nasser's star had just ascended as a luminary in the Middle East.

Nasser was born January 15, 1918, at Beni Mor, a village in Upper Egypt. His father was an employee in the post office. In his youth Nasser received a better than average education, first at a Cairo high school and then at the Egyptian military academy. He was graduated and commissioned as an officer in 1937 when he was only 19.

In 1948, when Egypt led the other Arab nations to challenge the right of Israel to exist as a nation, Nasser was assigned to the Faluga front. He gave a good account of himself. He was wounded in the shoulder but dubbed the "Tiger of Faluga" because of his pugnacious aggressiveness. He seemed to be a natural leader and the men under him referred to the handsome Nasser as "the Boss."

Under the rather simpering leadership of hefty, dissipated King Farouk of Egypt, the Arab war of 1948 collapsed. Later, Nasser became part of that segment of army officers who felt that King Farouk had to go.

By 1952, Nasser had successfully organized a secret coalition of young officers and they supported General Mohammed Naguib in ousting King Farouk that year. Nasser then became a competitor for leadership with General Naguib. An assassination attempt was made against Nasser's life in 1954 whereupon he immediately arrested General Naguib, confined him to his home, and openly took over.

No one can deny that Nasser captured the hearts of the Egyptian people. With a movie actor's face, a captivating smile, an athletic figure standing six feet two inches and weighing 200 pounds, Nasser projected a perfect public

Gamal Abdel Nasser, President of Egypt and head of the Arab League.

(UPI Photo)

image and a radical contrast to the fat, pornographic-loving King Farouk who had been ousted just two years before. Nevertheless, as Egypt was soon to discover, the worth of a political leader cannot be measured by his capacity to make feminine hearts palpitate. What was Nasser's program for Egypt? Here is the way one author describes it:

"Nasser's domestic economic programs began running into trouble almost as soon as they were undertaken. Advocate of a vague form of socialism, he launched a sweeping program of nationalizing Egypt's few productive facilities. He hoped, apparently, to transform a basically agricultural society into a regime based on state-owned and operated industry. But nationalization shattered Egypt's entrepreneurial [free enterprise] system, and since Nasser could provide neither efficient managers nor administration, the economy began to sag. He turned to the East and the West for economic help."[15]

The political confusion in the mind of Nasser then began to manifest itself. His only tangible foreign policy was based on an eventual war against Israel. He vowed the Jews would soon be driven into the Mediterranean. To acquire the Soviet weapons for such a campaign he deliberately engaged in vituperative vilification against the United States. Earlier the U.S. government had offered to help Nasser build the mighty Aswan dam, but by July 18, 1956, Nasser's wild charges were so saturated with polemic acid that the U.S. withdrew its offer. Nasser became furious and shortly afterwards nationalized the Suez Canal, claiming he would build the dam with its revenues. This of course, was ridiculous since the revenues were not even sufficient to offset Egypt's chronic trade deficits. Furthermore, England and France who owned the principal part of the stock in the Suez Canal, began deploying military forces in the Mediterranean basin to protect their rights.

---

15. Robert J. Donovan, *Israel's Fight for Survival*, pp. 31-32.

Nasser has never been one to undertake the solution of a single problem at a time. Right in the midst of this international crisis of 1956 he chose to enhance his political fortunes by announcing that he was preparing for an attack on Israel. Tanks, mobile guns and infantry rolled out across the Sinai desert toward Israel. Egyptian troops took over the entrance to the eastern horn of the Red Sea (the Aqaba Gulf) thereby cutting off essential shipments to Israel through her only southern port at Elath. Both Egypt and Syria began stepping up their exploratory guerilla raids on border settlements. The political climate had only one forecast—war!

It was on October 29, 1956, that Nasser received the greatest surprise of his military career. He awakened to discover that the Israelis had made a lightning attack on his Sinai forces during the night and had stampeded them into a complete rout. He learned that the Egyptian soldiers had been so terrified that they had taken off their shoes and fled in their bare feet. The Israelis afterwards sent trucks into the desert to gather up the tens of thousands of shoes and boots which the Egyptians had abandoned on the assumption they could run faster through the sand without them.

To make matters worse, French and British air units began attacking Egypt on October 31, and both nations landed ground troops near the end of the Suez Canal on November 5 and 6.

It was the United States that intervened to save Nasser's political skin. With an early defeat staring him in the face, Nasser found President Eisenhower and Secretary of State John Foster Dulles demanding an immediate cease fire. The Soviet Union vigorously concurred. This came as a great surprise to both France and England since a cease-fire would leave Nasser in possession of the Suez Canal. Nevertheless, the two UN giants forced their will upon all concerned including Israel. The U.S. insisted that

Israel retire from the Sinai Penninsula and rely on UN guarantees for her security.' Reluctantly, the Israelis complied but with strong misgivings which they did not hesitate to express.[16]

As the Israeli troops withdrew, Nasser insisted that UN buffer troops be installed between Israeli and Egyptian territory to prevent any future advance. The UN complied.

Nasser Moves Closer to the Soviet Union

Now, amazingly, instead of recognizing that the United States had been primarily responsible for helping him, Nasser made an abrupt left turn and became a virtual ally of the Soviet Union. He began holding conferences with pro-Communist regimes both east and west. He shipped arms to Communist guerillas in Algeria, the Congo and wherever else nearby Communist pockets developed. At the same time he accepted an accelerated program of Soviet aid to Egypt. Nasser had negotiated a Russian aid program in 1954 shortly after he came to power. Now it began to take on monumental proportions. First, the Russians came in to direct the building of the Aswan dam. Then they took from 800 to 1,000 officers per year from the Egyptian and Syrian armies to train in Russia. They shipped hundreds of millions of dollars worth of the latest Soviet weapons to Egypt with other military shipments going to Nasser's Arab allies.

Fortunately, a number of the Arab leaders saw that

---

16. Israel's Foreign Minister at that time was Mrs. Golda Meir. She said, "We are withdrawing from the Sinai Desert. We are negotiating various problems, because I think that it is the intention of the United Nations not only that we withdraw our forces, but it is quite important what happens when we withdraw our forces. . . . What happens later? Are the United Nations forces going to pull out in order to bring the Egyptian forces back exactly to the same place where they have been before so that we have the identical situation recreated that was there in the area before October 29, [1956]?" ("Israel and Egypt State Their Cases," U.S. News and World Report, December 14, 1956, p. 89.

Nasser was making a serious tactical mistake. He began getting strong resistance from some of them. These included King Hussein of Jordan, King Faisal of Saudi Arabia and the democratic leaders of Lebanon. When Nasser tried to put together a United Arab Republic in 1958 he was only successful in getting Syria to become a permanent member and Syria broke away after barely three years. Thereafter, Nasser had to rely primarily on the pontifical but weakly organized Arab League or use direct negotiations with Arab leaders in summit conferences to get united action.

On July 14, 1958, a crisis occurred in the Arab world when the Communist cadres of Iraq supported General Abdul Kassim in a violent one-day coup. Both the king and his prime minister were slain in cold blood. General Kassim then signed a pact with Nasser, established diplomatic relations with the USSR and other Communist states and entered into a series of agreements to get immediate shipments of Communist arms.

Arab leaders opposed to Nasser and his pro-Communist allies immediately asked the United States and Britain to help them prevent Communist coups in their own countries. Therefore, on July 15, 1958, U.S. Marines were landed in Lebanon. At the same time substantial British forces supported by fifty U.S. Navy jet fighters landed to secure the government of King Hussein in nearby Jordan. On July 17, 1958, Nasser flew to Moscow to confer with Nikita Khrushchev.

It was obvious by this time that Nasser was setting up relations with the Soviet Union which constituted a virtual military alliance. The increased supplies of Russian military aid together with grants, loans and technical assistance poured into Egypt. The western powers offered similar aid to Nasser's Arab opponents such as King Hussein and the Lebanese. At the same time everything possible was done to deter Nasser from looking upon the free nations as his enemies. Extremely liberal grants in food and economic aid were given to Nasser, particularly by the United States. A recent 1967 report from the State Department on Egypt says, ". . . the U.S. has provided the U.A.R. technical assistance, development and balance of payment loans and large quantities of agricultural commodities, especially wheat. U.S. aid. . .since World War II through June 30, 1966, when our last agreement expired totaled a little over $1 billion."[17]

It has now been disclosed that up until the middle of 1966 when Egypt-American relations collapsed, the United States had been shipping to Egypt nearly all of the 200,000 tons of food Nasser had to buy abroad in order to feed his people. In payment for this, the U.S. had accepted the extremely weak printing-press currency of Egypt. It was America's attempt to tell Nasser the U.S. wanted to be friends.

But there was one thing for which Nasser could never forgive the United States. That was the willingness of Americans to be as generous with Israel as they had been with Egypt. Any true friend of Nasser must be an enemy of Israel. Like the Soviet Union, for example. Although the USSR had been one of the first nations to recognize Israel in 1948, she had quickly cooled in her enthusiasm when it turned out that Israeli leaders like Ben Gurion and Weizmann (both of whom had been trained in Marxism during their youth) were actually vigorous advocates of freedom and strongly opposed to Communist policies. Therefore when Nasser asked for a united front against Israel, the Soviet Union responded with planes, tanks, missiles, trucks, rockets, mobile cannon and other equipment. Nasser openly declared that all of this equipment would be used to wipe Israel from the face of the earth.

---

17. Robert J. Donovan, *Israel's Fight for Survival*, p. 42.

The Fatal Arab Conferences of 1964

By 1964, Nasser apparently felt that the long-range objective of a war with Israel should be used as the magic glue to bring all the various Arab governments back into unity. Robert J. Donovan describes what happened:

"A serious effort at Arab unity came early in 1964, when Nasser made one of his remarkable policy reversals and invited all the Arabs back under one tent, to concentrate on the prime objective, Israel's elimination. This evolved into what became known as "Arab summitry," and a total of three summits were actually held. Several interesting and potentially strong Arab organizations emerged from [this] summitry, notably the United Arab Command. Budgets were set, contributions of the rich Arab oil states to the defense of poorer states such as Jordan and Syria were fixed, and the whole re-armament operation put on a tight schedule. The objective was to have a coordinated and integrated Arab army equipped and ready to fight Israel in 1970."[18]

Very shortly, however, Nasser began quarreling with King Faisal of Saudi Arabia who challenged Nasser's competence as a political and military leader. King Faisal pointed to Nasser's bungling attempt to establish a pro-Nasser regime among the Arabs in Yemen and scornfully baited Nasser with the fact that his 60,000 troops in Yemen who had been ruthless in their treatment of fellow Arabs, were still incapable of establishing any kind of stable government.

Nasser also saw several of his key supporters abroad being toppled from power. Like Nasser, they had all called themselves "neutrals" but had been pro-Communist and Soviet supported; nevertheless, they were gone. These included Algeria's Ben Bella, Ghana's Nkrumah and Indonesia's Sukarno.

---

18. *Ibid.*, pp. 38-39.

Nasser was soon observed making special concessions and overtures to the "hotheads" in the strongly pro-Communist government of Syria. This was the group of Arabs who had attended the summit conferences in 1964 and objected to a 1970 timetable for the Pan-Arabic attack on Israel. They wanted an immediate "war of liberation." They were in favor of financing several groups of Palestinian commandos who would be assigned to conduct a continuous series of sabotage raids inside Israel. The plan called for guerilla warfare similar to that used by the Red Chinese. By creating chaotic conditions in Jewish cities through extensive sabotage and terror tactics, they said Israel would be far easier to annihilate when the main attack took place.

By 1966, Nasser had obviously given this group of Syrian extremists the go-ahead signal and had abandoned the long range plan adopted by the conference of Arab leaders in 1964. As the Syrians commenced their 1966 raids on the border settlements of Israeli, other Arab leaders warned Nasser that this might lead to explosive provocation and trigger massive retaliation by Israel as in 1956. Although the formal defense pact between Egypt and Syria was not signed until later, Nasser announced that any attack on Syria would be considered an attack on Egypt.

Israel Makes a Tactical Error

By November, 1966, the Israeli government was in a state of maddening frustration. With Egypt's backing, the Syrians were committing sneak attacks on Israeli settlements with accelerated frequency. Some of the raids were far inside the Israeli border. The cannons from Golan Heights on the eastern side of Galilee were shooting again. King Hussein of Jordan warned the Syrians that they might be lighting a fuse for the whole Middle East, but the raids on Israel continued.

Diplomatically, Israel was in a trap. If she attacked Syria it would give Nasser the excuse he apparently wanted to immediately use his Soviet-built war machine to lower an exterminating blitzkrieg on Israel. So what was Israel to do? What about the UN?

The biggest frustration of all was the United Nations. There were fifty United Nations officials located at ten different posts on the Israel-Syrian border. Six posts were in Syria, four in Israel. Every incident coming to the attention of the UN officials was painstakingly recorded and then numerous copies of all reports were circulated through channels to UN headquarters in New York. *After that, absolutely nothing happened!* Israeli officials bit their lips as they recalled the profound assurances they had received in 1956 that if they would withdraw their forces they could definitely depend upon the UN peace-keeping agency to protect Israel from just such assaults. In hopes of dramatizing how much abuse Israel had absorbed over the years, the Israeli ambassador to the UN asked Secretary General U Thant to publish the official list of border incidents since 1949. There had been over 100,000. The Secretary General refused to publish the list on the ground that it was *too large to be usable!*

By November, 1966, Israel felt compelled to take some kind of action to emphatically impress upon the Arab world that these attacks were completely intolerable and could not be endured any longer. Since no direct attack could be made on Syria without risking a general war with Egypt, the Israeli leaders elected to attack a village in Jordan. To what extent this particular village may have been involved in acts of hostility toward Israel is not known, but since the vast majority of offenses were originating from Syria it seemed to be a most serious tactical error to select a defenseless village in Jordan for the purpose of making an example of it.[19]

---

19. Alex Benson, political writer for the *World Journal Tribune* says, "The Israeli

The name of the village was Es Samu. The Israeli forces crossed the border, ordered all of the people evacuated
from the village and then methodically destroyed the mud
huts in which the people were living. In the process
shooting broke out and the Arabs afterwards counted 134
wounded, 18 persons killed and 127 structures demolished.

Now the UN *did* take action. Without any reference to
the long series of Arab raids which had provoked the
attack, Israel was formally condemned by the United
Nations for an act of aggression. From the sidelines and
based on what information became public, it did appear
that the condemnation of Israel for this attack was
warranted. However, the over-all position of the United
Nations in the handling of the total problem was a
complete and cynical repudiation of everything set forth
in the first four articles of the UN charter. Israel got
nowhere in attempting to get a formal censure of Syria.
Many thought that following the Israeli attack King Hussein
of Jordan would have been more upset than anyone, but he
proved to be far more level-headed and philosophical
about the matter than the UN. He told his people that
the Israelis had been severely provoked. It was well-known
that King Hussein had done everything in his power to
dissuade Nasser and the Syrians from continuing this
provocation. Hussein therefore told his people that Israel
had felt compelled "to make a point" and now that it
was made everybody should learn a lesson from it and mind
their own business.

Immediately there was a political explosion inside Jordan. Nasser had planted well-organized groups in the refugee camps and these combined with leftist agitators to

attack was designed to be relatively bloodless—the villagers were ordered from
their homes before the village was obliterated. Despite Israeli precautions,
eighteen Jordanians were killed in action. Eshkol explained that the thrust was
designed as an object lesson to the Arabs and was in retaliation for numerous Arab
murders of Israeli citizens near the border." (Alex Benson, *48 Hour War*, New
York: IN Publishing Co., 1967, p. 88.)

raise a riotous demand that Hussein should abdicate. They also demanded that the government give the people guns to defend themselves. At first Hussein refused, but when the demonstrations and protests threatened civil war he authorized weapons to be distributed among border villages. King Hussein is well acquainted with the irrational mentality of mob action. His own father was assassinated and Hussein, himself, has expressed the opinion that very likely he may suffer the same fate.

Syria Steps Up the Tempo of Attacks

If the Syrian "hotheads" were supposed to learn any kind of lesson from the attack on Es Samu they failed to get the message. By January, Syria had moved Soviet T-34 tanks to the Golan Heights overlooking Galilee. On January 11, 1967, Israel announced that a two-hour tank battle had been fought along the border and one of the Syrian's T-34's had been destroyed. Soon after an artillery battle was fought between Israel and Syria with shells whistling across Huleh Valley in both directions. Afterwards Syria claimed to have knocked out three Israeli border posts, one arms and fuel depot and claimed they had frightened away Israeli fighter planes that tried to intervene.

On February 5, Israel used diplomatic channels to issue a stern warning to Syria. Syria was told that unless the raids and attacks on Israel ceased, there would be heavy retaliation. Ignoring this warning, Syria broke out with unusually heavy firepower in April, and when Israeli planes took to the air they discovered Syria's fleet of Soviet MIG-21's streaking down upon them. In the air battle which ensued Israel claimed to have shot down six MIG's while Syria claimed she had bagged five from Israel. Regardless of the score, it was obvious that the situation in the Middle East was approaching the boiling point.

Soviet Leaders Fan the Flames

It is now known that during this period the Soviet officials were feeding the Arab leaders faked intelligence reports designed to fan the flames of fanaticism. As the U.S. News and World Report summed it up on July 17, 1967:

"It is now definitely established by authoritative sources that a major Soviet blunder led to the Arab-Israeli war early in June.

"The Soviet Government, to further its purposes, faked intelligence reports, supplying those reports to the governments of Egypt and Syria, that Israel was massing troops to attack Syria.

"The Soviet purpose, these sources say, was political and somewhat limited. Russia hoped to create a crisis atmosphere that would unite the Arab nations, cause them to stop their squabbling and work together more closely."

Of course, both the Egyptians and the Syrians had intelligence forces of their own so they should have known that if there was any major deployment of Israel's military strength it was not concentrated on the border of Syria. The report continues, "Nasser and the Syrians either believed the faked intelligence reports or wanted to believe them."

Under the circumstances Nasser had no fear of the outcome of an early war with Israel. Statistically, the odds were overwhelmingly in his favor. For weeks "war" was what the demonstrators in Cairo had been demanding. So had the military. It seemed the right time to plot the course for the long-awaited annihilation of Israel. To set the stage, Nasser decided to follow the same pattern he had used in 1956. The first step was to clearly announce that the time had come for militant action. Over and over again the Cairo radio and Nasser himself would repeat the theme: "We intend to open a general assault against

Israel. This will be total war. Our basic aim is the destruction of Israel!"[20]

This ominous verbalization echoed what Syrian "hotheads" had been saying for months. The chief of state, Al-Attassi had proclaimed, "We raise the slogan of the people's liberation war. We want total war with no limits, a war that will destroy the Zionist base."[21]

Syrian defense minister Hafez Assad declared, "We shall never call for nor accept peace . . . We have resolved to drench this land with our blood, to oust you aggressors and throw you into the sea for good."[22]

Pushing the Crisis to the Brink

On May 8, 1967, Arab terrorists bombed a highway five miles inside Israel. On May 11, Israel delegate, Gideon Rafael, warned the UN that Israel cannot endure these attacks much longer and is "fully entitled to act in self-defense" if the Syrians do not cease and desist.

Nasser later asserted that on "May 13 we received accurate information that Israel was concentrating on the Syrian border huge armed forces of about 11 to 13 brigades."[23] When Nasser was assured by UN observers that this just wasn't so, he chose to ignore it. Nasser said he had it from an entirely reliable source that Israel intended to attack sometime after May 17. This "reliable information" later proved to have come from the phony Soviet intelligence reports which we have already mentioned.

On May 14 and 15 Egyptian troops began moving in force across the Sinai Peninsula to take up positions directly across from the Israeli border. Now Nasser was prepared to demand the removal of the UN troops assigned there.

20. "Israel," by James A. Michener, *Look* magazine, August 8, 1967, p. 65.
21. *Ibid.*
22. *Ibid.*
23. Robert J. Donovan, *Israel's Fight for Survival*, p. 66.

It will be recalled that in 1956 a UN peace-keeping force of token size had been installed along the Gaza strip, also at the mouth of the Aqaba Gulf (in Sharm el Sheikh) and at critical points along the border. Obviously, the strength of this army was infinitesimal compared to the legions Egypt was bringing into the field, but at least it was a symbol.

On May 16, 1967, Nasser had his General Fawzi who was assigned to the Gaza area deliver a letter to the commander of the UN forces. It requested that all UN troops vacate from the territory immediately.

For the next several days there was a great stir between Cairo and New York. Finally, Secretary U Thant agreed to their removal. This brought on a storm of protest both in and out of the UN. What was the Secretary General doing?

In Washington, D. C., a member of the majority party, Senator Henry M. Jackson, declared: "The Secretary General violated all canons of courage, good sense and responsibility by failing to take time to consult the General Assembly, which authorized the UN force, and the Security Council in order to weigh the legal contentions and to explore alternative ways of maintaining a UN peace-keeping presence in the area."[24]

By May 22, Secretary General U Thant felt impelled to fly to Cairo and discover just what was happening. However, when his plane stopped in Paris he was handed a dispatch which said Nasser had just taken the fatal step which Israel had always warned would be considered an act of war. As in 1956, Egypt had closed the Aqaba Gulf!

The northern end of the Red Sea terminates in two horns or gulfs. One is the Suez Gulf leading up to the Suez Canal and the other is the Aqaba Gulf leading up to the port of Elath which is Israel's only seaway outlet for connections with the southern hemisphere. Since

---

24. *Ibid.* p. 72.

Nasser had never allowed Israel to use the Suez Canal, Elath had been her only lifeline to Africa, India, Iran and the Far East. More important it is the port through which 90 percent of Israel's oil supply has to pass. As soon as the leaders of Israel learned that this gulf had been blockaded with mines, torpedo boats and artillery, the Israeli foreign minister told the UN that this action not only violated international law but it left Israel breathing with only one lung. British ships attempting to deliver their cargoes of oil to Elath were stopped by Egyptian artillery fire at the Straits of Tiran on the southern entrance to the gulf.

The major powers demanded an immediate cease-fire as well as the lifting of the blockade, but the Soviet Union threatened to use its veto power if the matter were put to a vote in the UN Security Council. It seemed obvious that so long as Nasser was gaining ground, the Soviet Union would block any attempt to invoke an effective cease-fire.

Nasser is Discovered Using Poison Gas in Yemen

It was at this critical juncture that a new dimension was added to the crisis by the disclosure that for at least several months and perhaps longer, Nasser had been experimenting with various types of poison gas in connection with the pacification of Yemen. This was particularly alarming to the Israelis because their intelligence officers had already learned that Nasser was transferring practically his entire Yemen force and all its equipment to the sourthern border of Israel.

The original charge against Nasser for using poison gas was directed to the United Nations by the people of Yemen and Saudi Arabia, both nations consisting of fellow

Arabs whom Nasser claimed he was trying to unite. One news columnist wrote: "The UN looked the other way when Nasser sent his troops into Yemen five years ago and as recently as May 28 [1967] used poison gas on innocent villagers . . . Saudi Arabia asked Thant [UN Secretary General] to appeal to the United Arab Republic to stop the merciless and illegal gassing but Thant refused." [25]

The International Red Cross took its toxicologists to Yemen, exhumed some of the bodies, made a careful examination, and then published its report. *U.S. News and World Report* summarized the story:

"Western intelligence officials say the Red Cross investigation confirmed what has been going on for two years or more. From these sources comes this account of Egyptian gas warfare, largely against civilians:

"Since last January, President Gamal Abdel Nasser's forces in Yemen have embarked on an intensified poison-gas campaign. Earlier gas attacks are said to have satisfied Egyptian leaders that world opinion would not be mobilized against them for this violation of the international agreement prohibiting use of gas. In January, these sources say, Egyptians for the first time in history used lethal nerve gases in an air attack on two Yemen villages—at Hadda on January 4 and at Kitaf on January 5.

"More than 200 civilians were said to have been killed in Kitaf.

"In April, Egypt was reported to have used mustard gas against three villages held by Yemeni Royalists.

"Then, on May 10, Egyptian pilots flying Soviet-built aircraft carried out a gas attack on the village of Gadafa. Fifteen persons were killed.

"It was on the same day that 75 were killed in Gahar, in the attack which the Red Cross investigated and confirmed. On May 17, Egyptian raiders returned to Gadafa

---

25. "Why UN Is Sick," by columnist Vera Glaser, *Deseret News*, Salt Lake City, Utah, editorial page, June 12, 1967.

from another poison-gas attack which reportedly killed 96 persons sheltered in a cave.

"When Yemeni Royalists asked for Red Cross Assistance, Egyptian bombers returned to the gassed villages and dropped high-explosive bombs in an effort to obliterate traces of the gas raids.

"On May 15, Egyptian bombers attacked two Red Cross vehicles en route to the gassed villages. All the Red Cross equipment was destroyed and a Yemeni Red Cross worker was wounded.

"Yemeni Royalists report two attacks during June in the Jaul region. There were said to have been no human casualties, but all livestock in the area reportedly was killed. . . . Intelligence experts say that the Egyptians, probably with the aid of German scientists, have developed a range of poison-gas weapons.

"Nasser's Army, sent to Yemen to help put down the Royalist uprising, has been stalled for several years. Now it is believed, the poison-gas attacks were ordered by frustrated Egyptians in an effort to terrorize the Royalists into submission."[26]

And if Nasser would take this cruel and extreme action against a nation of his own people, what could he be expected to do against the Jews in an all-out war against Israel?

The Onrushing Floodtide of the Final Week

Israel's premier, Levi Eshkol, had always been known as a "moderate" politician and one who was capable of absorbing tremendous pressure without taking precipitous action. However, the shocking news of Nasser's reckless, genocidal use of poison gas against his own people plus the rapidly rising tide of overwhelming, calamitous cir-

26. "In Detail—Nasser's Gas War," *U.S. News and World Report*, July 10, 1967, p. 9.

cumstances which were closing in around Israel, stirred the leaders of practically all political factions in the Jewish state to raise a united voice of urgent warning, "Premier Eshkol, don't wait too long!"

Actually, Premier Eshkol was under tremendous outside pressure from the United States and Britain to take no defensive, overt action. The U.S. State Department and British Foreign Office assured Eshkol that Russia would cooperate with them in forcing restraint upon Nasser. But on May 28th, ten Soviet warships left their bases in the Black Sea and steamed through the Bosphorus to strengthen the Soviet fleet of 16 naval vessels and submarines already stationed in the Mediterranean.

Nasser immediately hailed this latest manifestation of tangible Soviet support and at the same time bitterly denounced the United States as the major supporter of Israel and therefore the principal enemy of the Arab World.

On May 29, U.S. officials inadvertently exposed the fact that in this crisis, at least, they really had no significant leverage with Russia and not much more with the various western allies. A U.S. demand that the Aqaba Gulf be opened forthwith was ignored. An attempt to get the major maritime powers to join the U.S. in sending warships up the Red Sea to open the Aqaba Gulf by force was equally unsuccessful. Israel watched these gestures of diplomatic shadow-boxing with apprehensive anxiety. It seemed obvious that the United States could help Israel merely as a counter-weight in keeping Russia from entering the war as a direct participant. The promised possibility of using so-called "big power" pressure to force Nasser to exercise restraint emerged as a clearly discredited miasma of diplomatic delusion. Premier Eshkol recognized that no matter how painful it was to admit it, Israel must face the fact that she was being rapidly abandoned and would have to discover her own devices to save herself from the impending Egyptian-Syrian blitz.

In fact, the odds against Israel surviving were so over-whelming that even anti-Nasser Arabs finally capitulated and began closing ranks and giving token support to the Nasser campaign. The last and most significant of these was King Hussein.

Among all the Arab rulers, Israel had looked upon King Hussein of Jordan as the most moderate and the most likely Arab with whom an equitable settlement could be worked out. Furthermore, since Jordan faced Israel on its extended eastern border, this meant that so long as King Hussein refused to collaborate with Nasser the threatened attack against Israel could only be delivered from the north and the south.

But by May 30, the pressure from the hundreds of thousands of Jordanian refugees together with the political pressure coming from Nasser, forced Hussein to retreat. Nasser persuaded the advisers of Hussein that since the Arab league was now about to annihilate Israel, this would be Jordan's last chance to climb aboard the victory train and share in the fruits of the campaign. Consequently, on May 30, King Hussein flew to Cairo and, much to the sorrow of many Americans and others who admired the young king, embraced Nasser (whose Cairo radio had been calling him "a Hashemite harlot"[27]) and turned over his rugged Arab legion of 50,000 fighters to Egyptian commanders.

Immediately Egyptian planes began making overflights and practice runs on Israel's five airfields. Two Egyptian commando divisions took up a position facing Israel from Old Jerusalem. Over 900 Egyptian tanks dug in on the Sinai border to the south of Israel, and sporadic mortar fire began setting Israeli wheat fields ablaze. The 300,000 Arab refugees in the Gaza Strip had been inflamed by an organization among them known as the Palestine Liberation Organization and these began a day-and-night chant for

---

27. *Israel's Swift Victory*, a special edition of *Life* magazine, June 23, 1967, p. 15.

"War now!" Because this band of warhawks had threatened a campaign of total terrorism and extinction for all Jews it is interesting to note the source of its political orientation:

"The Palestine Liberation Organization was founded by one Ahmed Shukairy, a 60-year-old ultra-left Palestine lawyer with an Egyptian passport and self-claimed ties with Russia and Communist China. Shukairy dates his Palestine Liberation Organization back to the early 1950's, but it made no particular impact until a decade later. His army is estimated to contain some 10,000 to 15,000 men and is purportedly organized for guerilla warfare in Israel. Palestine Liberation Army units have been trained in Syria, Egypt and Iraq, and are armed with Russian and Red Chinese light weapons. Shukairy's 'soldiers' slipped into some of the Gaza and Sinai positions abandoned by the United Nations Emergency Force when it was withdrawn at Nasser's demand from Egyptian territory. On the eve of the war, June 4, 1967, Shukairy was trumpeting, 'We will wipe Israel off the face of the map and no Jew will remain alive.' "[28]

Israel's Precarious Position as of Sunday, June 4, 1967

By this time the outlook for Israel was so dubious that *U.S. News and World Report* summarized the well-nigh impossible position in which Israel now found herself:

"Israel is a small enclave of 2.7 million people—without abundant natural resources—lying on the Mediterranean and surrounded by hostile Arabs.

"Arab powers, on the other hand, control a vast territory that includes a large portion of the oil resources of the Western world . . . .

---

28. Robert J. Donovan, *Israel's Fight for Survival*, p. 45.

"There are more than 50 million Arabs [Egypt, Syria, Jordan, Iraq, Lebanon and Saudi Arabia] commited to a sort of 'holy crusade' to the goal of getting rid of Israel— with no time limit set. These Arabs often are divided among themselves on just about every issue—except the one of Israel's destruction. On that they are almost fanatically united.

"Israel, at the same time, is considered by military men to be highly vulnerable to Arab attack if the country is left on its own for self-defense.

"In terms of geography, Israel as a nation possesses no natural barriers to invasion by land. Most of Israel's strategic points are within 40 miles of Arab territory. The vitally important city of Tel Aviv is only 13 miles from the Jordan border.

"Seven miles above Tel Aviv, at the town of Herziliya, the Jordanian border comes to within 10 miles of Israel's coast.

"In the South, at the head of the Gulf of Aqaba, the Israeli seaport of Eilat [Elath] is only three and a half miles from the Jordanian port of Aqaba.

"No Israel city is more than a few minutes away from Arab airfields, which are loaded with Soviet-made jets. No other country is more vulnerable than is Israel to damage by ground-to-ground rockets, if not by airborne bombs.

"Israeli military leaders live with the ever-present realization that their country could be cut in half by a thrust from Jordan to the sea.

"Military strategists say the Arab planning probably is based on a three-power attack mounted by Egypt, Syria and Jordan—including saturation bombing and rocketing— designed to destroy Israel before the U.S. or any other friendly force could come to the rescue."[29]

And apparently this is exactly what would have hap-

---

29. "If Egypt Does Fight Israel—Who Wins?" *U.S. News and World Report*, pp. 33-34.

pened if Israel had taken the advice of "patient waiting" which she was getting from the U.S. State Department and other well-meaning friends. But Israel and her military leaders turned out to be greater realists and therefore more decisive strategists than the U.S. diplomats and others who had so often fumbled in their attempts to cope with Communist-supported aggression against free peoples.

The Israelis decided to go it alone. On Sunday afternoon, June 4, 1967, her leaders determined to defy the Soviet Union and her puppet Arab League and independently launch a stunning blow against the Pan-Arabic colossus. Nasser had already announced that he was ready to go for broke and that negotiated peace was completely out of the question.[30] Very well, if there must be war the Israeli leaders determined that *they*, not Nasser, would decide the time and place where the war would be fought.

---

30. Robert J. Donovan, *Israel's Fight for Survival*, p. 158.

PART II

THE MIRACLE WAR

Levi Eshkol, Prime Minister of Israel at the time of the Arab-Israel
War in 1967.

DAVID AND GOLIATH
—A MODERN VERSION

It seemed amazingly singular that so many parallels emerged between the Israeli-Egyptian conflict of 1967 and the original duel between David, the young Jew, and Goliath, the gigantic Philistine.

In the case of young David, he knew he could not match Goliath sword for sword and spear for spear so he resorted to a tactic involving all the strategic elements of speed, simplicity and surprise.

Dressed in a light tunic which allowed him great flexibility of movement, David used a weapon which permitted him to remain at a distance and strike down his opponent from the air. By this means he did not expose himself to close in-fighting until the giant was sprawled upon the ground. Then David rushed forth to finish the job with Goliath's own sword.

In many of its essentials, Israeli leaders utilized the same tactics in 1967 against Egypt. Their strategy was to open up with a hard-hitting and completely crippling blow from the air. Then, when Egypt was left stunned and compelled to fight on the ground, they planned to close in for the *coup de grace* with tanks, infantry and mobile artillery, thereby smashing the enemy before he had time to recover.

Of course, there is a great difference between a combat involving two gladiators and an all-out war between military forces comprising the combined strength of a million men. But even here the Israeli generals hoped to keep the fight between the two nations of Israel and

(UPI Photo)

Moshe Dayan, hero of the 1956 campaign and Minister of Defense for Israel during the 1967 campaign.

Egypt rather than involve the whole Arab league. The Israelis reasoned that if it had not been for Nasser's intemperate passions and political ambitions the threat of all-out war would never have arisen. Therefore they identified Egypt as the real enemy in this conflict with Nasser in the bully role of a blustering Goliath. It was the Israeli plan to deliver a massive, debilitating blow to Egypt's air forces (deployed on twenty-five airfields from Damascus to Luxor) and then appeal to Syria, Jordan and the other Arab states to stay out of the fight because without his air power, Nasser would be doomed. They reasoned that only a suicide mentality would want to launch a military ground action when it was obvious that the skies were completely controlled by Jewish jets.

But what about the Soviet Union? It was later disclosed that the Israeli leaders were relying upon the overwhelming superiority of America's Mediterranean-based Sixth Fleet to discourage any reckless tendencies on the part of the blustering Soviet warships or submarines to unlimber their hardware.

Israel's One-Eyed General—Moshe Dayan

The defense of diminutive Israel was in the hands of a famous Jewish General, one-eyed Moshe Dayan. Thirteen years before he had started building and modernizing the country's military forces. In 1956 he had master-planned the successful campaign which had so humiliated the Egyptians on the Sinai peninsula. On June 1, 1967, Premier Levi Eshkol asked Moshe Dayan to take over again. To all Israel, Dayan was a symbol.

". . .Dayan represented not only military triumph; he was a *sabra*. Dayan, that meant, was of the new generation, born on Israeli soil, unblemished by the painful experiences of growing up in Europe, cocky and aggressive,

proud of his country not merely as a haven for the perse-
cuted and a sentimental reincarnation of a Bible story, but
as a dynamic, progressive, self-sufficient force. Dayan was
not a transformed European like Eshkol and Ben-Gurion
and the other great men who founded the new state on the
soil of Palestine. He was an Israeli through and through
and, as such, he was an important symbol to the Israeli
people."[1]

Dayan was born on May 20, 1915, in a communal
village (called a *kibbutz*) which was located below sea
level in the Jordan valley south of the Sea of Galilee.
At the age of six his family moved to a more swampy and
primitive area to help build a new cooperative settlement
called Nahalal. It was at Nahalal that Moshe Dayan learned to plow while carrying a rifle on his back to protect
himself from Arab attacks. Still, he liked many of the
Arabs, started to learn their language, and eventually
achieved the ability to speak Arabic fluently.

At the age of 12, Dayan already knew what it meant to
stand sentry duty against marauding Bedouins, and by the
time he was 14, this young *Sabra* (native-born) was
learning to be a professional soldier in Israel's volunteer
defense army called the Haganah.

While still a teen-ager, Dayan volunteered for
commando duty under Captain Orde Charles Wingate
of the British army. Captain Wingate was sent to Palestine
to stop Arab-Jewish clashes along the border and he did
this by organizing vigilantes into special night squads who
prowled up and down the border in the darkness. When
Dayan reached 22 he had become Wingate's second in
command.

By this time, however, Britain's need for Arabian oil
together with other factors had led to a new political
policy of restricting Jewish immigration and placating

---

1. Robert J. Donovan, *Israel's Fight for Survival*, p. 83.

the Arabs. When this was announced the Jews were deeply resentful, feeling this was a repudiation of Britain's former commitments. As tensions grew, Britain became fearful that the commando units Wingate had organized might be used against Britain. Wingate was recalled. These antici- pated fears turned out to be justified. As soon as Wingate was gone, Dayan formed a commando unit within the Haganah, and taught his volunteers everything he had learned from Wingate. Jewish reprisal action soon became so hot that the shocked British War Office outlawed the Jewish defense army, the Haganah, and issued orders that Dayan must be captured. He was apprehended in 1939 and sentenced to five years in prison. In two years he was released. By that time World War II was spreading its tentacles across three continents and the Nazi puppet government of the Vichy French was in control of Syria just to the north of Palestine. Britain desperately needed a few dare-devils to perform advance intelligence work inside Syria prior to attack. They chose Dayan to lead them. The young Jew led 50 commandos into Syria where, disguised as Arabs, they gathered the vital information. Dayan was then made the commander of the British troops which launched the campaign to capture Syria.

"Later in the war, during a battle for Lebanon's Litani River, Dayan was holding a telescope to his left eye when a bullet caught the eyeglass with a glancing blow, driving it into his eye socket. The black patch he has worn over his eye ever since has become his trademark as a leader."[2]

When World War II was over, Dayan returned to farming although he continued in the Haganah reserve as a lieutenant colonel. In 1948 when the British mandate over Palestine was about to end and the surrounding Arab countries said they would annihilate Israel rather than permit the Jews to set up an independent country, Dayan

---

2. *Ibid.*, p. 85.

was called back to active duty. In the war that followed Dayan moved up fast. As a brigade commander he led a group of jeeps armed with machine guns in a dash across the desert to clear the Negev. His forces later captured the important Arab towns of Lydda and Er Ramie. This resulted in his being made the chief officer to command the siege of Jerusalem. When the Arabs finally said they wanted peace, it was Dayan, as the chief military delegate for Israel, who signed the armistice with Jordan on April 19, 1949.

Thereafter, Dayan remained in the Israeli army until 1952 when he was assigned to attend the senior staff officer's school in England. This was considered a singular honor for a man who had advanced no further than agricultural high school at Nahalal. After his graduation with distinction, Dayan was made the Israeli Chief of Staff with the rank of major general.

The Israeli armed forces soon discovered they had a tough, new commander. He made every officer train as either a commando or a paratrooper. Dayan chose to be a paratrooper himself and on one of his jumps in 1955 broke a leg.

Dayan streamlined, modernized and beefed up the Israeli defense forces, using principles laid down by the classical German strategist, Von Clausewitz. He also adopted and implemented tactics developed by the United States airborne troops. As we have already mentioned, Dayan built the structure for the staggering victory over Egypt in 1956. In this campaign he demonstrated the value of his uncompromising demand for speed, simplicity, and surprise together with preparations for the initial attack being made at night.

After 1956, Dayan hoped the Egyptians had learned the futility of fighting, and therefore he left the army to enter politics. He belonged to the party of David Ben-Gurion and thereby became part of the political opposition to the current premier, Levi Eshkol, who succeeded Ben-Gurion. As a result, when the 1967 crisis began to shape up, Eshkol found the people clamoring for Dayan under circumstances that were politically embarrassing to the premier. However, he confidentially allowed Dayan to tour Israeli defenses to see if the commander-in-chief, Major General Itzhak Rabin, had done a good job. On June 1, when the crisis had reached the boiling stage, Eshkol asked Dayan to enter the Cabinet as minister of defense and run the war.

The Dayan-Rabin Strategy

But what kind of a defense should a nation raise when she stands on the brink of being burned to a cinder? Both generals agreed that their defense must be a shattering offense. Dayan found that Major General Rabin had tuned up the nation's fighting machine to the highest pitch of readiness. Unfortunately, however, the politicians were battling each other as to just how this machine should be used. Some wanted Israel's striking power used merely as a threat. Some wanted to restrict military action to the seizure of the Gaza strip and then use it as a bargaining tool to force the Egyptians to open the Aqaba Gulf. Some wanted to do nothing but wait for diplomacy and world opinion to save Israel. Others wanted to throw the responsibility of saving Israel on the United States.

Dayan scrapped the lot. Privately, he told the government officials that Israel must seize the whole Sinai peninsula exactly as was done in 1956. Publicly, Dayan announced that the Israeli Jews were determined, if necessary, to take on the defense of Israel alone. He said they did not want the soldiers of any other country "getting killed here in order to secure our safety."[3]

---

3. *Ibid.*, p. 87.

The announcement of this lone-wolf policy was as auda-
cious as it was desperate. But Dayan meant it and General Itzhak Rabin backed him up. The nation was put on
a total mobilization basis. One out of every ten Israelis
was in uniform, including women as well as men. (A comparable effort by the United States would raise an army
of 20,000,000!) The very young and the very old poured
in to fill jobs left vacant by the called-up reservists.
Every resource of the country was on a war footing. Even
ice cream trucks had their assignments.

The Dayan-Rabin strategy was based on the legal and
military recognition of the fact that Egypt had already
started a shooting war by using her artillery to close the
Aqaba Gulf. From the beginning, Israel had warned Egypt
that this would be an intolerable "act of war." Therefore, at this moment it was Israel's military task to "react"
before Nasser interpreted prolonged delay as weakness and
descended on Israel with a blitzkrieg of consuming incen-
diaries, block busters and perhaps even poison gas. Both
Dayan and Rabin were determined that the "doves" and
"wrist-slappers" must now step aside to make way for men
who had already risked their lives a hundred times for
Israel and knew exactly how to deal with deliberate acts
of war and blatant tyrant-talk which threatened to exterminate a whole nation. Israel's offensive action was going
to be massive, staggering, decisive.

Israel's Citizen Army

When they were finally given the green light, Dayan
and Rabin had the monumental task of whipping Israel's
citizen army into a mammoth, one-shot striking force. For
Israel it would have to be all or nothing at all. There
would be no second chance. For such a desperate gamble,
Dayan and Rabin had reason to be thankful for the govern-

ment's long-term policy of "total mobilization in time of war."

Israel had always accepted the threatened war from the ring of hostile Arab states as a genuine possibility. It was therefore customary to devote 10 percent of Israel's 4 billion-dollar gross national product to defense preparations. And it was customary for the Jewish leaders to insist that they get their money's worth. Their regular army consisted of only 60,000 men. These depended upon 204,000 sharply trained reservists to make Israel's defense machinery operate. The reservists were paid only while in training or actually fighting and their pay was small.

Under King David the country was divided into twelve districts and for one month during the year each district had to provide the standing army needed to protect the nation. Each of these districts paid for the support of its own soldiers during their month of service, including their food, so David's army was never a serious tax burden to the country except in time of war when all the districts had to send their troops simultaneously.[4]

The same kind of frugality has characterized the military policies of modern Israel. All youth, whether boys or girls, are required to enter the service as conscripts sometime between the ages of 17 or 18. The girls serve from 20 to 24 months and the young men from 26 to 30 months. The wages for both girls and boys during their tour of duty is $5.00 per month!

The only Israelis excluded from universal military training are Arabs, young mothers, the insane, and *women* who take an oath that military service volates their religious principles. Jewish men who live under the protection of Israel's citizen army are not allowed to claim they are conscientious objectors. On the other hand, Arabs, whether male or female, are not required to serve in the Israeli

4. See W. Cleon Skousen, *The Fourth Thousand Years*, Bookcraft, Salt Lake City, 1966, p. 183.

armed services since they might be forced to fight against their own relatives.

Only after the youth have served as conscripts can they volunteer for the regular army. And only after a youth has completed his transcript training as a plain GI can he be appointed an officer or even a senior sergeant. In actual combat, Israeli officers *lead* their men and therefore the Jews pride themselves in the fact that when there is a shooting war the officers take it right along with their men. The officers have more than their share of casualties. as statistics from the 1967 campaign later showed.

Following basic service as a conscript, a Jewish boy or girl is released from active training and assigned to a frontline reserve until age 39. After that, assignment is to a home guard or civil defense unit until the age of 50. Reservists must take thirty days of field training every year, plus one day a month for weapons training and target practice. Sergeants are required to put in six additional training periods each month and reserve officers must put in twelve.

In order to provide instant mobilization, each reserve unit has its equipment where it is likely to be used. It is the job of the regulars to keep weapons clean, occasionally warm up jeep engines and spot-check them regularly, test radio equipment and make sure that routine equipment such as fire extinguishers, batteries, first aid kits and drug packs are fully operative and ready for instant use.

Mobilization in Israel extends beyond manpower. It covers every resource in the nation. Israel soldiers ride to battle in the same buses they might ordinarily use for transportation to work. A reservist who is a civilian truck driver will be mobilized right along with his truck. The same is true of all civilians with private aircraft, private boats, heavy mechanical equipment, etc.

Even ice cream trucks from Tel Aviv and Haifa are made available to be plastered with mud (for camouflage) and sent into the desert carrying rations and supplies.

Instant mobilization requires code signals for the various units. Thus, during the 1967 crisis all kinds of codes began showing up on movie screens and appearing on the commercial radio stations. These were codes like, "Open Window," "Electric Boiler," "Men at work," and "Wedding March." Each code phrase represented secret mobilization orders to various military units.

The Dayan-Rabin Strategy in Operation

The Dayan-Rabin plan called for two vast, volatile and dangerous projects to be executed in the pre-dawn darkness of Monday, June 5, 1967. The first was "operation frogmen." On the evening of June 4, as a purple curtain of darkness settled over the Mediterranean, Israel's frogmen were already lining up along the coast of Egypt ready to strike shortly after midnight. Their assignment was to sabotage, sink or otherwise disable Egypt's extremely powerful ship-to-shore missile delivery system as well as her flotilla of seaborne rocket launchers. These, by themselves, could make an ashheap of Tel Aviv and Haifa.

The second project was a pre-dawn raid on every important Arab air base from Syria to Central Egypt. Insofar as possible there must be a total emasculation of Arab air power and the bombing of all the land-based missile pads which the Soviet Union had built for her Arab allies.

While this was going on, there was to be little sleep for Israeli's citizen army. The tank battalions and mobile artillery units were to remain poised on each of Israel's borders ready to charge across at a moment's notice. The major attack was to be against Gaza where Egypt had concentrated her armament strength and where the fanatical Palestine Liberation Army had threatened to invade Israel and massacre every Jew on sight. The Israeli armies on the Lebanon, Syrian and Jordan fronts were simply designed for holding action in hopes that the impact of the air assault would be sufficient to dissuade these countries from entering the war.

As the Arabs went to bed on Sunday night, June 4, 1967, they never would have believed the kind of world to which they would awaken on Monday morning.

Monday, June 5, 1967—the First Day

For the Egyptians, it all began like some horrible nightmare in the middle of the night. From far out over the Mediterranean to the north and northwest (not, you will note, from the east) came the flying scorpions of Israel. It was too dark to see the star of David painted on their tails. They came in low at a point where Israeli intelligence operators told them they would not be detected by Egyptian radar. In fact, one Egyptian pilot later admitted, "When the Israeli planes came over that morning we were all sitting at mess having coffee. The radio was turned off."[5]

The most sophisticated electronic apparatus was aboard the Israeli planes to guide them to their targets. The Jewish pilots were young but zealously dedicated. Their average age was 23. They had been told that they must make every single bomb and rocket count. Intelligence experts had briefed them in minute detail concerning the bases they were to hit. They knew the precise location of the planes and the ones to go after first. The Jewish flyers were even told which planes were dummies so they would not waste fire-power on them.

At great personal risk to themselves, most of the young pilots elected to come into the target area as

5. *U.S. News and World Report*, June 27, 1967, p. 14.

slowly as possible so as to make their bomb drops and rocket strafing as effective as possible. Some of the pilots even made their approaches with flaps down and wheels extended in order to cut their speed.

Photographs after the war revealed the unbelievable accuracy of the Israeli air strikes. Even Washington experts found it hard to believe.

The press suggested that Israel must have had some kind of "secret bomb" because the parked Egyptian planes were hit dead center leaving other nearby installations practically untouched. U.S. military authorities speculated that Israel was using something similar to the American Bullpup air-to-ground missile with television guidance. In any event, during somewhere between one to three hours of bombing and strafing, the backbone of the Egyptian air force was pulverized.

As the blazing summer sun rose slowly over the bleak, sterile peaks of the distant desert mountains, its harsh, bright light first silhouetted, then illuminated, the garish, gnarled skeletons of twisted metal which had once been the pride of the Pan-Arabian air force. A pall of smoke hung low on the still morning air. To Gamal Abdel Nasser's high and boastful ambitions had come the plague of a sudden death.

Egyptian Air Force officials went rushing about frantically seeking to discover just how damaging the pre-dawn raid had been to their mighty armada. The evidence was bewildering, devastating, heartbreaking. From Syria to Luxor, 387 precious and extravagantly expensive planes had been blown to smithereens or burned to cinders in one mammoth holocaust of phosphorous and TNT. Before the day was over the tally of smashed planes would reach 410.

In Cairo the Egyptian populace had no idea what was really happening. Civilians awakened before dawn to hear the earth-shaking booming of bombs and rattling of anti-aircraft guns. They turned on their radios to hear excited announcers cry out, "Israel has attacked!" Then they heard Cairo radio trumpet to the Egyptian fighters their stirring call to arms: "Destroy! Ruin! Liberate!" the radio blared. "Wo to Israel, your hour has arrived. The Arab nation is on its way to render its account. O Israel, this is your end!

"Every Arab must take revenge for 1948, must cross the Armistice lines from all directions and head for Tel Aviv. We shall drive out of existence the shame of Zionism. Rescue the looted Palestine! Hit everywhere til the end!

"There is no room for Israel in Palestine. This is your responsibility, O Arab soldiers! Israel, taste death!"[6]

Operation Frogmen

When Egyptian generals learned that their control of the skies was next to obliterated, they desperately turned to the Egyptian navy to order a hard-hitting blitz against Israeli population centers. This was a most critical but magnificent opportunity for the Navy to show what it could do with its ship-to-shore missiles and powerful Russian-made rockets. But they soon discovered that Israeli's nighttime "operation frogmen" had been as ravaging as their air attack. As the London Times correspondent later wrote:

"Led by Yochai Bin-Nun, the 43-year-old former commander-in-chief of the Israel Navy, the commandos attacked in the small hours of June 5. Their main objective was Ras al Tin, the naval anchorage of Alexandria, but they also attacked other naval installations along Egypt's northern coast as far as Port Said, and raided Port Tawficq, south of Suez.

---

6. James A. Michener, "Israel, A Nation too Young to Die," *Look* magazine, August 8, 1967, p. 72.

"Combined units of frogmen and paratroops trained for marine warfare were so effective that they dealt with the most powerful navy in the Middle East as ruthlessly and fast as their air force colleagues attacking the Soviet MIGS on the ground.

"All but two of the Egyptian submarine fleet were crippled; more important, the small but potentially lethal flotilla of high-speed missile-carrying patrol boats was destroyed by limpet mines. It seems that no one of them succeeded in firing a shot throughout the war.

"The commando raid thus relieved the ground troops of one of their major worries. Because of Israel's long coastline and slim hinterland she was vulnerable to rocket attack from the sea."[7]

Invasion of the Gaza Strip and Sinai

When photographs were taken during the early daylight hours they revealed that the Pan-Arabian air force had been whittled down to a stick. Within a few hours the Israelis had suddenly acquired a decisive ratio of air superiority. Israeli generals assigned to ground operations openly cheered. Now they at least had a fighting chance against Egypt's mighty arsenal of tanks.

As mentioned earlier, the primary ground assault was to be aimed at the heart of the Gaza strip and then fan out to drive a wedge across the Sinai desert toward the Suez Canal. The Gaza front was by far the most heavily fortified section of the whole Sinai-Negev border. Egyptian generals had not set up their line of attack back in the desert where they were favored by natural terrain but had driven 900 of their 1200 Russian tanks right down to Israel's border as though they were expecting to crash down on the Jews like a lion on a mouse. The ratio of

---

7. "Raids by Israel Frogmen Paralyzed Nasser's Navy," *Miami Herald,* June 27, 1967.

(UPI Photo)

Some of the fiercest fighting was in the Gaza Strip, but once the Israeli armor had broken free it moved swiftly across the desert toward the Suez Canal.

Egyptian tank superiority over Israel was more than two to one.

From Gaza southward to Elath the Sinai-Negev front covers 117 miles. The Egyptians had over 100,000 of their best equipped troops dug in along this border. Other thousands were dug in all along the Gaza border. In fact Gaza constituted the natural shield protecting the main road along the Mediterranean which led to Egypt. The Gaza Strip also contained the camps of more than 300,000 Arab refugees, all of whom had formerly lived in Israel. These had not only been inflamed sufficiently to demand that Nasser launch an immediate "war of liberation," but they had formed suicide squads and trained whole cadres of troops for guerilla warfare.

It was approximately 8 A.M. that the battalions of Israeli armament received their terse orders to smash across the heavily mined border. Their orders were to breach the Egyptian defenses wherever holes could be punched in the Gaza or Sinai lines and then speed across the desert day and night toward Egypt. Dayan had told them, "Don't stop until you reach the Suez Canal!"

For the most part, Israel's initial ground assault was made without the benefit of substantial air cover. Israel's air forces were being refueled and reloaded with bombs and rockets following their victorious night raids. It was not until later that the welcomed wings of Israel's French-made planes came roaring down the Negev. Meanwhile, the ground battle on the desert was a far cry from the swift, easy night victories enjoyed by the air force.

In spite of the speed and initial shock with which Israel's ground forces struck, they found the Egyptian tanks and troops securely dug in and preened for total war. The Egyptians put up a tough, tenacious and effective resistance. Had it not been for the later pounding by rocket-loaded Israeli planes, the Arab tanks and artillery might have prolonged the war indefinitely.

As we have already mentioned, the Egyptian tanks greatly outnumbered those of Israel and they were heavily insulated and equipped to resist the desert heat so they could fight prolonged battles. This had been a critical weakness of the Egyptian tanks in 1956 when Nasser's men frequently gave up in the middle of an engagement because they were being roasted to death inside their mobile iron ovens. In 1967 the Egyptian staying power was significantly stronger. Tank battles as great as that of El Alamein during World War II, erupted. In some places the fighting became so desperate that tanks fought muzzle to muzzle for hours throughout the early part of the first day. Then the Israeli planes began to arrive. This made the difference. Phosphorous bombs and high explosives turned the Egyptian tanks into metal coffins. The spectacle of seeing those giant moving fortresses literally blow apart as Israeli rockets struck them, petrified the discipline of the Egyptian tank corps. They began jumping out and running from their tanks as though they had the kiss of death implanted on them.

By the end of the day Israel had not only captured the festering political sliver of Gaza which had been pricking her tender underside so long, but her advanced armament had penetrated 30 miles into the Sinai desert and was commencing to engage important Egyptian defense forts along the Mediterranean. In the process, the Israelis had taken thousands of prisoners and had captured hundreds of Soviet-built tanks. Some of them were so new they hadn't even been painted or camouflaged for battle action. All of the captured tanks which would still run were quickly given a star of David, new Jewish crews, and were sent scampering back into the desert to fight alongside Israel's U.S. and British tanks. It was like slaying Goliath with his own sword.

Israel Fails in Her Attempt to Contain the War

While all of this had been going on the Israeli leaders had been keeping diplomatic channels humming in their attempts to prevent the war from spreading.

Shortly after the first reports verified the remarkable success of the pre-dawn air raids, Israeli leaders made assurances to Jordan and Syria that no ground action would be launched against their territories unless they themselves began overt military action against Israel.

Israel's Foreign Minister, Abba Eban, told the United Nations on Tuesday:

"In accordance with the policy to contain the conflict I yesterday invited General Bull, the chairman of the Truce Supervision Organization, to inform the heads of the Jordanian State that Israel had no desire to expand the conflict beyond the unfortunate dimensions that it had already assumed and that if Israel were not attacked by Jordan, it would not attack, and would act only in self defense. It reached my ears that this message had been duly and faithfully conveyed and received. Nevertheless, Jordan decided to join the Egyptian posture against Israel and opened artillery attacks across the whole frontier, including Jerusalem."[8]

At the same time, Premier Levi Eshkol made an appeal to the Syrian officials not to take action which would compel Israel to retaliate against their country. Syria answered by bombing Megiddo from the air and bombing Deganya with artillery fire. Then long-range cannon rifles were used to pulverize Israel's Kibbutz Ein Hamifrats and Koordoni.

Nevertheless, no immediate action was taken against Syria. "Holding action only" was the order for both Syria

---

8. Alex Benson, *48 Hour War*, New York: The Publishing Corp., 1967, pp. 167-168.

and Jordan as far as the Israeli leaders were concerned.
It was hoped that both would cool off when they realized
how devastating Israel's air raids had been against Egypt's
Pan-Arabian sky strength.

But the war would not remain "contained."

Jordan's powerful and well-trained Arab legion was the
first to crash through into Israel and thereby create a
completely new dimension in the war.

The Battle for Jerusalem Begins

As of 1947 the Old City of Jerusalem had been occupied
by Jews, Arabs, Christians, Armenians and many other
ethnical and religious groups. However, during the Arab-
Israeli war of 1948 the Jews were bombed and burned out
of their homes in the old Jewish quarter near the famous
temple wailing wall, most of them were compelled to flee
from Jerusalem and take up residence on the higher regions
to the west. On these heights overlooking the Old City,
the Israelis built their own "new" Jerusalem with a new
Hebrew University, a new parliament building, a modern
business center, several theaters and concert halls, new
homes, hotels and hundreds of modern apartment houses.
By 1967 the population had reached well over 200,000.

Between the two Jerusalems, the United Nations established a narrow, barbed wire, fenced-in, "No Man's Land"
with its bomb-gutted buildings deliberately left along that
wretched streak of desolation as a reminder of the violent
fighting of 1948. The only crossing from Israel to Jordan
was at the famous Mandelbaum Gate near Old Jerusalem's
U.S. Consulate. Here Jordan officials allowed Arabs to cross
back and forth but no Jews, with extremely rare exceptions,
were permitted to come into Jordan. All tourists were
required to have a certificate verifying their non-Jewish
faith.

The exclusion of the Jews from Old Jerusalem violated the 1949 armistice agreement, but the United Nations failed to provide a remedy. For 19 years the promise of "Jewish access to the wailing wall" remained an empty and sterile pledge (therefore an open and running sore on the Jewish soul) just like so many other guarantees the Israelis had received from the UN.

For this very reason it is undoubtedly a fact that when the Egyptian supreme command ordered the Arab Legion of Jordan to blast across the border and open a new front against Israel they committed the most serious mistake of the entire war. They thereby unleashed pent up Jewish resentment germinated by nineteen years of Arab religious abuse which had deprived this people of its right to worship at its most sacred shrine. For the Arabs, the results were calamitous.

The Opening Round

According to observers, it was approximately 11 A.M. on the first day of the war that the Jordanians launched their attack. There had been sporadic border fire prior to this time on both sides but nothing had occurred to indicate a full-scale offensive until now. The stage had been set earlier in the day. At 6:30 A.M. a TU-16 Soviet-made bomber had violated Israeli airspace just north of Elath to transport Egyptian general Abdel Moneim Riad and his staff to the Jordan Capital at Amman. There General Riad took over the command of King Hussein's army. The bomber was followed by 10 turbojet Antonov transports carrying military equipment and two Egyptian commando units of 350 men each. Anyone observing what was happening would have had no doubt that a major assault was in the making.

As we have already noted, Israel had promised no ground action against Jordan if this eastern neighbor

did not start an offensive against Israel. However, three
hours after the campaign opened in Sinai, the new
Egyptian commander triggered the Jordanians into an all-
out offensive from Jerusalem. It began with heavy shelling.
News reporters summarized what happened:

"The mortar and artillery bombardment from the
Jordanian sector was intense. No part of the city escaped.
More than six hundred buildings in the Israeli sector were
damaged. Shells landed near Prime Minister Eshkol's home.
Glass panes in the Israel Museum were blasted out by
concussion from exploding shells. The Church of the
Dormition, southwest of the old city and said to be
the scene of Christ's Last Supper, was hit early. A shell
punched a hole in the church dome."[9]

In this kind of a situation the Israeli capital was
extremely vulnerable. The 1948 armistice had left Israel's
"new" Jerusalem at the eastern end of a long, finger-
like corridor with Jordan hills surrounding it on three
sides. The corridor permits little or no military maneuvering space. At one point the corridor is barely four
miles wide. The Israelis would never have settled for such
an obvious geographical booby trap had not the United
Nations assured them of "protection."

In this hour when protection was completely lacking,
the Jordanian guns were able to pound on the Israeli
capital with deadly effect. The city's casualties jumped
to over a thousand in the opening hours of the war.

Arabs Capture UN Headquarters

Of course, Israel immediately returned the Jordanian
fire, but the Jewish commander is said to have gambled
against any general engagement—hoping that King Hussein
was "merely paying his respects to Arab unity," and that

---

9. Robert J. Donovan, *Israel's Fight for Survival*, p. 115.

the bombardment was merely a political gesture. It was 2:30 P.M. when the commander realized he had been mistaken. Through his binoculars he could see an advance contingent of the Arab Legion pushing quickly across the UN "No Man's Land" and invading Israel.

On the border the Jordanians encountered no resistance. They moved along the UN corridor until they came to the UN headquarters, called the Government House. This was the first captured and then the troops moved over into the suburbs of Israel. General Uzi Narkiss, head of Israel's Central Command, immediately ordered a counter-offensive.

As of that moment the Jordanians were enjoying a spirit of complete jubilation. Americans caught in the Old City by the hostilities noted that all during these early hours Radio Cairo and the local Jordanian radio crackled continuously with excited announcements of a whole series of glorious Arab victories. Ben Neal, a 23-year-old tourist from Mineola, Texas was staying at the Al Arab Hotel near Jerusalem's Damascus Gate. The proprietor joyously announced, "We will be in Tel Aviv tomorrow. We have already shot down 1,000 Israeli planes!"[10]

It took the Israelis a little while to get their counter-offensive going. Only 5,000 soldiers were in Jerusalem. The remainder had been drained off for the big punch into the Sinai-Gaza campaign. Now Israeli generals were forced to redeploy back to Jerusalem some of their badly needed troops and armament from the southern sector. While these were on the way the Jewish sector commander sent three Israeli companies, supported by two tanks and several cannon-mounted jeeps, to recapture the UN headquarters and rescue the Norwegian general, Odd Bull. There was a stiff, uphill fight for a period of an hour before

---

10. Sanche de Gramont, "Battle of Jerusalem," *Saturday Evening Post*, August 12, 1967, p. 71.

the UN headquarters were recaptured. Even so, the UN general seemed less than appreciative of what the Israelis had done. Over his strong protests, General Odd Bull (that really is his name) was evacuated with 50 members of his staff to the greater safety of the President Hotel on the Israeli side of Jerusalem.

Preparing a Counter-Attack

In preparation for a general counter-attack, two brigades of mobile artillery and paratroopers were ordered up to Jerusalem. As the 10th Armored Brigade moved up into the narrow corridor they found the roads mined. The first tank was blown up, but the second tank simply pushed it off the road and the brigade proceeded. The brigade of paratroopers had been on the border expecting to be flown in behind the Egyptian lines on the Sinai Front. Suddenly here they were being assigned to fight for their Holy City of Old Jerusalem!

Before an all-out counter-offensive could be launched, however, the Jewish central command felt that Israel's over-worked air force should be brought in to bomb the major defenses along the Jordanian border. Throughout the day these plucky 23-year-old Israeli pilots had been deeply involved in the desperate tank battles being fought all along the Negev-Sinai-Gaza front. It was therefore after midnight before a substantial number of them could be reloaded with gas and rockets for redeployment to Jerusalem.

Meanwhile, the Jewish civilian population and especially the Jewish troops wondered how the war was going.

It is interesting that all during the first day of fighting and while the Egyptians were broadcasting voluminous reports of magnificent victories, the Israeli government was telling its people virtually nothing. No one but the military commanders and the top government officials knew what a historical change the events of this day had brought to the world. Even the 120 members of Israel's parliament, the Knesset, who had met Monday night for the swearing in of their new cabinet officers, were generally tense and apprehensive. Only when David Ben-Gurion suddenly came in to announce that photographs showed 362 Arab planes had been destroyed, did their spirits begin to pick up. Later, the tally was increased. As they began to perceive the full implications of these reports, the law makers of Israel finally saw themselves and their country in a completely new perspective. Not even the bombs and shells falling around the blacked-out parliament building could prevent them from celebrating. Rounds of toasts were drunk with uplifted glasses of lemonade!

Meanwhile, as fast as Israeli reinforcements began arriving in "New" Jerusalem, they were briefed and dug in for heavy fighting. The Jordanians had built concrete bunkers along the border and all roads were heavily mined. In addition, the Jordanian mortars and cannon rifles mounted on the summits of the surrounding hills meant that the battle for Jerusalem was going to be ferocious and deadly.

As Monday, June 5, 1967, came to a close, the Israeli supreme command could tabulate some phenomenal plus marks for the first day of the war. The back of the Pan-Arabian air force had been broken, Gaza had been breached and her most important towns occupied, tank battles had been successfully fought and three spearheads of Israeli armament had broken into the open stretches of the Sinai desert.

At Jerusalem the Arab forces had elected to fight and the enemy was already joined. The initiative was still with the Arabs but Israeli soldiers had recaptured the UN headquarters and reinforcements had arrived ready to commence the liberation of Old Jerusalem as soon as Israeli bombers had softened up the frontier so troops could cross. Altogether, it had been a most remarkable and amazing day.

Tuesday, June 6th—the Second Day of the War

If residents of Jerusalem on either side of the border thought they were going to get any sleep after the first day of the war they were soon aware of their mistake. Both Arabs and Jews were rudely awakened shortly after midnight by the thunderous explosions from bombs and rockets. The Israeli air force had arrived.

Using high precision, night-time, electronic gear, the Israeli pilots began a methodical bombardment of the eight mile border adjacent to the Holy City. Special precautions were taken to keep from damaging the shrines of various religious faiths. Nevertheless, shrapnel and bomb fragments fell in a heavy hail upon border sanctuaries such as the Garden Tomb. Dr. Matter, its caretaker, was forced to take his wife and adopted daughter from the family residence and seek refuge inside the sacred tomb, itself.

While the Israeli Air Force was bombing and strafing strategic strongholds, the newly-arrived paratroopers made their way through the debris to clear away any remaining resistance. Everywhere the fighting was fierce throughout the night. One Israeli unit had 50 killed and many more wounded as it crossed the heavily mined No Man's Land and touched the explosive Jordanian border on the other side. It was necessary for them to come in spraying machinegun fire and throwing hand grenades.

By dawn, highly amplified loud speakers as well as Israeli radio broadcasts were warning the Jordanian populace to stay indoors because anyone peering out of windows would be considered a sniper and brought under immediate fire. White cloths were ordered displayed out-

(UPI Photo)

The Battle of Jerusalem brought heavy fighting to the Holy City and left the streets cluttered with the rubble of war.

side houses to indicate that the occupants had heard the messages and would guarantee no resistance.

One Jordanian stronghold which the paratroopers knew would block their advance at the Mandelbaum Gate was a large reinforced concrete bunker. However, Israeli commandos took to the rooftops and came down to the rear. They entered the bunker through the kitchen and after several rapid bursts of machinegun fire the bunker was silenced.

This was the day in which approximately 15,000 Jordanians were killed. The Israeli soldiers later called the Arab Legion of Jordan the toughest resistance of the war. Every type of strategy was employed by the bombed-out Arab troops as they retreated house by house and often room by room. One of their favorite tricks was to throw off their uniforms, beneath which were pajamas. Or they would quickly don business suits. They would also hide their guns and after the Israeli troops had by-passed them they would grab up their weapons to trap the out-flanked Israelis with a deadly stream of automatic bullets. However, this strategy backfired. It forced the Israelis to shoot some innocent persons who were dressed the same way.

One of these was Dr. Matter at the Garden Tomb. Because this particular shrine is only a few hundred yards from the Mandelbaum Gate, it was reached early Tuesday morning during the house-to-house fighting. As mentioned earlier, Dr. Matter had taken his wife and young adopted daughter into the tomb to sleep so they would be safe from the bombs. About 7 A.M. the bell at the garden entrance rang and when Dr. Matter opened the door he was confronted by six Israeli soldiers who had been fighting all night. Dr. Matter said, "Shalom!" (Peace be unto you). But they mistook him for a disguised Arab soldier and a burst of gunfire killed him instantly. They immediately sprayed the interior of the garden with their

automatic weapons, but suddenly stopped when the young
daughter of Dr. Matter ran screaming from the tomb.
She cried out, "You have killed my Daddy! You have
killed my Daddy!" The soldiers looked around, decided
this must be a civilian establishment, and left. Such
is the grizzly work of war.

The Israelis Put the Pincers
on Jerusalem

The Israeli central command had decided that the
battle of Jerusalem should follow the same tactics as those
used by the Roman general, Titus, when he conquered
Jerusalem in 70 A.D. Although difficult to accomplish, it
resulted from a tight pincers movement surrounding the
entire city. It was designed to secure all the high places
overlooking Jerusalem and control every road leading into
it. After that the city could be invaded by direct assault.

Modern warfare permitted the two-thronged thrust
around the city to be made by tanks so the early hours of
Tuesday morning revealed Israeli-owned Sherman and Patton tanks commencing the encircling movement. Behind
each battery of tanks came the paratroopers. The pincer
movement to the south ran into mined roads and nests of
anti-tank guns. Air force support helped to breach the
resistance but, even so, every advance had to be achieved
house by house, street by street and hill by hill. An Israeli
sergeant-major described the paratrooper and commando
action on this front as follows:

"You go into a room, and it leads to another room.
There are steps going up to yet another room, or steps
going down. And so on and so on. Anywhere in this
maze, a suicide squad sniper may lurk. Some of them have
thrown away their uniforms and have put on pajamas."[11]

---

11. Robert J. Donovan, *Israel's Fight for Survival*, p. 118.

The pincer movement toward the northern side of the city moved a little faster at first and the paratroops had difficulty keeping up. Then the Jordanian cannonading came down like a curtain of fire. This contingent was trying to reach Mount Scopus.

Mount Scopus is practically a continuation of the Mount of Olives and lies northeast of the city. It was here on this high vantage point that Titus had built the head-quarters for his Roman legions nineteen centuries before. But for these Israeli troops Mount Scopus held far more recent significance. It was here, prior to the Palestinian war of 1948, that the Jews had built their first Hebrew University, and it was here that they had built their famous Hadasseh Hospital. After the war the armistice lines left these two institutions far inside the Jordanian border but were designated Israeli territory. For 19 years Mount Scopus had stood like a Jewish island in a hostile Jordanian sea waiting for a permanent peace. The armistice agree-ment had also permitted the hospital and university to be garrisoned by 120 troops and re-supplied by a special caravan from Israel every two weeks. But for all practical purposes these institutions had been isolated and extremely difficult to use.

At around noon on Monday when the Jordanians opened up their first offensive, this Jewish enclave on Mount Scopus began receiving tremendous shelling. Most of it came from the Mount of Olives and a fortified position near the former palace of Germany's Kaiser Wilhelm. Counter-shelling from Israel against the Mount of Olives resulted in some of the bullets criss-crossing the section occupied by the beautiful Intercontinental Hotel. Monday evening an American, Ted Yates of NBC was one of those killed during the exchange of fire.

Now, on Tuesday, as the tanks and paratroopers made their slow, tedious course up toward Mount Scopus under heavy Jordanian shell-fire, the casualties were numerous.

Helicopters were used to transport the wounded to Hadasseh Hospital on Mount Scopus. During this war Hadasseh would treat around eight hundred wounded men (including 40 Jordanian soldiers) and although one-fourth of them required major surgery, only three died. In the maternity ward, five babies were born during the same period so the balance was on the side of life rather than death.

It was the Israeli Air Force which finally opened up the pathway for the tanks by slamming bombs into the Jordanian gun positions until they were silenced. By late afternoon Moshe Dayan hurried up along the northern sector to encourage his forces and ended up having tea on Mount Scopus.

Meanwhile, down in the city the Israeli forces finally smashed through what the soldiers called Jordan's "Maginot Line" and began taking up new positions preparatory to the final occupation of the whole of Jerusalem. Members of the press who were huddled together by government orders at Jordan's National Hotel, suddenly saw tanks sporting the star of David rattling down the cobblestone streets. They could scarcely believe it. Neither could some of the Arabs. One tank stopped to ask an Arab youth for directions. He told them. It turned out that the soldiers were asking for directions to Rockefeller's Palestine Museum which houses Jordan's archaelogical treasures. The Israeli tanks had orders to protect them. An observing Armenian businessman asked the Arab youth what had been said. "I think they're Iraqui tanks come to help us," said the boy. "They speak Arabic, but with a funny accent."

Minutes later, the blue and white Star of David banner suddenly broke out and floated free above the high tower of the Palestine Archaelogical Museum. The few Jews living in sight of it cheered, wept, prayed. Later, as nightfall darkened Jerusalem's narrow, crooked streets,

Israeli tanks and paratroops took up their assigned positions ready for the final assault which was scheduled for early Wednesday morning.

World Attention Is Focused on the Middle East

But nightfall in the Middle East meant it was only early afternoon in New York City. The achievements of two full days of fighting were already in the headlines and the Jewish population (the largest of any city in the world) was hysterically jubilant. However, at the United Nations there was an ominous uproar. Millions of Americans stayed glued to their television sets as they watched the delegates from Russia, Egypt, Syria and the Pan-Arabian entente ventilate their frustrated rage in blistering polemics. The war was not even half over and already the score was adding up frightfully fast for the Arabs.

The press reported that by Tuesday night Jerusalem was on the verge of complete occupation. Fast mobile armament units were already leaving other forces to mop up the city so these batteries of tanks and armed jeeps could race southward toward Bethlehem and Hebron.

Just above Tel Aviv, Israel had not only saved her territory from being cut in two at the narrow ten-mile waistline, but she had pushed Jordan forces back in a hard-punching operation that was carrying her tanks and artillery to the very gates of Nablus—the most important northern Palestine-Arabian city—the site of Jordan's big university and the center of her intellectual life.

Out across the Sinai desert, Israel had captured or destroyed nearly 700 tanks and thousands of trucks, jeeps and automotive-mounted-cannon. The dead and captured ran into thousands. Military roads built by the Egyptians for a fast blitz against Israel had become choked with miles of Egypt's wrecked and abandoned military equipment from Russia—millions upon millions of dollars worth. Late on Tuesday the Israeli tanks had largely broken loose and were using their radar and night-fighting equipment to race toward the Suez Canal on a thirty-mile front.

Nasser Is Caught Attempting to Create a Myth

In the midst of all this the Israeli government recorded a radio-telephone conversation between Nasser and King Hussein which completely exposed a fallacious alibi that Nasser had conjured up to explain the devastating defeat which his leadership had brought to the Arab world. Israeli leaders played the tape for UN officials and published translations of it so the world press would clearly know the duplicity of Nasser in his latest and most scurrilous barrage of deceptive propaganda against the United States and Great Britain. The official transcript went as follows:

"Hello—His Majesty is ready? The President is coming.

"Hello, Amman, is His Majesty ready?

"Hello, His Honor the President is ready.

"How are you? I hear His Majesty, the brother wants to know if the fighting is going on along all the fronts.

"Yes. Shall we include also the United States? Do you know of this, shall we announce that the U.S. is cooperating with Israel?

"Hello, I do not hear, the connection is the worst—the line between you and the palace of the King from which the King is speaking is bad."

After these preliminaries Nasser and King Hussein were finally connected and the following conversation was recorded:

NASSER: Hello, will we say the U.S. and England or just the U.S.?

HUSSEIN: The U.S. and England.

NASSER: Does Britain have aircraft carriers?

HUSSEIN: [answer unintelligible].

NASSER: Good. King Hussein will make an announcement and I will make an announcement. Thank you. Do not give up. Yes. Hello, good morning brother. Yes. I hear.

HUSSEIN: Mr. President, if you have something or any idea at all . . . at any time.

NASSER: We are fighting with all our strength and we have battles going on on every front all night and if we had any trouble in the fighting, it does not matter, we will overcome despite this. God is with us. Will His Majesty make an announcement on the participation of the Americans and the British?

HUSSEIN: [answer not intelligible].

NASSER: By God, I say that I will make an announcement and you will make an announcement and we will see to it that the Syrians will make an announcement that American and British airplanes are taking part against us from aircraft carriers. We will issue an announcement. We will stress the matter. We will drive the point home.

HUSSEIN: Good. All right.

NASSER: Your Majesty, do you agree?

HUSSEIN: [answer not clear].

NASSER: A thousand thanks. Do not give up. We are with you with all our hearts and we are flying our planes over Israel today. Our planes are striking at Israel's airfields since morning.

HUSSEIN: A thousand thanks. Be well.[12]

This conversation demonstrated the amazing lengths to which these Arab leaders felt compelled to go in order to

---

12. *Ibid.*, pp. 109-110; Associated Press dispatch, "Israel Says Charges Trumped-Up," *Salt Lake Tribune*, June 9, 1967, p. 6A.

save face after the scorching humiliation they had suffered at the hands of Israel. In Nasser's thrashing about for an alibi perhaps it was almost inevitable that he would eventually pounce upon his traditional propaganda scarecrows— the U.S. and Britain—and pin upon them the badge of everlasting shame for bringing down upon his head this monstrous catastrophe.

Accordingly, Arab representatives promptly appeared before the United Nations to denounce the knife-in-the-back attacks by the "imperialistic powers," the United States and Great Britain. As Nasser, himself, would later say in his famous resignation speech:

"On the morning of last Monday, June 5, the enemy struck. If we say now it was a stronger blow than we had expected we must say at the same time, and with assurance, that it was much stronger than his resources allowed.

"Also, British aircraft raided, in broad daylight, positions on the Syrian and Egyptian front, in addition to operations by a number of American aircraft reconnoitering some of our positions. The inevitable result was that our land forces, fighting a most violent and brave battle in the open desert, found that their air cover was inadequate in face of decisive superiority.

"It can be said without fear of exaggeration that the ENEMY WAS OPERATING AN AIR FORCE THREE TIMES ITS NORMAL STRENGTH. . . . What is now established is that American and British aircraft carriers were off the enemy's shores, helping his war effort."

It turned out, of course, that Nasser and Hussein had no proof whatever for their charges. Both the U.S. and Britain were able to account for all planes and prove that not one of them was even near the area. But for home consumption, Nasser had made his point. As far as vast multitudes of Arabs were concerned their beloved leader had spoken and a myth had been fixed in their minds as a permanent historical fact. As we shall see later, it saved Nasser from political suicide.

Now it was Russia's turn to try to save face. To do this she took her polemics to the UN arena.

Pandemonium at the United Nations

There is no doubt but what the Arab-Israeli war will remain a permanent blemish on the history of the United Nations. In twenty-two years of its existence nothing had been more damaging to its image From the middle of May the whole world had watched as this international convocation of political authority convulsed itself for weeks in frustrated negation of everything it was created to provide. People could see that as a "town hall of the world" where each nation could mount the stump and state its case, the UN was useful. But as a genuine "union of peace-loving nations" combined against war-mongering nations, its performance was preposterous.

Actually, its crude contradictions and agonizing frustrations had been built into this organization from its inception.

The original promoters of the UN had really wanted a "world organization" with all nations participating regardless of their attitudes on war, subversion, economics, revolution, politics or any other subject. Understandably, this created widespread suspicion that the foundation was being laid for a one-world government which could fall into the hands of a Communist leadership. The UN promoters therefore took a different approach. They popularized the idea that the UN would be restricted to a "union of peace loving nations." To make this crystal clear, Article 2 of the Charter provided that all member-nations must guarantee that they will "settle their international disputes by peaceful means." All members were further required by this Article to "refrain in their international relations from the threat or use of force against the territorial in-

tegrity or political independence of any state." Article 4
provided that membership was open to "all other peace-
loving states" who would accept the obligations of the
charter. In other words, it was to be an exclusive club
of good neighbor nations who would commit themselves
to settle all their disputes exclusively by peaceful
means. And Article 6 provided that any member which
"persistently violated the principles contained in the
present Charter may be expelled from the organization."
Theoretically and philosophically it made a lot of sense.

How the United Nations
Became Disunited

But having given the United Nations a wholesome
image, the original promoters did something which professional politicians do so often. They set about to promote the very opposite of what they had promised. Long
before the final draft of the charter was even presented
for approval they had laid the foundation for a "world
organization" rather than restrict it to a union of peace-
loving nations. In spite of what the Charter specifically
stated, they set about to bring into the UN the revolutionary nations, the conspiratorial nations, the war-mongering nations. This was sold to the leaders of the free
world on the basis that it would subject these aggressive,
revolutionary powers like the Soviet Union and her satellites to the pressure of the world community. It was promised that membership would mellow them, civilize them,
control them.

What it actually did was to vitiate the whole foundation of the UN Charter. It compelled the organization to
become a conglomorate of hostile political forces. Actually,
there is much which can be said in favor of an international
arena where all nations can have a voice. In fact, if this

were merely a debating society it would be of no particular
threat to anyone. But such a structure takes on a totally
different complexion if massive authority is going to be
turned over to this agency and nations are asked to give
up their right to settle disputes except through this powerful structure. In that case you have not just "a town hall
of the world for international debates" but a huge jugger-
naut of executive and legislative authority which in the
hands of the wrong people, can rob free men of liberty,
justice and the defense of their natural rights. This is
what happened 22 years ago when the functions and philosophy of the United Nations was deliberately shifted
from a union of peace-loving nations to that of a house
divided—an institution where liberty and slavery were
yoked together under one roof and great power was dele-
gated to whichever group could gain control of this institution.

The introduction of compromises necessary to accomo-
date the war-making nations not only involved a contemptuous disregard of Charter provisions but it actually nulli-
fied the whole framework of the UN as a "union of peace-
loving nations." No longer could they function as a union
for peace because they had brought in members who represented disunion and war. In fact, by granting membership to the very nations which were threatening the peace
of the world, it gave them spectacular advantages they
had never had before. It allowed the war-mongering nations to come in and exploit the peace-making machinery
of the UN to their own selfish advantage at that very moment they were subverting and conquering other peoples.
If the student is looking for the key to the frustrations and
failures of the UN during more than two decades of its
existence, this is it.

The UN Performance in the Arab-Israeli Conflict

Nothing better illustrates the complete helplessness of the UN in a time of crisis than the collapse of its peace-keeping role in the Arab-Israeli crisis.

Here was a fantastic situation where a whole cadre of the UN's powerful war-mongering members had openly and blatantly announced that they were going to annihilate one of the UN's tiny, weaker members. In its moment of agony when Israel needed protection from an illegal and immoral cataclysm of destruction, the United Nations not only failed to censure, penalize or prohibit its Charter-violating members from committing this contemplated massacre, but its Secretary General removed whatever UN peace-keeping forces happened to be in the area. And he did it without consulting the Security Council or calling in the General Assembly.

What is worse, at the moment Secretary General U Thant took this rash and impetuous action, he had in his possession information from the sovereign head of an Arab state (King Faisal of Saudi Arabia) that Nasser was using poison gas in Yemen. As mentioned earlier, the International Red Cross had verified this atrocity. Had the Secretary General been functioning on the principles of the Charter instead of trying to accommodate the various war-mongering members of his organization, he could have tipped Nasser back on his heels by the simple expedient of announcing to the world that Egypt would be charged with a crime against humanity—the multiple use of lethal gas as an instrument of war. This would have fractionalized the Arab League, discredited Nasser in the world community and deflated his imperious threat to exterminate Israel. The crisis would have passed.

As it turned out, however, the tiny enclave of Israel

found herself abandoned to destruction. Instead of functioning as a union of peace-loving nations, the members of the UN Security Council pitched about in a continuous cycle of parliamentary convulsions. And the greatest war-maker of them all, the Soviet Union, cast its grotesque shadow over the lot; threatening to use its monolithic veto to sabotage anything constructive the Council might try to do to help Israel. Russia's flagrant violations of all her commitments as a member of the UN was partic-ularly evident after Nasser had used his artillery at the Straits of Tiran to illegally close the Aqaba Gulf. Day after day all attempts to get a cease-fire resolution were subverted by the USSR.

But by Tuesday afternoon, June 6, 1967, everything had changed.

By this time Israel had fought and overwhelmingly won the initial phase of her miracle war. Egypt and Jordan were flat on their backs and Syria soon would be. The Soviet Union was faced with the traumatic calamity of losing from two to three billion dollars in Arabian military investments. In 48 hours Israel had gone from one of the weakest nations in the Mediterranean Middle East to one of the strongest. And Israel was not through. Military experts prognosticated that at the rate things were going it was entirely feasible that within another 48 hours Israeli troops could be in Cairo, Damascus and Amman!

This was enough for Russia. Across the periphery of the watching world she sent out the cry of the wounded bear: "Cease fire! Cease fire!"

Television cameras on prime time showed Federenko of the Soviet Union urgently supporting a cease-fire reso-lution.

The duplicity of the war-mongering Soviets in this whole tragic fiasco was demonstrated by Federenko's refusal to allow the Security Council to be convened for a vote until he was absolutely positive there was no hope.

The chairman of the Security Council had its members standing by and ready for instant call as early as 10:30 A.M. on Tuesday. Federenko would not permit it. Instead, he engaged in a heated debate with the U.S. Ambassador. He claimed he would not support a cease-fire regardless of Russia's commitments under the Charter, unless Israel would agree to withdraw to her original lines. The U.S. held out for a simple cease-fire. For six hours Federenko remained bellicose and defiant. But as the calamitous reports continued to pour in from Soviet consulates all over the Middle East, he finally capitulated. For Federenko and the Moscow master-planners, it was doomsday.

Actually, the cease-fire resolution was nothing in and of itself but a scrap of paper. It had no enforcement machinery behind it whatever. It simply called upon the combatants to stop where they were. Everything depended upon whether or not the Israelis and Arabs would accept it.

Israel was the first to be heard from.

An English-Speaking Hebrew Wins a Top TV Rating

The man the Israelis sent over to speak for them was a total stranger to most Americans. His name was Abba Eban. It was announced that he was the Foreign Minister for the government of Israel. As Americans watched their TVs they found themselves getting acquainted with a man who was to leave a dramatic and lasting impression upon the whole world.

All those who knew Abba Eban realized that he came to the forum of the United Nations with exceptionally high credentials. Members of the Middle East diplomatic community knew that Eban had never counted himself an enemy of the Arabs. He was among the foremost of the Israeli leaders who had consistently advocated a policy of patience and endurance during the provocative guerilla incidents on the Arab-Israeli borders. He had expressed the utmost confidence that eventually the Arab hotheads would come to their senses and cooperate for peace.

As for the masses of the Arab people, Abba Eban expressed a kindred feeling for them. Even before Israel was made a state, Eban became the chief instructor of Arabic culture in Jerusalem. This Jewish institution was called, "The Middle East Center of Arabic Studies," and Eban declared that here was a chance to build bridges between the Arabs and the Jews.

In 1946, he became an official of the Jewish Agency for Palestine and had charge of Arab-Jewish problems in the agency's political department. Eban served as a liaison officer to the UN Special Commission on Palestine and energetically tried to iron out the tensions and complaints which continually arose on both sides.

In 1947-48, when Israel's case needed to be presented at the United Nations, Eban was one of its most eloquent and acceptable special pleaders. He was in a position to present facts which Arab leaders could not refute. Until Israel became an independent nation, Eban served as the UN representative for Ben Gurion's provisional government. After Israel was admitted to the UN in 1949, he became the head of Israel's UN delegation.

In 1950, Abba Eban took an additional assignment of being Israel's ambassador to the United States. He was still a young man, only 35, and the youngest ambassador in Washington.

In 1959, Eban resigned his diplomatic posts in order to seek election to Israel's parliament (the Knesset). He ran as a member of the popular Mapai party and won his post. Premier Levi Eshkol, head of the party, then made him a member of his cabinet. Through the years, one of Eban's foremost boosters and mentors had been Mrs. Golda Meir. When she resigned as Foreign Minister of Israel in January, 1966, Eban was appointed to succeed her. It was in this capacity that he now appeared before the United Nations.

Abba Eban as Seen by Soviet-Arab Leaders

As the Russian and Arab leaders saw Abba Eban take over the Security Council rostrum they must have had some peculiar feelings. In recent years it was this man, along with Levi Eshkol, who had been in closest liaison with Russian and Arab officials. The policy of the Mapai party had been one of conciliation with Russia. Politically, the Eshkol-Eban wing of the Mapai party had been left-leaning and therefore its policies tended to magnetize toward other leftist governments including, to some extent, the Soviets. Except for outright Communists (of which there are comparatively few in Israel), Eshkol and Eban had been the best diplomatic contacts the Soviet-Arab bloc had in Israel.

Furthermore, there are $2\frac{1}{2}$ million Jews in Russia, and Israel looks upon it as the last big population pool from which Israel can gather numbers in the years ahead. Eshkol and Eban had been earnestly seeking permission from the Soviet to allow these Russian Jews to migrate to Palestine. Their pleas, however, only brought insulting rebuffs from the Communist bosses in the Kremlin and a renewed persecution of the Jews in Russia. Still Eshkol and Eban had persisted.

At long last, after the Russian-sponsored Arab hostilities had reached an intolerable point, some members of the Mapai party became disgusted with this soft, crow-eating posture of Eshkol and Eban. Under the leadership of Ben Gurion and Moshe Dayan they broke away and formed a political group of their own called the Rafi party.

(UPI Photo)

Abba Eban, Foreign Minister of Israel, addressing the U.N. Security Council.

Although the Mapai party was able to beat the Rafi's two to one in the 1965 parliamentary elections, the subsequent escalation of tensions between the Israelis and the Russian-armed Arabs rapidly gravitated public support behind Ben Gurion and Dayan. This created such an explosive political pressure that Eshkol and Eban had to bring Dayan into the government as Minister of Defense on June 1, 1967. This was done in order to assure the people that the Mapai leaders were not going to compromise and equivocate so long that Israel would lose her rapidly deteriorating thread-thin chance for survival.

One can well imagine the heated conversations between Abba Eban and his contacts among the Russian-Arab bloc as he warned them not to push Israel so far that the Mapai party could no longer keep its finger in the dike. He had warned them that if Jewish anguish were pressed to the breaking point the flood of Jewish indignation would come like a smothering deluge of defensive destruction. Both the Russians and the Arab leaders had held these warnings in contemptuous disdain—until now.

Now, the very man who had risked his entire political career to try to maintain a bridge of friendship with them had come to say, "I told you so!"

The Arabs and Russians could see that Eban was in no mood to coddle them tonight. He was there to make them squirm. They would not listen before, now they had to listen.

And what of the pontifical United Nations that had abandoned Israel in her hour of terror? He would make them squirm, too. Israel was in no need of a cease-fire. If she conceded to one, it would be an act of outright generosity. Every hour that passed, Israel's victorious troops were adding territory to her conquest. Cairo, Damascus and Amman lay literally naked, defenseless and trembling before her. Why stop now? Before Israel was ready to give her answer on the cease-fire there were some scores to be settled, a number of issues to be reviewed, and some ugly, incriminating facts to be spread across the record.

So Abba Eban began his speech.

Tens of millions watched him on TV or listened by radio as he presented what was to be later hailed as a classic example of superb yet temperate eloquence. No Roman orator ever had such an audience, nor a greater impact. A magazine article later carried the headline: "Israel's Surprise Weapon—Envoy Eban."

Eban Presents the Case for Israel

Eban delivered his talk in excellent Cambridge English and the full text will be found in many magazines and books.

First, he declared that the latest report from the war front clearly showed that Israel had consummated her rendezvous with destiny and a glorious victory was now assured.

Second, he emphasized that the action taken by Israel was something she was compelled to do because of a viciously hostile encirclement by overwhelming forces of destruction which had moved up to Israel's very gates.

Third, Eban said the war became inevitable when Egypt committed a deliberate act of war by forcibly blockading the Aqaba Gulf and leaving Israel economically gasping with only one lung.

Fourth, he said that when Israel's margin of security had been reduced to zero, she struck, but she did everything possible to keep the war from spreading beyond Sinai.

Fifth, he said that the decision of Jordan and Syria to bomb and cannonade Israel came as a great disappointment to the Jewish leaders and made the spreading of the war inescapable.

Sixth, Eban stated that an even greater disappointment had been the conduct of the United Nations. Referring to the hasty removal of the UN peace-keeping troops by U Thant, Eban shot out, "What is the use of a United Nations presence if it is, in effect, an umbrella which is taken away as soon as it begins to rain?" He pointed out that the whole peace-keeping mission of the UN had been opened to question by the serious derelictions of the UN in the current crisis.

Seventh, he expressed the hope that the Arabs would now sit down with the Israelis and work out their mutual problems face to face rather than cat-walk half way around the world to jangle in endless debates at the United Nations. Said Eban, "men and nations do behave wisely once they have exhausted all other alternatives."

Eighth, Abba Eban now came to the crucial point of his talk. He said that Israel welcomed the cease-fire resolution and would heartily support it providing certain conditions were met.

1. The Arabs must recognize Israel as a sovereign political entity. "It would seem to me," he said, "that after 3,000 years ·the time has arrived to accept Israel's nationhood as a fact. Here is the only State in the International community which has the same territory, speaks the same language and upholds the same faith as it did 3,000 years ago."

2. The Arabs must agree that all existing or future problems will be solved by peaceful means and not by constantly resorting to big or little wars. He said the combatants in this war must solve their problems by "direct contacts. They must find their way to each other. After all, when there is conflict between them they come together face to face. Why should they not come together face to face to solve the conflict?"

Ninth, Abba Eban said Israel does not want the "big powers" supporting one country against another as they have in the past. Israel would like to see them pledge to supporting principles which will be good for all nations: ". . . not to be for one State against other States, but to be for peace, against war; for free commerce, against belligerency; for the pacific settlement of disputes, against violent irredentist threats; in other words, to exercise an even-handed support for the integrity and independence of States and for the rights of States under the Charter of the United Nations and other sources of international law."

Tenth, Eban closed by sweeping away the wild slanders of the Soviet representative, Federenko, who had spoken just a short time before. Eban said: "But surely world opinion, before whose tribunal this debate unrolls, can solve this question [of who caused this war] by posing certain problems to itself. Who was it that attempted to destroy a neighboring state in 1948, Israel or its neighbors? Who now closes an international waterway to the port of a neighboring State, Israel or the United Arab Republic? Does Israel refuse to negotiate a peace settlement with the Arab States, or do they refuse to do so with it? Who disrupted the 1957 pattern of stability, Israel or Egypt? Did troops of Egypt, Syria, Jordan, Iraq, Lebanon, Kuwait and Algeria surround Israel in this menacing confrontation, or has any distinguished representative seen some vast Israeli colossus surrounding the area between Morocco and Kuwait?"

Having made his point, Eban closed his speech on a philosophical note. Said he, "Israel in recent days has proved its steadfastness and vigor. It is now willing to demonstrate its instinct for peace. Let us build a new system of relationships from the wreckage of the old. Let us discern across the darkness the vision of a better and brighter dawn."

The Arab Leaders Take
a Defiant Stand

Now the world waited to hear what the Arab leaders would say. Syria came first. Her spokesman was George J. Tomeh. To the amazement of all who were watching, Tomeh completely evaded the issue of the cease-fire resolution. Instead, his talk was the well-grooved assortment of bitter denunciations against Israel. The psychological atmosphere in the Security Council had cooled during Eban's speech, but now it began heating up again. It reached the scorching stage when Tomeh decided to close by heaping vituperative abuse on the United States and England for throwing their forces into the war on Israeli's side.

This was more than Arthur J. Goldberg the U.S. Ambassador, could stand. Taking to the microphone he collectively rebuked the Arabs for concocting such a slanderous fabrication and then challenged the Security Council to take an inspection tour of the Sixth Fleet where they could see for themselves that neither ships nor planes belonging to the U.S. were involved. He called for the Arab leaders to bring proof of their charges.

"Put up or shut up," he angrily told Tomeh.

The Arabs continued to give speeches and debate but not one of them was willing to concede support of the cease-fire resolution. Iraq's Foreign Minister, Pachachi, made reference to the resolution but called it, "a surrender to Israel." That's the way the Security Council session ended Tuesday night. Israel had offered to accept the cease-fire if the Arabs met her requested guarantees, but the Arab nations were declining the offer. The war would go on.

Just to make certain that no one would have any doubts as to the way Nasser and his associates felt toward the Americans, Egypt announced that she was breaking off diplomatic relations with the United States. All Americans were ordered out of Egypt. All Arabian oil going to the United States was ordered cut off. Britain was also struck from further diplomatic relations with Egypt and placed under an Arabian oil embargo. Then to show his indignation and independence toward the rest of the western world, Nasser summarily banned all international shipping through his domain. He closed down the Suez Canal.

But by the time the UN Security Council debates had terminated in New York, dawn was creeping over the Middle East. The third day of the war was about to commence.

Wednesday, June 7, the Third Day of the War

As the early streaks of morning light turned the desert skies of the eastern Mediterranean into indigo blue, there was a quickening of heartbeats all along the Arab-Israeli war fronts. Sleepless Arab regulars tried to shake off their weariness as they prepared for a last-ditch stand. Israeli reservists who only a few days before had been working in stores, factories and at farm chores, fingered their automatic weapons nervously, knowing this was the "big day."

It was at Jerusalem where the focus of Israeli aspirations rode on a tide of explosive emotional anticipation. Perhaps it would be difficult for most goyim (gentiles) to understand the feelings of the Jews at this moment. It was the feeling which had surged through the Crusaders in 1099 A.D. when they captured this city from the Moslems. It was the rapture which General E. H. Allenby and his British troops felt in 1917 when they captured this city from the Turks. Now the Jews had their chance. For them this was a highly poignant moment.

It will be recalled that the Israelis had been driven from the holy city during the Palestine war in 1948 when the Arabs had evicted them with heavy casualties. Previously, the United Nations had proclaimed Jerusalem an "international city" where all nations and faiths would have representation and free access, but the Palestine Arabs had said, "Death to the Jews!" and driven them out. For 19 years Jordan Arabs had assumed exclusive political occupation of the city.

During the war the old Jewish quarter in Jerusalem was bombed and burned, but later most of it was rebuilt and occupied by the Arabs. By 1967 only here and there could any fragments of the old Jewish community be found.

It was one of the strange coincidences of history that in 1967 the three Israelis who were in charge of Jerusalem's recapture had been officers over the Jewish forces in 1948 when the city was lost. Back in 1948, Mordecai Gur had fought as a company commander under Brigade Commander Itzhak Rabin. By 1967, Mordecai Gur was a Brigade Commander himself and Rabin had moved up to commander in chief of all Israeli forces. In between them was a sector commander, Uzi Narkiss, who, like both Gur and Rabin, had been born in Jerusalem and had fought for the defense of the city in 1948. These three now combined their ingenuity to regain possession of their native city.

Severe handicaps were voluntarily assumed by the Israeli commanders as they plotted their attack. They decided to throw their paratroops into the Old City without either air protection or tank fire. This was so that none of the holy places belonging to Jews, Christians or Moslems would be damaged. This decision, while later applauded by the leaders of many faiths, cost the Israelis heavily in their number of dead and wounded. But even the troops agreed that this was the only way to do it.

The Capture of Old Jerusalem

The most dangerous Arab artillery outpost left in Jerusalem by Wednesday morning was on Mount Scopus near
Jordan's August Victoria Hospital. To destroy this Arab
entrenchment without damaging the hospital, Israeli
fighter planes dropped cannisters of napalm on the pre-
fabricated barracks and then Israeli infantry crept along
behind tanks to take the hill. Observers noted the "drill
school" tactics of the Israeli forces as their assignment
was executed. First came the tanks with the infantry in
clusters behind mortars. They formed a diamond pattern
on the hill. Gradually, they pushed forward each of their
positions until finally, when they were almost at the top,
they formed into a straight line and with a great shout
made their charge.

The collapse of this last Jordanian artillery outpost
was the signal for the troops in Jerusalem to begin their
siege of the Old City.

The attack was two-pronged. Tuesday evening tanks
had been used to protect paratroopers as they took up a
position by the Dung Gate on the southern wall of the Old
City. Tanks had also been used to get Israeli paratroopers
over to St. Stephen's gate on the east wall. It was obvious
what the Israelis were trying to do. These two prongs were
projected from the closest possible entrances to the great
32-acre temple square. If the attack were successful they
would converge not far from the famous Dome of the Rock
mosque which covers the traditional site of Solomon's
Temple. It is immediately adjacent to the famous
"wailing wall" which the Jews treat as a sacred shrine
because it formed part of the original wall of ancient
times.

The feelings of the Israeli paratroopers waiting for
their orders to attack may be best appreciated if it is
realized that each year during Passover, Jews around the

world had ended their prayers with the exclamation, "Next year in Jerusalem!" For centuries they had been saying it. Altogether, it had been nearly 1900 years since the Jews had been deprived of possession of their sacred temple block in Jerusalem and it had been 19 years since they were deprived of access to the wailing wall. That is how important this moment was in the lives of these Israeli troops.

When the order was given to attack, the rapid sequence of events was carefully chronicled by Sanche de Gramont in his dramatic "Battle for Jerusalem." He writes:

"As the last Jordanian high point collapsed (on Mount Scopus), paratroopers attacked the old city through St. Stephen's Gate, in the eastern wall, and the Dung Gate in the southern. They were joined by four militia rifle companies recruited in Jerusalem. The Via Dolorosa, the route Christ followed with the cross, goes through St. Stephen's Gate and continues uphill, past the station of the Flagellation and the Ecce Homo station, and this was one of the routes the Israelis now followed into the old city. Directly across from the Ecce Homo station, which is a convent today, the Jordanians were entrenched inside an elementary school. There were also Jordanian snipers atop a minaret across from the 12th century Crusader Church of St. Anne, built over the pool where Christ cured the paralytic. Israeli jets circled above it but held their fire, as did the tanks.

"The paratroopers, deprived of air support, suffered heavy losses. They were combat-weary and nervous as they rushed through St. Stephen's Gate. One fired a burst at something that moved on the right. It was a seminarian opening the door of St. Anne's, just inside the gate. He was shot in the foot. Half the paratroopers proceeded up the Via Dolorosa to mop up the Jordanians in the school. The rest cut left to join those who had come in through the Dung Gate on the broad esplanade of the

Mosque of Omar [Dome of the Rock]. By this time small groups of civilians were starting to surface, approaching the Israelis in the stealthy, hesitant manner of an alley cat suddenly face to face with a large and growling dog. White flags began to appear at windows.

"Jim Neal, the young Texan in the Al Arab Hotel near the Damascus Gate, was in the hotel lobby on Wednesday morning when the owner, who had been so confident of victory, came in weeping. 'All Arab kings are bad,' he said. He removed portraits of Hussein and Nasser that hung behind the reception desk and tore them up. 'It was so quiet,' Neal says, 'that I didn't realize the Israelis had moved in until I saw them below my window. The Arabs wanted me to stay in the hotel and protect them. 'We know what we would do to the Israelis, and we don't want them to do the same to us,' they said.'"

Israeli Troops Knew They Were Fulfilling Prophecy

"Organized resistance collapsed swiftly in the old city, but snipers remained a danger for days. . . . Besides snipers, there was the peril of simple emotion itself. 'My men were walking about the old city as in a dream,' a platoon leader says. 'Tears rolled down their faces. They did not even bother to take cover. They had realized the two-thousand-year-old prophecy of recovering Jerusalem.'

"The emotional rush to the Wailing Wall was an example of this peril. Every Israeli knows what 'Article Eight' is. It is the paragraph in the 1948 armistice agreement that guarantees them access to the Wailing Wall. The 19-year violation of Article Eight has rankled perhaps more than any other single Arab harassment. Many of the soldiers who stormed the old city were infants in 1948 and had never seen the wall. When they

(UPI Photo)

Victorious Israeli troops chant prayers of thanksgiving at the famous Wailing Wall of the Jews—said to be the only remnant of the Second Temple not destroyed by the Romans in 70 A.D.

broke into a run crossing the Mosque of Omar esplanade
and scurried down an exposed flight of narrow steps—
which soon became a prime target for Jordanian snipers—
they were reactng to some deep archetypal stimulus.
They touched the wall and sobbed, as their ancestors had,
when victory should have made them exult. . . .

"The mournful bleating of the shofar sounded. Un-
shaven, red-eyed soldiers, their combat uniforms stained
with sweat and blood, donned their skullcaps, opened
small leather-bound prayer books and rocked back and
forth as they chanted: 'Thank the Lord, for the Lord has
been kind.' Beyond the wall heavy firing could still be
heard."[13]

Five minutes after the Wailing Wall had been reached
by the Israelis, the Arab governor of Jerusalem appeared
with a Moslem priest or Kadi and certain other top
officials of the city to assure the Israelis there would be
no more shooting. Some soldiers placed a wooden box
at the foot of the Wailing Wall containing the scrolls
of the Bible. Others went up and down the nearby streets
with loudspeakers saying to the people in Arabic, "Please
obey orders. You will not be harmed. Stay in your
homes. Lay your arms on your doorsteps."

Shortly after the walled area was secured, Israeli Prime
Minister Eshkol arrived wih General Dayan. They were
jubilant. They joined with the soldiers in the
first formal service at the Wailing Wall which was conducted by Rabbi Shlomo Goren, senior chaplain for the
Israeli armed forces.

"We have taken the City of God," intoned the grey-
haired, uniformed Rabbi. "WE ARE ENTERING THE
MESSIANIC ERA FOR THE JEWISH PEOPLE. And I
promise to the Christian world that we are responsible
for, we will take care of, the holy places of all religions

---

13. Sanche de Gramont, "Battle for Jerusalem," *Saturday Evening Post*, August 12,
    1967, p. 75.

here. For all people, I promise them, we will take care."[14]

The scattered remnants of the few Jewish residents who had clung to such a fragile existence in Jordan-Jerusalem since 1948, now dared to come forth with food and drink to refresh the Israeli troops. Some of them were highly orthodox Jews with curls at their temples who had always looked upon Israeli Jews as political Zionists rather than spiritual Jews and therefore an affront to the Jewish religion. But unexpectedly things were different. No matter how irreligious the majority of the Israelis may have seemed from an orthodox point of view, the fact remained that here they were doing something the spiritual, orthodox Jews had not done. The Israelis were fulfilling prophecy!

Flight of the Arabs

The suddenness of the Israeli victory in Jerusalem left the Jordanian Arabs benumbed. For two days and nights they had heard the Cairo radio proclaiming that Israel had been cut in two at its narrow waist, that Tel Aviv had been bombed into a smoldering ashheap, that the Arabs were winning on all fronts. Now they looked about them to see Israeli tanks, Israeli planes and Israeli soldiers. And it was terrifyingly obvious that except for occasional sniper-fire, all Arab resistance had been silenced.

A Jordanian judge had taken his wife and family into a barricaded apartment to sit out the war. When he heard his radio announce that it was practically over and Israel had won he almost went hysterical. "But we were winning," he said. "It was supposed to end before reaching Jerusalem."[15]

---

14. Robert J. Donovan, *Israel's Fight for Survival*, p. 120.
15. Sanche de Gramont, "Battle for Jerusalem," *Saturday Evening Post*, August 12, 1967, p. 75.

The judge was not alone in his feelings. As it gradually dawned on the consciousness of the Palestinian Arabs
that their contemplated victory had been turned into a
rout, there was a wild, frenzied scramble by tens of
thousands to escape the avenging angels of Judah. Nineteen
years of inflammatory propaganda had created a monstrous
image of the Jews. The news of an Israeli breakthrough
was enough to send them into a screaming panic as they
rushed toward the Jordan River in an attempt to flee
from the expected reign of Israeli terror.

The moving tide of escaping civilians was further
swollen by additional thousands from the refugee camps
which were located in Jordan Valley. All these began
pouring pell mell across the Jordan River into the virtual
wastelands of eastern Jordan.

Some of the fleeing civilians from villages lying on the
borders of Israel said they had been driven from their
homes and that their villages had been demolished by
advancing Jewish troops. In certain cases, this was true.
There were villages like Qualquilya, for example, which
had harbored sabotage and guerilla units that had preyed
upon Jewish farmers and workers for nearly two decades.
Israeli forces did to these villages what the Arabs had
threatened to do to the whole Israeli nation—obliterated
them. This was not done, however, until the inhabitants
had been allowed time to evacuate—a gesture of mercy
the Arab Legion had not expected to concede to the
Jews.

Fleeing Arabs Expose Their Inner Conscience

There is no doubt but what a number of these Arab
villages on the border of Israel had reason to believe
that there would be vengeful reprisal from the Jewish
armies. Instances of provocation which they had heaped

on the heads of the Jews through the years were witnessed by the well-known author, James A. Michener, while he was in Israel doing research for *The Source*. Actually, Michener had no particular love for the Jews. He wrote:

"I must point out at the beginning that I hold no special brief for either the Israelis or Jews in general. I have lived too long among them to retain any starry-eyed visions. They are ordinary people marred by ordinary weaknesses and bolstered by the courage that ordinary men of all nations and races can at times draw upon. I worked among Muslims [Arab Moslems] for ten years before I ever set foot in Israel, and on at least fifty percent of the characteristics by which men and societies are judged, I like Muslims at least as well as I like the Jews."[16]

As a professional researcher, however, Michener was shocked by the completely irresponsible and virulent hate which continually manifest itself in the feelings of the Arab leaders toward the Jews. At first he tried to shrug it off as merely "politics" but then he finally decided they really meant it.

"Especially appalling to me," he wrote, "were five different times when some Arab head of state announced that he was going to blow up the city in which I sat working. I took even those threats without panic, for I have seen a good deal of war and bombing and do not frighten easily, but I must admit that when the Arab leaders narrowed down their target to the hotel in which I was sitting, and when on two occasions they gave a specific timetable for dispatching their rockets, I felt shivers run up my spine. I lived for more than a year under these constant threats."[17]

But the Jews were getting more than mere threats. "Israel's apprehension," Michener continues, "was not a

16. James A. Michener, "Israel, A Nation Too Young to Die," *Look*, August 8, 1967,
    p. 65.
17. *Ibid.*, pp. 64-65.

paper one. In addition to threats, there were constant incursions into Israel, constant shootings across the borders, constant intrusion by groups as large as squadrons or small companies. If I went to do some research on the old synagogue at Korazam, I was somewhat taken aback to find that one day later, a pitched battle had been fought there and two Israeli civilians had been killed. If I went on a picnic to the Sea of Galilee, I was a bit shaken when two days later, there was a bombardment of Israeli boats. If I visited the kibbutz at Dan and waded upstream to the cool spring that forms one of the headwaters of the River Jordan, I was frightened to learn that, shortly before, a man had been lost doing that. And when I moved to Jerusalem [the Israeli's "new" Jerusalem] to work in the libraries there, I was sorrowful when children told me I must not walk down this ally by the Persian synagogue; gunfire had been coming in from the rooftops [on the Jordan side] only 50 feet away."[18]

This had been the situation all along the border from north to south. Speaking of the Syria-Israeli border, Michener wrote, "From the high hills that Syria occupied to the east, gun positions pumped in random shots at workers on the Israeli farms. From protected emplacements along the shore of the Sea of Galilee, Syrian guns fired point-blank at Israeli fishermen. And night after night, marauding parties crept over the border to mine, to murder, to destroy."[19]

Through the years the Jews had stormed across the border every so often to try to teach the Arabs a lesson, but the attacks had continued. Finally, as we mentioned earlier, the United Nations had recorded over 100,000 separate border incidents. If the UN observers could not keep the peace, they at least kept a tabulation of the events which eventually led to war.

18. *Ibid.*, p. 65.
19. *Ibid.*, p. 67.

All of this will help the reader appreciate the feelings of the Arabs in that fateful week of June, 1967, when they saw their own armies collapsing and the Jews breaking through upon them like a floodtide. Their hysteria as they raced toward the Jordan River was contagious and other thousands from the hinterland joined them. The Jordanian government at Amman estimated that during the six-day war nearly 200,000 Palestine Arabs were believed to have swarmed across to the eastern side. For a poverty-stricken nation like Jordan this amounted to a compounded calamity, and massive human suffering was predicted. However, as the war slowed to a conclusion a few days later, the Israeli government announced that Palestine Arabs wishing to do so could return to their homes.

Major Raanan Lurie's Story

By Wednesday mid-morning it was obvious to Israeli leaders that Jordan was beaten and would no doubt call for a cease-fire at any moment. Four key positions needed to be firmly fixed under Israeli military control if Israel was to avoid arbitrary and unnatural boundaries similar to those which had exposed her villages and valleys to attacks in the past. Three of these were on the verge of capitulation—Jericho in the Jordan River region, Bethlehem on the heights just south of Jerusalem, and Hebron on the heights of Judah, further south. This left Nablus, second largest city in Jordanian Palestine, unaccounted for. At this point Nablus was not even being approached by any Israeli forces. The man who was assigned to take it was Major Raanan Lurie.

Lurie was a professional portrait painter who was caught by the war at Expo 67 in Montreal, Canada—some 6,000 miles from home. Leaving his family in Montreal Lurie flew home and landed at Lydda airport on May 29th.

A jeep met him there containing everything he needed for combat readiness—uniform, gun, everything. Three hours after he landed he was in the trenches facing the Jordan border at the most critical front Israel had to defend—the Israeli waistline just above Tel Aviv where the distance between Jordan and the Mediterranean is only ten miles wide.

Lurie had spent six years training his infantry company of reservists. They were a combination of ex-paratroopers and young students. Some of them were neighbors from his home town of Herzliya. This company along with several others received what could have been a suicide assignment. Major Lurie was told to dig his men in and hold the position against the Jordan and Iraqi armies no matter what the cost. Furthermore, he was told that all Israeli armament resources would be concentrated in the south so he could expect no help.

During the few days before the war broke out, Lurie had his men digging like gophers. He knew what Russian mortars could do to his men. He dug them in the ground so deep his men began to complain but he bullied them until they had completed the job.

Early Monday morning, June 5, Lurie watched Jordan trucks hurriedly gathering up all the peasants from the fields. That was a bad sign. Fifteen minutes later the heavy shelling began. The Arabs were using 81-mm and 120-mm mortars and howitzers. Israeli artillery responded immediately and soon the air was whistling with flying iron going both ways. Lurie's men were now grateful to their leatherneck Major who had forced them deep into the ground. Not a man was lost.

Lurie had one worry, however, his men didn't know about. Poison gas. He was not allowed to tell his men, but he had been told in a special briefing just before the war started that the Arab leaders possessed poison gas and were expected to use it. He was also told that Israel had no equipment to protect the men from the gas. Therefore certain commanding officers such as Lurie were told to get out in the open with walkie-talkies where they could see the Arab shells drop. If the shells began to spout visible fumes the observing officer was to advise head-quarters so that companies in other areas could be moved out and saved.

Russians Discovered Directing Arab Artillery

Major Lurie learned from his signal corps that Arab artillery was being directed in a language which was not Arabic. It was soon discovered to be Russian. Major Lurie wrote:

"By radio we could detect Russian voices directing the Arab artillery. The first Russian voice was that of a woman, and when I heard it I assigned a Russian-speaking soldier to the radio unit to intercept and translate the Russian commands. We believed that the Russians directing the fire were with the Iraqi brigade facing us."[20]

So far as is known these were the only Russians who allowed themselves to get directly involved or exposed. None were detected in the Sinai theater. However, in the Korean war it was several years before investigators discovered and finally proved the fact that Russian generals and officers had commanded the entire North Korean campaign.

A top Communist intelligence officer, Pawel Monat, defected to the West and described the whole operation in which he played an important part.[21] He revealed that the North Korean invasion in June, 1950, was master-

---

20. Major Raanan Lurie, "With a Troop Commander on the Point," *Israel's Swift Victory*, special edition of *Life*, June, 1967, p. 64.
21. See Pawel Monat, "Russians in Korea: the Hidden Bosses," *Life*, June, 1960, pp. 76-102.

minded by Russian General Alexei Antonov in Moscow and
directed in the field by General Terenty F. Shtykov who
went to North Korea disguised as Russia's "Ambassador."

The war was run by several thousand Russians—military
officers, MIG pilots, engineers, technicians. He stated that
on one raid by U.S. planes, 60 Russians were killed. They
were immediately buried to avoid detection. In fact he
describes how great pains were taken to keep the West
from discovering who was running the war: "Most of
the Russians were outfitted in Chinese 'volunteer' uniforms.
To avoid capture, they stayed as far back from the front
as possible. Even when the fighting was stabilized, they
seldom ventured farther forward than a corps command
post, some 20 miles behind the lines. North Korean units
with Russians attached to them had top priority orders
to evacuate the Russians to safer rear areas immediately
in the event of a U.N. breakthrough."[22]

The West was led to believe that the genius of the
war was the North Korean Premier, Kim Il Sung, but
Monat states: "The Premier of North Korea, Kim Il Sung,
also lived and worked under Soviet direction at the high
command headquarters. As a wartime leader, Kim was
hardly a standout. He was fat and rather dull, but since
he was under complete control of the Russians, he did
not need much personality. Kim was never allowed to
make a decision or a public announcement without the
Soviet ambassador's express permission. All North Korean
military orders were drafted in Russian and had to be
initialed by a Russian officer to become effective."[23]

Many of these Russian orders were captured at Seoul.
thereby corroborating Monat's disclosures.

The most significant element of this plot, and the part
which applies to current problems, is the fact that right
while Russia was running the Korean war she was pumping

22. *Ibid.*, p. 76.
23. *Ibid.*, p. 77.

promises to western diplomats that she would use Soviet influence to try to persuade the North Korean leaders to use prudence, keep the war within bounds, etc. and etc. Precisely as Americans were being told late in May, 1967, that Russia would do everything possible to keep Nasser from taking direct military action against Israel. U.S. diplomats relied on these pretensions and put tremendous pressure on Israel to keep her from responding defensively, even after Egypt had commenced using artillery fire to close the Aqaba gulf. Tragically, western diplomats, particularly those of U.S. and Britain, have fallen for this pretended cooperation for several decades. It became the basis for the U.S. "no win" policy in Viet Nam just as it became the basis for the U.S. "no win" policy in Korea. Diplomats led themselves into thinking that they were somehow bargaining with the Russians eye-ball to eye-ball.

Fortunately, Israel saw through this whole tissue of fraudulant pretensions and conducted herself accordingly. In the process, Jewish officers like Major Lurie uncovered the bloody paw of the bear performing its ugly work in the Arab-Israeli conflict exactly the way it did in Korea.

Major Lurie Is Commanded to Push Toward Nablus

It was Wednesday morning on the third day of the war that Major Lurie was called to sector headquarters and told to head for Nablus. He formed his own company into a spearhead with the supporting infantry following in the rear. Actually, it wasn't much of a spearhead but it got the job done. It consisted of two jeeps carrying Major Lurie and four men with machine guns plus two ancient (but refurbished) American tanks which rumbled along behind. They took the first two villages of Tulkarm and Dannaba with surprisingly little resistance, then charged up into the high hills of Samaria toward Nablus.

Nablus is located in the saddle between Mount Ebal on the north and Mount Gerizim to the south. The ancient city of this place was called Sheckem in the Bible. Here the Patriarch Jacob purchased a plot of land and dug a well for his flocks. In New Testament times it was visited by Jesus on the notable occasion when he conversed with the woman of Samaria. This is where Jacob's only daughter was kidnapped and ravished. Here is where his sons avenged her disgrace by destroying every male in the village. It was not far from here that Joseph was kidnapped at Dothan and sold into slavery. When the Israelites came up out of Egypt they brought Joseph's bones with them and buried them in this place. Joshua brought all of the armies of Israel to this spot to bid them farewell after their long battles for the liberation of Palestine. Later Shechem became the capital city of the Northern ten tribes and it was here that both Elijah and Elisha carried out their ministries. In Roman times the Emperor Vespasian changed the name to Neapolis but the sound became corrupted so for many centuries it has been called Nablus. It was here that the Jordanians built their national university and set up their center of intellectual life. Now it was about to change hands again.

However, as Major Lurie was proceeding toward his goal he received an urgent command from sector headquarters to detour from his capture of Nablus in order to occupy a road junction at Ramin, some ten miles distance. "I don't care how you reach this place," the commander said, "but you have to get there. As long as I get one Israeli solder there it's okay. But we have to be there."[24]

---

24. *Israel's Swift Victory*, special edition of *Life*, June, 1967, p. 64.

A Cease-Fire Comes to the Jordanian Front

This was a clear signal that Jordan was about to accept Israel's previous invitation to a cease-fire. Jewish leaders felt that Israel's occupation of certain key spots prior to the cease-fire was vital to Israel's future peace. Major Lurie did not know it, but the UN Security Council had already passed a resolution demanding that the combatants stop shooting that afternoon by 4 P.M., New York time.

Of course Jordan had been beaten so badly that her guns were already reduced to virtual silence but the Israeli leaders wanted to be in a position of occupational strength before the deadline so they could safely announce a formal cease-fire and invite Jordan to do the same. This is why Major Lurie had been directed to take Ramin while a much stronger force was brought down from the north to take Nablus.

This undoubtedly saved Lurie's life. Thirty powerful Jordanian tanks were sitting outside Nablus just waiting for the first contingent of Israeli troops. But instead of Major Lurie arriving on the scene with his two little jeeps and his two outdated tanks, the Israeli air force arrived. The sudden strike from the sky wiped out the entire Nablus tank brigade and left the city completely open to occupation. As Israeli tanks moved in immediately from their base to the north, they found the people turning out into the streets to joyously welcome them. The Arabs thought these were Iraqi tanks which had come to rescue them. Such are the incongruities of war.

When the people realized what was really happening they quickly disappeared from the streets and the city became very quiet.

About this same time a sector commander in charge of the battle of Bethlehem advised central headquarters that the city of Christ's nativity was back in Jewish hands.

Equally good news came from the Gulf of Aqaba. Since the Egyptians had used force to close this Gulf and it was the principal cause of the war, the Israelis expected stiff resistance. A simultaneous assault by land, sea and air was scheduled for Wednesday. Commando units reached the target first and discovered to their amazement that the Egyptian base was completely deserted. The Arabs had fled north into the desert. The paratroopers arrived about this time and were ready to drop when they were advised that this part of the war was already over. Sharm El Sheikh was soon in the hands of Israeli commandos and the Gulf of Aqaba was once more restored to its status as an international seaway for the ships of all nations.

It was just seventeen minutes before 5 P.M. and forty seven minutes after the deadline, that Abba Eban advised the UN Security Council that all was quiet on the Jordan front. All Israeli guns had been silenced. King Hussein later accused the Jews of prolonging the war for several hours after the Jordanians were ready for a truce. This may have been true. In any event, the Jewish attitude was that since the Jordanians had initiated the attack on Jerusalem and refused a cease-fire offer of the day before, it was now the prerogative of the Jews to terminate hostilities at a time and place most conducive to their own advantage. That moment had arrived. As between Jordan and Israel this war was over. And for 15,000 Jordanians their *Jehad* or Holy War was over. They were dead.

Almost immediately bulldozers moved into the old Jewish section not far from the wailing wall and commenced to clear the area of the ramshackled stone houses which the Arabs had hastily constructed from the rubble after the Jews were bombed and burned out in 1948.

One-eyed General Dayan announced that Jerusalem would never be relinquished by the Jews again. It was placed under a unified administrative authority and soon both "new" Jerusalem and the Old City were functioning as a single metropolis. As far as the Jews were concerned, it would never be divided again.

Egypt's Debacle on the Desert

Wednesday was the day of total terror for Egypt's armor brigades fighting frantically to escape across the upper half of Sinai's blistering desert. Temperatures hit 120 degrees. No longer were the Egyptian tanks and heavy mobile artillery fighting coordinated, organized battles. Every brigade commander was an island unto himself. Egyptian communications were so completely disrupted that officers in the field tuned in on Nasser's Cairo radio hoping to get some idea of what was going on. The billowing waves of propaganda pouring from it were of no help whatever.

Commanders heard their own situation being described with such complete distortion and inaccuracy that they knew they could never trust Cairo's reports about other fronts. In disgust they turned back to the task of blindly fighting their way westward toward their only remaining refuge—the Suez Canal.

The race for the Suez was one of maddening frustration. Nothing had been done to prepare the Egyptians for massive retreat. And even if there had been preparations, the unorthodox tactics of the Israelis would have made them obsolete. Instead of attacking head on, the Israelis operated their armament like a fleet at sea. They came in on their enemy from all sides. A glimpse into the all-out, no-holds-barred punches which the Israelis delivered to Egypt's Russian-built brigades may be gained from the following statement of a Jewish Brigadier-General:

"We operated many troops together—armor, paratroops, infantry, artillery, engineers. At this particular point the

(UPI Photo)

Israeli troops survey compound where Egyptian captives are searched and stripped only hours after Egyptian leaders had promised that their forces would annihilate Israel.

enemy had an infantry brigade and about 90 tanks, with 6 regiments of artillery. We opened the attack with para-troops who fell upon the Egyptian artillery from the rear. Then our infantry made a frontal assault, while tanks penetrated the enemy line to the north and attacked from the rear. With our tanks behind them and our armored troops now hitting them from the front, the enemy was trapped. The fighting began in the evening at 10:30 and continued until six the next morning."[25]

General Israel Tal was in charge of all this. His assign-ment was "tanks and armor." He is described as "a wiry little Galilean with the oblong face of a cocky Mediter-ranean beach-comber: quizzical mouth, cynical brown eyes, and a disrespect for authority. He was, all the same, commanding armor. Like other field commanders, he led his men. 'There is no order in this army like *forward* he said. 'Officers say only *follow me.*' In cold print that sounds like bravado but Brigadier-General Tal was not a boastful man. On foot he moved with the peculiar heel-and-toe stride of a desert commando, and when he talked he rested his hands on hips and stared at his questioner with a face innocent of expression and eyes that never flickered. He was 43 when he got command of the division that was to smash through the fortified lines of the Egyptian First Divison. . . ."[26]

For him, the real test had come on Monday and Tues-day when his armament brigades had to break through the concrete bunkers and 2 to 1 ratio of Egyptian tanks and cannons massed along the Gaza Strip district. Once the Egyptian "Maginot Line" was punctured and smashed he knew his tanks could "get their tail up" and, like fleet desert stallions, churn the burning sands as they charged toward the Suez. By Wednesday this was hap-pening.

25. William Stevenson, *Strike Zion!* New York: Bantam Books, 1967, p. 67.
26. *Ibid.*, p. 58.

General Tal hit so hard and moved so fast that another Jewish commander, General Yoffee, was afraid of being over-run. He said, "My division, an armored mobile division, had to penetrate through very difficult terrain which everyone will tell you is impossible, and to come to the rear of the enemy and try to do two things: stop reinforcements going in to the main defense, and try to catch anybody running away." He succeeded in his assignment by spearheading recklessly across a trackless sea of sand dunes which stretched for miles across Sinai. In taking up his position he suddenly realized the danger of being mistaken for the enemy as General Tal's tanks came rumbling into the heart of Sinai shooting everything in sight. Yoffee continues, "I can tell you it was a very dramatic moment standing there with the force, trying to coordinate so Tal in his momentum would not collide with my armor."[27]

Tal, like General Patton in World War II, used his tanks and mobile artillery for fast, hard-hitting thrusts on a broad, multi-pronged front. Tal used three prongs. One went along the coast following the Sinai railroad and the ancient thoroughfare from Egypt to Palestine which was undoubtedly used by Mary and Joseph as they fled with Jesus. A second prong was launched on a parallel line further south. It passed through Abu Aweigila and pushed westward across the caravan route that used to lead from Beer Sheba to Egypt. The third prong, even further south, had the critical task of cutting off the escape route of the Egyptians through Mitla Pass. There is a range of bleak desert mountains a few miles east of the Suez with only three passes to the lower plain which extends along the Canal. The Israeli armor used strenuous night maneuvers to over-run the bulk of the Egyptian forces and seal off these passes. This bottled up the main Egyptian task force on the desert. As Tal explained later, "Our main purpose was to destroy the enemy's

---

27. *Ibid.*, p. 47.

divisions and not to occupy as much territory as possible."28

Once these passes were occupied the Egyptians sent out heavy relief brigades from Suez to break the wedge of Jewish tanks and guns, but the Israelis held. This allowed the Israeli airforce to promptly move in with rockets and napalm to decimate the bottled-up Egyptian forces on the desert.

The destruction was selective. Since the Israelis were anxious to capture as much equipment as possible for their own use, they first bombed gasoline trucks. With no fuel supply, the lumbering iron giants soon came to a standstill. However, Egyptian tanks actually engaged in battle with Israeli contingents and were pounded to pieces. Where Nasser's tank columns were pushing west trying to escape, the Israeli pilots would bomb two or three lead tanks. In most cases the crews in the remaining tanks would assume this was about to be their own fate, so up would go their hatches and out they would climb to flee across the desert on foot. In this manner several hundred Egyptian tanks and thousands of their mobile units were captured and added to the more antiquated and patched-up armament of Israel. Every Israeli unit carried white paint to emblazon the Star of David on captured Egyptian equipment.

The Closing Hours of Wednesday

During the day the helpless position of the Arab League on all fronts had reached such a hopeless stage that Nasser realized the Arab world must be prepared for the terrible news which could not be held back much longer. Most of Wednesday the government radio stations in Cairo, Jordan-Jerusalem and Damascus had been describing glorious

---

28. *Ibid.*, p. 58.

victories. As late as 12:15 P.M. Wednesday the screeching
plea from the Jordan station had been, "Kill the Jews
wherever you find them. Kill them with your arms, with
your hands, with your nails and teeth."[29] But by Wednesday evening Cairo radio was beginning to talk
continually about a sweeping avalanche of destruction
being poured in on the Egyptian forces by the Americans
and British. This myth had been wind-tested the day
before in the United Nations and pricked like a bubble,
but, no matter, Nasser would now sell it to his own people
as a historical fact.

By Wednesday night, King Hussein of Jordan was bitter.
Not only had his valiant Arab Legion been cut to ribbons
while fighting under Egyptian generals, but Nasser's
leadership had proven to be as much of a buffoonery in
1967 as it was in 1956. The 32-year-old Hussein said the
next day, "I have been continually awake for three days.
Do not be misled by my appearance to suppose there is
any other reason for the way I look [unshaven, etc.] . . . .
After my meeting with Nasser I thought we would be now
ready for the battle of liberation . . . I was again let
down."[30]

Hussein wanted the people to know that the disgrace
of being forced into a cease-fire late Wednesday was the
direct result of the failure of Egypt to provide promised
support. Perhaps he did not know that this was the
history of Egypt long before Nasser became its modern
Pharaoh. Twenty-six centuries earlier the prophet Isaiah
had declared to the rulers of his day, "Woe to them that
go down to Egypt for help. . . . Lo, thou trustest in the
staff of this broken reed, on Egypt; whereon if a man lean,
it will go into his hand, and pierce it: so is Pharaoh king
of Egypt to all that trust in him."[31] Here was one passage

---

29. *Ibid.*, p. 70.
30. *Ibid.*, p. 72.
31. Isaiah 30:2; 36:6.

in the Jewish scripture with which King Hussein could heartily agree.

So, as the third day of the war came to its close the Jewish leaders found themselves in complete control of all Biblical Palestine; Jordan was out of the war; Israeli armor was converging on the Suez Canal and six whole divisions of Egypt's best-equipped mechanized army were trapped on the Sinai desert.

Thursday, June 8, the Fourth Day of the War

The Sinai campaign came to its explosive conclusion in two mighty tank battles—one at Mitla Pass which leads to the Port of Suez, and the other at El Quantara further north. Both were hard fought because the Egyptians were now using all that remained of their badly battered airforce to smash the persistent onslaught of Israeli armor. An extremely tense situation erupted at Mitla Pass early Thursday.

As previously mentioned, General Abraham Yoffe had been ordered to streak through the sand dunes with his lighter mobile units and head off the fleeing Egyptians. About eighteen miles east of the Suez Canal, the bleached highlands stretch north and south like a huge desert skeleton with its spine permitting passageways in only three places. Yoffe out-ran the fleeing Egyptians and sealed off these escape routes. General Tal then reinforced his position with tanks and guns.

The next problem was to snake through one or more of these passes to reach the Suez Canal. But the Egyptians had anticipated this advance and had therefore dug in a hundred tanks with supporting mobile equipment to plug up Mitla Pass. The result was one of the major battles of the entire war. It was fought in the air and on the ground. General Tal describes it:

"It took us six hours to cover five kilometers in the subsequent move toward the Canal, with the enemy attempting to delay us with a force of one hundred tanks. We killed forty tanks and it was here the enemy was broken. This battle along a very narrow axis was conducted by sniping methods because sand dunes hemmed us in. Only three tanks led all the time. The gunners were firing up to ranges of 3,000 meters, and very accurately. The Egyptians were positioned to see us first and were always the first to fire, and for three hours there was bitter fighting between their planes and our land forces. Then our planes intervened."[32]

Later photographs of Mitla Pass showed the amazing scene of apocalyptic destruction which had descended on the Egyptians. It had left the charred remains of tanks, jeeps, half-tracks and cannon stretched along the tortuous pass for a dozen miles.

Once General Yoffe and General Tal had bulldozed their way through this pass they ordered all brigades to proceed toward Suez. Before long the commander of an Israeli column urgently radioed to General Yoffe:

"Request permission to wash feet . . . in the Suez Canal!"

Russians Once More Discovered Directing Military Action

While the battle of Mitla Pass was raging, a similar struggle had locked Israeli-Egyptian forces in a ground and air battle at El Qantara. This is an Egyptian town located a few miles south of the Mediterranean at a point where the Gaza railroad crosses the Suez Canal. Over 1,000 tanks were involved in the frantic furor of this last-ditch stand as the Egyptians tried to hold back the Israeli forces from seizing this vital link to the Suez.

<hr>

32. William Stevenson, *Strike Zion*, p. 78.

It was during this battle that Commander Amost Unger, 21, intercepted radio commands in Russian directed to the Egyptian tank officers. Once again Russian commanders were exposed participating in the campaign.

We have already mentioned the experience of Major Raanan Lurie who accidentally detected the Russian personnel commanding Jordan and Iraqi artillery units up along the Jordan front.

The Sinai campaign had exposed the Russians also. On Monday and Tuesday when Israeli tanks were making their first breakthrough along the Gaza strip, Captain David Petel, a paratrooper who speaks Russian, reported intercepting messages from the Russians who were giving orders to the Egyptian tanks fighting at Khan Yunis.[33] By Thursday, as we have seen, when the forces had retreated to El Qantara, the Russians were still issuing orders.

Had there been time and opportunity no doubt Israeli intelligence agents could have picked up a continuous pattern of Russian participation all along the line. And no doubt it would have revealed, just as the evidence now shows concerning the Korean War, that the Russians were not merely advisors, but were actually in command.

The Israeli Attack on the USS Liberty

While this struggle was filling the Suez air with the smell of cordite, napalm and burning fuel oil a different kind of drama was taking place twelve to fifteen miles off the Sinai coast where a U.S. communications vessel was drifting slowly through the Mediterranean Sea. No American ship was supposed to have been in these waters. American naval commanders had reported to both Israel

---

33. Associated Press commemorative edition, *Lightning Out of Israel*, Englewood Cliffs, N.J.: Prentice-Hall, 1967, p. 120.

and Egypt the exact whereabouts of every U.S. vessel—except this one.[34]

To the observing Israeli pilots and naval personnel it was obvious that this was a highly sophisticated ship with elaborate electronic gear for picking up even the weakest radio signals as they came through from the nearby battle front. The question was, why was the ship there and why was it being kept under wraps? The Israelis later claimed that a ship similar to this one and flying the American flag was used by Egypt as a decoy during the 1956 campaign.

In any event, for approximately five hours the Israelis kept this vessel under surveillance. Then suddenly the Israelis attacked. Five or six bombing, strafing and rocket runs were made against the ship with two or more planes participating. Three motor torpedo boats also attacked and one explosion left a gaping hole in the side of the ship.

This vessel turned out to be the USS *Liberty*.

The attack resulted in 34 American sailors killed and 75 wounded. It was the biggest news in the headlines of Thursday's papers around the world.

Immediately after the attack, several inquiries were made from the personnel of the Israeli torpedo boats and two helicopters concerning the number of casualties and the need for help. The distraught captain of the American vessel refused aid and headed the crippled ship to sea. He had already radioed an S.O.S. to the Sixth Fleet and fighter planes from the aircraft carriers were dispatched to protect the *Liberty* from further attack. Washington heated up the "hot line" to Moscow to advise that the American planes were in the air merely to convoy the stricken vessel to safety.

When Washington released the news that the *Liberty* had been attacked, the air was filled with indignant protests. But even before the public knew of the attack, Israel

---

34. Robert J. Donovan, *Israel's Fight for Survival*, p. 143.

had apologized and offered full compensation. After that a blanket of mystery seemed to settle down around the whole affair.

It seemed apparent that Washington had some reason for not wishing to make a big issue out of the attack. Robert J. Donovan gave this analysis:

"The 11,000-ton vessel was an unusual ship. Actually, it was a spy ship, crammed with electronics equipment, designed for the complex espionage business of the modern age. Her forest of antennae were a tangle of steel sensors. Their electronic fingers could pluck from the air the messages passing around the world in scores of codes and dozens of languages. Equipped with her own computers, she could decode or break cryptographic languages considered unbreakable by the governments which send them. When the *Liberty* was attacked, it was intercepting battlefield messages from both Egyptian and Israeli forces in the Sinai battle, as well as unknown higher-level messages between governments."[35]

It was disclosed that among those who were killed aboard the *Liberty* was an officer of the National Security Agency, the highly secret governmental agency dealing with codes, ciphers and communications gathered from all over the world for U.S. intelligence evaluation.

So, for all practical purposes the attack on the *Liberty* was laid to rest as just another casualty of the war. It was obvious that there was much more to the story than either country desired at the moment to publicly discuss.

Americans Are Caught in the Cairo War Fever

It will be recalled that as early as Tuesday, Egyptian officials had launched a propaganda attack against the United States by accusing it of joining Israel in the war

35. *Ibid.*, pp. 142-143.

and using its fighter jets to bomb Arab-League territory. However, it was not until Wednesday that the full brunt of the propaganda began to hit the Arab masses.

Egypt had also led the parade of Arab states in breaking off diplomatic relations with the United States so this meant that all Americans were required to leave Egypt. By Thursday the exodus of Americans from all Arab countries was in full swing. Their departure was accompanied by widespread violence as the Egyptian propaganda ministry churned out its charge that the U.S. was to blame for most of the catastrophic debacle which had come to the Arab League as a result of this war.

Arab mobs sacked and burned the U.S. consulate in Alexandria, Egypt, and damaged U.S. installations in Tripoli and Beghazi of Libya; in Baghdad and Basra of Iraq; in Damascus of Syria; in Beirut of Lebanon; in Khartoum of Sudan, in Sanaa of Yemen and in Tunis of Tunisia. However, mobs were held at bay by soldiers and police in Amman of Jordan and also in Algiers. Another mob was held back from attacking the U.S. embassy in Beirut after it had previously damaged American property in other parts of the city.

Those of us who had enjoyed the warm hospitality of the people of Damascus, Amman, Beirut and Cairo only a few weeks before could scarcely comprehend the newspaper accounts of the sudden and vehement Arab hostility which had descended on Americans in the Middle East. It was only later that we learned what Nasser's propaganda had done.

Thomas Thompson, Paris bureau chief for *Life* magazine was caught in the melee and described his experiences in an article entitled, "U.S. Humiliation—a Diary from Cairo."[36]

"All over the country Americans are being rounded up and ordered to leave—oilmen in the far reaches of the

---

36. *Israel's Swift Victory*, special edition of *Life*, June, 1967, pp. 70-71.

blistering desert, students, missionaries, tourists wandering through the temples at Luxor, bird collectors, beatniks, residents who have spent their lives in Cairo."[37]

The first violence was at Alexandria, Egypt: "In Alexandria a howling rabble overpowers the guard outside the American consulate and bursts in, knocking Consul General David Fritzlan out of the way and pushing him and his aides into the room-sized consulate vault. They drench the furniture and equipment with kerosene and then toss in Molotov cocktails. The offices are gutted. For more than half an hour the consul is trapped inside the vault, not knowing the fire is raging outside. Four consulate automobiles parked on the grounds are burned, and the mob then turns to the handsome, splendidly equipped USIS library. The building quickly goes up in flame. The consul and his staff are taken to the police station where they are held two hours 'for your own protection.' In all of this, there is not a single expression of sympathy or regret, despite the fact that the consul has lived in Alexandria for three years and enjoyed good relations with the official community."[38]

The hysteria of mobs in the street was no worse than the provocative and inflammatory statements coming from the official government radio in Cairo. One of its announcers shouted, "We are killing the Israelis, O America, and we will now kill you Americans, too!"[39]

I could not help but contemplate the vicious consequences of this cruel trick Nasser was playing on his own people. In their native innocence, Arabs admire and respect Americans. Only the "Big Lie" technique reminiscent of Hitler's days could have produced such a tide of hate and terror. But just as Robespierre died on his own guillotine, and just as Hitler, Mussolini and scores of

37. *Ibid.*, p. 70.

38. *Ibid.*

39. "We Will Kill You Americans, Too!" *U.S. News and World Report*, June 26, 1967, p. 30.

other tyrants who bullied and deceived their people fell foul of their own snares, by the same token, any historian could safely predict that Nasser's poison gas and venal propaganda would eventually catch up with him. I made a mental note that when things calmed down and I returned to Egypt, I would want to remember the Egyptian people as I had known them in the past—as friends.

Egypt Gives Up

It will be recalled that during the early part of Thursday morning, Egypt had rallied the last remnants of her tattered air force in order to support hundreds of tanks in a last-ditch counter-attack east of the Suez Canal. The Egyptians had frantically hoped they could stop the Israelis at Mitla Pass and El Qantara. Both had failed.

Meanwhile, in New York City, a war of words was taking place at the United Nations. The U.S. had introduced a resolution calling for a general cease-fire similar to the resolution of Tuesday, June 6. The United States proposed a resolution calling for a simple cease-fire which could be followed by a negotiated peace based on principles which would provide a permanent settlement between the Arabs and the Jews. However, the Soviet spokesman would have none of it. Federenko introduced a resolution calling upon Israel to abandon all her gains and withdraw to her original boundaries. He further demanded that she be condemned as "an aggressor."

Throughout the debate, El Kony, the Egyptian delegate, supported the Russian position, denouncing the United States and saying there could never be a cease-fire until Israel agreed to withdraw. In fact, El Kony was just about to take over the Security Council rostrum for a major address when he was called out for an urgent long distance telephone call. It was Cairo. The Egyptian foreign minister was on the line. El Kony listened. A few moments later he returned to the Security Council and passed word to the presiding officer that he would not speak. He scribbled a brief message and passed it to the Secretary General. Observers wondered why El Kony seemed so deeply disturbed. It was later disclosed that he was too emotionally upset to read his own message.

U Thant therefore asked for permission to speak and then read from the piece of paper which El Kony had given him. It said:

"I have the honor to inform you, upon instructions of my government, that it has decided to accept the cease-fire call as it has been prescribed by the resolutions of the Council on 5 and 6 June, 1967, on the condition that the other party cease-fire."[40]

So that was it. Israel's victory over Egypt had become official.

Astonished and grief-stricken, the various Arab delegates buried their heads in their hands. Even the British and American officials shook their heads in amazement. Russia's Federenko sat silently and stone-countenanced. It was as though the whole UN Security Council were momentarily engrossed in contemplating the kaleidoscopic course of events which, in 72 hours, had changed the whole balance of political power in the eastern Mediterranean. After merely four days of lightning war, tiny Israel stood astraddle her enemy. The giant was on the ground, stunned, disabled.

But the Israeli leaders had no intention of slaying Goliath. They simply said they wanted to rehabilitate him—to seek, if possible, to make a good, compatible, cooperative neighbor out of him. Of course, only the future could reveal the pragmatic possibilities of such a hope. Meanwhile, the nation of Israel held its lightning swift sword pointed at the throat of the Arab League.

Jewish armor stood poised along the full length of the

---

40. Robert J. Donovan, *Israel's Fight for Survival*, p. 144.

Suez Canal ready to drive on to Cairo should the word be
given. The entire Sinai peninsula was now under Jewish
command. The Aqaba Gulf had been reoccupied and
opened for navigation. The Holy City had been pre-
empted and pacified. Jewish troops held everything west
of the Jordan River. Syria alone remained in the fight.
She, too, had offered to accept the cease-fire but had continued shooting. This was all the excuse the Israelis needed
for a decisive blow against her. No Arab state had been
more inflammatory and provocative than Syria.

When the Security Council adjourned its proceedings
shortly before midnight in New York City, the dawn of a
new day had commenced in the Middle East. This was to
be Syria's day.

Friday, June 9, the Fifth Day of the War

As we have already mentioned, the Jewish leaders had
hoped they could persuade the Syrian government to stay
out of the war. The Syrians had answered with bombs and
artillery. They were determined to fight both in the sky
and on the ground.

Nevertheless, the policy of Israel during the first four
days of the war was to avoid a direct confrontation with
Syria until the more deadly threat to the south had been
handled. Following this strategy, Jordan was forced into a
cease-fire on Wednesday, Egypt followed on Thursday, and
now Israel was ready to regroup her military resources and
prepare for a direct attack on Syria.

A glance at the map will help explain why there had
been such a festering abscess of tension between Israel and
Syria down through the years. It will be noted that the
headwaters of the Jordan which bring water down from
Mount Hermon to the Sea of Galilee, pass through a slit

in the earth's crust called, at this point, Huleh Valley. This valley was demilitarized after the war of 1948-49 and Jewish farmers thereafter asserted their claim for the peaceful settlement of this valley. To do this, the Jews had to rely upon the armistice agreement which guaranteed that no military activity could take place in this region. Almost immediately, however, the settlers began to be cannonaded at regular intervals from the Golan Heights of Syria.

The Golan Heights consist of a range of wilderness mountains which rise steeply to the east of the Huleh Valley. These highlands comprised a perfect overview of the Jewish settlements, and for nineteen years the Syrians had used them to torment the Jewish villages and farms in the valley below. The miracle was that the Israeli settlements had survived at all. In spite of shelling, sniping and crop-burning the Jews had stayed there. The reason was water.

The Israelis knew from the beginning that the sterile Negev desert in Southern Palestine could never be conquered by either Arab or Jew until the precious water of the Jordan could be diverted and brought down to irrigate its thirsty but fertile soil. Concerning this, William Stevenson writes, "Past attempts to win Syrian cooperation in the development of the Jordan River had failed. And the headwaters were essential to any further growth of the cultivated lands extending out of Huleh Valley."[41] The development of the headwaters region was also essential before water could be drained off in major quantities to develop the Negev.

The Jews therefore unilaterally created a reclamation project in Huleh Valley involving some 15,000 acres. It was designed to drain Lake Huleh, increase the flow of the Jordan headwaters into the Sea of Galilee, and thereby make more water available for everybody farther south.

---

41. William Stevenson, *Strike Zion!* p. 83.

Syria did everything possible to sabotage this project. Stevenson continues:

"A plan to share the waters between Lebanon, Syria, Jordan and Israel was prepared by a special U.S. envoy, but only Israel pursued it—the Arabs refusing to participate on the grounds that it would in effect confirm Israel's right to the valley."[42]

Refusing to be held back by Arab obstinacy, the Israelis went ahead and build underground aqueducts large enough to accommodate an automobile. In 1965 pumping stations on the shores of Galilee began pouring sparkling, fresh water from this source onto the Negev desert 130 miles south. The Arabs then began digging an open ditch on their side to carry the water to their own parched land. At the same time they began shelling the underground area where they thought the Israeli pumping stations were located. UN observers noted the attack and recorded it, but no action was taken to condemn Syria or stop the shooting. It was apparent to almost everyone, even to Syria, that one day Israel would become sufficiently provoked to retaliate. In anticipation of such a day, the Syrians had spent great quantities of time and money fortifying the Golan Heights which extend along the Syrian side of Huleh Valley for 48 miles. On the face of these steep slopes the Syrians built a maze of camouflaged trenches and bunkers. These were protected by a lining of black, volcanic rock and cement. The exterior was covered with steel, dirt and a heavy overgrowth of wild grass. The trenches were eight feet in depth and generally three feet wide. These led back to a network of caverns in Golan Heights which piled up against the desert sky some 3,000 feet.

Heavy Russian mortars and burrowed-in tanks provided Syria's firepower all along this border. Militarily speaking, this natural barrier of fortified highlands constituted a long

42. *Ibid.*, pp. 83-84.

series of impregnable Gibraltars.

When the war first broke out on June 5, 1967, the Syrians began bombarding Huleh Valley and the settlements around Galilee with incessant mortar fire. Residents of the Jewish Kibbutzim and other Jewish farm projects went into their shelters and remained pinned down day after day. Thinly spread military forces combined with the peasants to provide the necessary "holding action" until reinforcements could arrive from the south. Jewish cannon tried to answer the Syrian guns shot for shot.

The general cease-fire on Thursday brought a temporary lull along the Israeli-Syrian border, but by Friday morning the Syrians were charged with violating the truce by deliberately shelling sixteen settlements. General Moshe Dayan, the Israeli minister of defense, immediately ordered the subjugation and occupation of the Syrian highlands and a broad penetration into Syria of at least twelve miles.

The Israeli Forces Invade Syria

This counter-attack opened up with heavy artillery fire from tanks and cannon plus napalm bombing by the airforce. The latter was designed to flush out the trenches and catacombs. Armored brigades then began moving forward—one at each end of the Syria-Israeli border while a flanking brigade crept forward in between.

The brigade on the north end of the border succeeded in fighting its way up the Syrian slopes and crossed into Syria at 11:30 A.M. To achieve this, engineers had to go ahead of the tanks blasting out a roadway. Where possible they were preceded by farm tractors equipped with homemade steel flails to explode the many mines. Throughout this steep climb the fighting was fierce. The two brigades spearheading their assault farther south also met powerful resistance. Military authorities who visited the region after the war were amazed that the Israelis ever made it. No

(UPI Photo)

The body of an Egyptian soldier lies between two wrecked trucks
near the Gaza-El Arish Road, June 8.

(UPI Photo)

On the Sinai Peninsula the skeleton of an Egyptian tank bears mute
witness to the ferocity of the conflict.

amount of bombing and shelling could have dislodged the Arabs. It was the furious frontal assault by Israeli infantry willing to engage in hand-to-hand combat which made the difference. As in Sinai, the genius of Israeli strategy was using multi-operational assaults with tanks, cannon, infantry and air force all combined to blast, bomb, clear mines, build roads and inch their way up the jagged slopes regardless of the cost. Associated Press dispatches described some of the action:

"Supporting tanks were slowed by the heavy fire from the trenches and bunkers, and by the mines sowed on the approaches. It became a job for the infantry, a dirty job of face-to-face fighting, and cutting through the coils of barbed wire. Finally Israeli troops made it to the trenches and cornered the Syrians inside and the fighting was furious. It took three hours to dig them out. The Israeli troops pushed through the catacombs to the command post, an underground post with kerosene lanterns, tables and chairs, maps on the walls, and sleeping rooms lined with double bunks and dull green footlockers. This one complex held 120 men. And there were hundreds of them along the Syrian ridges leading to snow-streaked Mount Hermon. . . .

"South of these battles, Israeli infantry and paratroop units struck in a series of frontal assaults. They pierced the Syrian defense line at Jalibna, Dradra, Tel Hilel and Darbeshiya. Two prongs of this drive blasted out bridgeheads at Darbeshiya in the north and the customs house in the south. Then they stopped for the night, to reorganize, refuel and resupply."[43]

Arab Leaders Enmeshed in Political Shambles

The imminent fall of Syria merely added to the disgrace of the whole top cadre of Arab leaders.[44] Rumors of

---

43. Associated Press commemorative edition, *Lightning Out of Israel*, pp. 129-130.

dethronement, military coups and seizure of power by dissident forces were rampant. Western analysts predicted the early political demise of leaders in all of the three major combatant nations—Egypt, Jordan and Syria. It seemed quite obvious that no political leadership could survive very long after such a colossal catastrophe.

No one sensed this pending retribution of doom more than Gamal Abdel Nasser. When a war is lost, politicians, like soldiers, turn from the common effort and strive only to save themselves. This now became Nasser's total obsession. For many hours the whole central administration of Egypt seemed caught in a leaderless paralysis while Nasser met with close personal advisors to formulate an escape from political oblivion. As a result, military leadership was left to its own confused devices. There was no mobilization of resources to provide Red Cross assistance to thousands of Egyptians trapped without food or water on the merciless Sinai desert. There seemed to be no directed effort to relieve the suffering and shock of the scattered bands of troops who managed to survive the war and straggle into border settlements.

Americans and Europeans who were war-marooned on board boats at Port Said or along the Suez Canal could scarcely comprehend the indifference with which the Egyptian soldiers were received by their own people as they staggered back from the Sinai front.

"They looked like broken dolls," said Beverly Johnstone of Boston. "Some were covered from head to foot with blisters. I saw one man with an arm dangling, and blood congealed on his face and bare legs, fall like a ninepin. Almost all the men were covered head to foot in light sand and they looked like ghosts."[45]

William Stevenson writes, "There was no evidence that Egypt which was complaining about alleged Israeli indiffer-

---

44. William Stevenson, *Strike Zion*, p. 81.
45. *Ibid.*, p. 76.

ence to the defeated troops, had prepared for their reception."[46]

Lt. Joseph Lucas of the British Army who was aboard one of the ships and remembered how the civilians of Britain had rallied to save the men at Dunkirk, looked in amazement at the poor devils who had been sent off to war by Nasser with such huzzas but were now ignored as they returned in defeat. He said, "They just wandered off down the streets with their arms stretched out. Against the bare landscape they looked bigger than life . . . they come over the dunes, and there we were, lounging on the ship's rail, and it seemed the most awful confrontation. It was like Exodus in reverse."[47]

Meanwhile, Nasser was preparing to appear before his people on TV. It was to be his first public appearance and his first official statement since the outbreak of the war.

He knew that nothing but a stroke of tactical genius could save him, but he believed his understanding of the Arab mentality plus his proven dexterity in manipulating their feelings was sufficient to pull off the master stroke he needed.

Nasser's intention was to force the Egyptian people to either acclaim him or disown him. Every precaution was taken to prevent the latter. To insure adequate emotional manipulation and crowd control, carefully briefed partisans were scattered everywhere. Cairo radio and the government controlled press were plied with propaganda to whip the people into a fervor. Nasser's idea was to formally relinquish his dictatorial power and then have the people massively demand that he take it back again. When the stage was set, Nasser made his appearance.

Nasser Resigns!

In spite of everything else that was happening at the

46. *Ibid.*
47. *Ibid.*

moment, Nasser's dramatic and unexpected resignation was the big news story throughout the world on Friday, June 9, 1967. His speech was brilliantly composed and carefully calculated to create widespread sympathy. It epitomized humility, self-sacrifice and most important of all, a willingness to personally assume complete responsibility for all that had happened. Here is the way it started:

"Brothers, we have been accustomed together in times of victory and in times of stress, in the sweet hours and in the bitter hours, to speak with open hearts and to tell each other the facts, confident that through this means alone we can always find our sound direction however low the light.

"We cannot hide from ourselves the fact that we have met with a grave setback in the last few days. But I am confident that all of us can in a short time overcome our difficult situation. To do this we shall need much patience, much wisdom and moral courage, and ability for devoted work.

"Brothers . . . we should look at what happened in order to follow developments and the way they proceeded until they reached this stage."[48]

At this point, Nasser launched into special pleading by presenting his version of the war which he wanted the people to believe.

First of all, he gave full credence to the phony Soviet intelligence reports delivered in the second week of May which we have already alluded to and which claimed that Israel was about to launch an attack against Syria. Concerning this, Nasser said,

"Even our friends in the Soviet Union told the parliamentary delegation which was visiting Moscow early last month that there was a calculated intention. It was our duty not to accept this in silence. In addition to its being a question of Arab brotherhood, it was also a matter of

---

48. Alex Benson, *48 Hour War*, p. 179.

national security. Who starts with Syria will finish with Egypt."[49]

It was somewhat ironical that while Nasser was saying these words, Israel was just finishing with Syria, and Egypt where the Israelis had started, was already finished.

Nasser now did his best to present Egypt in a defensive position. He explained that all the provocative acts which he initiated were purely for self-defense. His demand that the UN peace-keeping forces be removed, his closing of the Aqaba Gulf by artillery fire, the implanting of tanks, cannon and infantry at the borders of Israel, the stepped-up provocation of guerilla warfare inside Israel and the cannonading of her villages in violation of the armistice agreement—all these were glossed over with the supreme artistic flourish of a modern Machiavelli. What required comment was referred to with deference, the rest was ignored. Throughout his speech Nasser was employing one of the oldest tricks in the aggressor's bag of magic. In cold reality he was accusing a threatened nation which defends itself of breaching the peace. To prove his own innocence he cited the fact that both President Johnson and the Soviet Ambassador had urged him not to be the one to strike the first blow. What he failed to point out was the fact that these warnings against further aggressive action came after Nasser had already struck the first blow by closing the Aqaba Gulf and forcibly cutting off 90% of Israel's oil supply.

Then came his comments on Israel's attack.

At this point Nasser wanted to leave no doubt about Egypt's ability to wipe Israel off the face of the map. It was simply that the United States and Britain had prevented it. In bold and sweeping charges Nasser repeated what had already been discredited in the United Nations debates. He made the United States and Britain the black culprits who had robbed the Arab League of its oppor-

---
49. *Ibid.*

tunity for vengeance on Israel. "What is now established," he declared, "is that American and British aircraft carriers were off the enemy's shores, helping his war effort."[50] No attempt was made to support the charge with any proof. It was enough that Nasser had spoken.

Concerning Russia and her satellites he simply stated, "There were great nations outside the Arab world which gave us moral support which cannot be estimated, but the conspiracy was bigger and stronger."[51]

He commended the valiant Arab armies which he said had done their best against terrible odds. Then he made specific reference to King Hussein of Jordan which carried a hidden barb. Hussein had already told the world how disappointed he had been in Egypt's leadership. Nasser now decided to spread the blame for the defeat of Jordan by stating that the Jordanian Arab Army had fought bravely "under the command of King Hussein." This was a cruel twist of the facts since it was Nasser who had used every possible pressure on Hussein and forced him to turn over his troops to the command of Nasser's generals.

Nasser was now ready to wind up his speech on a highly dramatic note. He had firmly fixed the blame for the Arab catastrophe on the Israeli-U.S.-British conspiracy so he could not admit his own guilt in provoking the present disaster without fear of being believed or convicted. In the most abject humility he faced his people and declared:

"We now reach an important point in this soul-searching by asking ourselves: Does this mean we do not assume responsibility for the consequences of this setback? I tell you truthfully that I am ready to assume the entire responsibility."[52]

Then came his political bombshell. In a quiet and

---

50. *Ibid.*, p. 180.
51. *Ibid.*, p. 181.
52. *Ibid.*, p. 182.

restrained voice he announced, "I have taken a decision with which I want you to help me. I have decided to give up completely and finally every official post and every political role and to return to the ranks of the public to do my duty with them like every other citizen."[53]

There it was. Nasser had resigned!

The remainder of his talk was a point by point reminder to the Egyptian people of the singular achievements of the Nasser administration. Seizing the Suez Canal in 1956 was mentioned (the fact that he would have lost it had not the U.S. intervened in Egypt's behalf was *not* mentioned.) The people were reminded of the half-completed Aswan Dam as though it were an accomplished fact. He pointed out the development of industry, electric power, oil development and other improvements. The fact that American money had contributed substantially to make many of these possible was conveniently forgotten. The fact that for many years thousands of Egyptians had kept from starving through the distribution of surplus American food was also forgotten. All gains were Nasser's and Nasser was resigning.

Barely had the Egyptian leader left the air before the streets were packed with shouting, chanting, cheering multitudes. "Nasser! Nasser! Nasser!" they cried. "You are our leader! Return to power!"

It was an amazing and interesting demonstration of the ancient science of large-scale political manipulation and the massive application of hypnotic crowd psychology. Observers in Cairo who scarcely an hour before had been predicting the early fall of Nasser now began realizing that they had underestimated the shrewd sagacity of this Egyptian leader. There was no doubt about it, Nasser had apparently saved his political career.

---

53. *Ibid.*

Saturday, June 10, the Sixth Day of the War

In his resignation speech, Nasser had nominated as his successor the Egyptian Vice President, Zakariah Mohieddin. Had Mohieddin become the new leader of Egypt, it would have augured well for Israel.

This was one Arab leader who had no sense of inferiority, nor did he feel the need to constantly over-compensate by building some kind of hero image for himself. He was far less antagonistic toward the West and had a sense of social justice with which the Jews felt considerable empathy. He was born wealthy but had always been sensitive to the needs of the poor. He voluntarily and unobtrusively gave up much of his land when the government called for "agrarian reform." He was in favor of dividing the large estates among the peasants providing they knew how to work the land. Over the years he had developed more amiable relations with the Israelis than any of the Arab leaders. The Jews felt he understood them.

Politically, Mohieddin had enemies. He represented the interests of the disinherited masses rather than the sheik clique. He broke the power of the Moslem Brotherhood while he was serving as Minister of the Interior in 1954, and in his capacity as the chief law enforcement official of the government, he gained a reputation for removing restraints rather than imposing them.

In 1965 he became Prime Minister and "his policies put the economy into better condition than it had been for a long time. Six bumbling directors of public enterprises were toppled and efficiency crept into a bureaucracy which had sheltered too many freeloaders."[54] In 1966, Mohieddin was swept aside and replaced by hard-core Nasser nationalists. Nevertheless, he remained popular in the

---

54. William Stevenson, *Strike Zion!* pp. 105-106.

eyes of the people and a logical choice for Nasser's successor.

But in the 1967 crisis Moheiddin's prospect of moving into Egypt's top spot was short lived. Even though he heard the announcement of his name as Nasser's nomination for a successor, Mohieddin observed Nasser immediately doing everything in his power to prevent it. As soon as the resignation speech was over, he saw government trucks bringing in a virtual army of Nasser partisans to demand withdrawal of the resignation. They chanted that the father of the nation must stay at his post. Mohieddin saw Nasser's tightly-controlled cabinet vote unanimously to reject the resignation. Then, without a single dissent, the rubber-stamp national assembly voted to do the same.

Reflecting a spirit of abject humility, Nasser suddenly announced that he would bow to the will of the people. The resignation was summarily withdrawn.

Final Phase of the Syrian Campaign

Meanwhile, the forces of Israel were chopping their way up the last vestiges of the Golan Heights and were preparing for a final charge toward Damascus. First, however, the Syrian striking power had to be cut off, encircled and destroyed. As we have already seen, one prong of the Israeli power thrust scrapped and scrabbled its way to the top of the Syrian ridge by Friday night. However, the main Israeli forces fighting up and down the 48-mile Syrian border did not make the summit until Saturday. Casualties were heavy. Advances were often carved out of the 3,000-foot hogback yard by yard, bunker by bunker and boulder by boulder.

Even before the morning sun had climbed high enough to surmount the ridge and send its bright shafts down across the fields of ripened grain, Huleh Valley was trembling with the roar of falling bombs and exploding shells.

The Syrian positions were scoured with napalm. Artillery fire dislodged machine-gun nests and implanted cannon. Within an hour after the bombardment began, the infantry, tanks, bazooka-jeeps and half-tracks were on the move again.

The armored force up north slashed the fortifications at Tel Hamra and then cleared the residual resistance on up to the Lebanon border before turning east toward Massada. Simultaneously, a strong Israeli force moved up from Tel Katzir at the southeast corner of the Sea of Galilee. Its assignment was to occupy the heavily fortified Tewfik mountains and then, after ascending to the highland plateau, push on around to form a pincer prong which would meet the prong from the north. This assault proved so successful that paratroopers had to be helicoptered up onto the plateau to cut off the Syrian retreat.

But in many places the Syrians fought ferociously. Once they had been rooted out of the security of their caves, trenches and tunnels along the border they fell back and holed-up in every conceivable place. From improvised barricades they fought with a tenacity equal to the Jews. The Crusader's castle near Kalat Namrud is crumbling in ruins yet it took a continuous stream of air attacks by the Israeli jets to dislodge the Arab soldiers who had taken refuge there. At Tel Kafar, more than two hours of bombing and mortar fire were required to soften the Syrian resistance sufficiently to permit a direct assault by Israeli infantry. Even so, the Arabs held on bitterly and during the attack the Israeli battalion commander was killed.

By early afternoon it was plain that the spirit of resistance was breaking up. Syrian soldiers sensed what was happening and abandoned their posts. Some fled toward Damascus, others tore off their uniforms in order to hide among the populace. Many of them surrendered or were captured.

Immediately the pace of the Israeli armor accelerated

as the northern and southern prongs raced toward each other in order to cut off the Syrian escape route. Their orders were to capture the main body of the Syrian forces and destroy their Russian-made equipment.

Some units remained behind, however, to mop up and secure the Syrian ridge against any future counter-attack. Who could tell what the future might bring? Surely the Soviet Union would not take this defeat without some sort of heavy recrimination. The Jewish leaders felt they must take no chances. Every installation had to go. They concentrated especially on the fortifications overlooking Israeli farming communities. These demolition operations had to be accomplished in four to six hours since a cease-fire could come at any moment. The Associated Press reported, "With devastating thoroughness, the Israelis scourged the area that had been a spring-board for terrorists who had raided the kibbutzim (communal villages) since 1948. And with a vengeance they blew up the concrete and stone forts where Russian-made cannon and mortars were trained on the Israeli border."[55]

Mid-afternoon found the advance Israeli columns from north and south rifling in toward El Qunaytirah so as to rendezvous by nightfall. They found the modernistic military headquarters of the Syrian high command abandoned and discovered that nearly all of the city's 30,000 inhabitants had fled.

Intelligence reports indicated that Damascus lay naked and defenseless just thirty miles away!

No doubt some of the Jewish troops expected that they might be ordered into a forced night march in order to capture the Syrian capital while the hysteria of defeat and fear held the population in its paralyzing grip. But this was not the goal of General Dayan. He did not seek the conquest of Arab capitals nor Moslem nations. He merely wished, 1-to destroy the Arab capacity to wage war, and

---

55. Associated Press commemorative edition, *Lightning Out of Israel*, p. 140.

2-to occupy those areas which made Israel vulnerable to attack. This had now been done. As far as Israel was concerned, the war was over.

It was also over for Syria. At 6:30 P.M. the Syrian leaders agreed to accept the provisions of the UN cease-fire.

The Tally

The eve of peace had come just about a week after the eve of the war. In that brief interval world history had suddenly lurched out in a significant, new direction. A tiny, beleaguered territory no larger than the state of Massachusetts with a population of less than three million had stood up to the mighty Soviet Union and her Arab allies, totaling 110 million. To be sure, the massive military might of the United States had theoretically check-mated that of Russia, but other than that, the fact remained that little David had taken on Goliath and won.

London's UPI reporter, K. C. Thaler, wrote, "Israel, only a week ago one of the smallest and most endangered nations in the Middle East, today stands as one of the most powerful in the area."[56]

In six days Israel had doubled her population and quadrupled her territory—going from 8,000 square miles to 34,000. The borders of Israel had been expanded south, east and southwest until they had reached natural boundaries which would be much more easy to defend. The famous temple-city of Jerusalem was back in Jewish hands for the first time since the days of Rome. In fact, by acquiring all of the territory west of the Jordan River, the Israeli government had not only come into possession of the sacred shrines of three world religions, but one of the most popular tourist attractions in the world as well.

---

56. *Deseret News*, Salt Lake City, June 12, 1967, p. 1.

Some would count these "spoils of war," but not the Israeli leaders. There were mountain-high burdens associated with each of these new acquisitions—over half a million Arab refugees, for example. To the Israelis these expanded boundaries meant more work and sacrifice, but in the long run they would be a gain. These by-products of the war had increased the national security of Israel, expanded the working base for an eventual Arab-Israeli peace, and had definitely hurtled Israel back into the main stream of world history.

However, to compel her Arab neighbors to reach this juncture of political reality had cost both Israel and the Arabs a lot of blood and wealth. As soon as the war was over Premier Levi Eshkol castigated the Arab leaders whose threats he had endured until it had practically emasculated his political career. To them he said:

"Israel fought only because you left us no choice. Reflect on your losses which Israel deeply regrets, on the money wasted which could have gone to the constructive development of your countries and on the benefits which could have arisen from yours and our cooperation." Then he pointed out that since 1952 the Arab peoples and Israel had spent ten billion dollars on arms. "Had these vast sums been applied to economic and social needs, millions of human beings who are steeped in poverty could by today have enjoyed an appropriate standard of living."[57]

The Arabs had suffered an estimated 35,000 dead and probably three times as many wounded. No one would ever know for sure. To avoid contagion and epidemics, Israeli bulldozers covered heaps of sand over the scattered bodies of Egypt's host who had fallen beneath the blazing desert sun of Sinai. Egyptian prisoners were released by the thousands to return to their homes. However, one military group was held for trading purposes. A UPI dis-

---

57. *Deseret News*, Salt Lake City, June 12, 1967, p. 1 and William Stevenson, *Strike Zion!* p. 112.

patch stated, "Israel said Wednesday that sixteen Israeli prisoners were known to be in enemy hands after the six-day Middle East war and offered to exchange 5,499 Arab prisoners for them. The Israelis also announced they had returned 6,000 prisoners to Egypt without negotiations in the past two days . . . Among the 6,000 repatriated Egyptians were 300 officers, including nine generals and ten colonels . . . The International Red Cross had confirmed that one Israeli pilot had been lynched in Egypt."[58]

It seemed rather fantastic that in a war in which Nasser had promised to exterminate $2\frac{1}{2}$ million Israelis, he had been beaten to a standstill and the Israelis had suffered merely 679 dead and 2,563 wounded. But every dead Israeli soldier was mourned as a monumental loss to Israel. This led William Stevenson to comment, "One suddenly realized the importance of human life to a small country struggling to make a go of things, nursing its human resources. That's why there were no victory parades, no dancing in the streets, none of the swaggering bouts of drunken laughter, no tickertape processions. The losses were light when weighed against the near destruction of a nation of nearly 2,500,000 and yet 679 fighting men and women were just 679 too many.[59]

In fact, the extent of Israel's losses in comparative terms may be better appreciated if it is realized that according to population ratios her 679 killed would have an impact equal to 51,604 deaths in the United States. Her 2,563 wounded is equal to the impact of 194,788 casualties in the U.S. population.

Were Russians Among the Captives?

As we have already observed, Israeli monitors were able to detect Russian voices giving commands on both

58. *Salt Lake Tribune*, June 15, 1967, p. 8A.
59. William Stevenson, *Strike Zion!* p. 88.

the Jordan and Sinai fronts. On Friday, June 9, they were detected on the Syrian front.

"Israeli commanders in the Tel Aviv war room listened with something more than grim satisfaction to the alarmed flurry of two-day radio conversations which their monitors were picking up from Syrian transmitters. Heavy Russian voices were heard instructing Arab tank men on how to scramble out of the T-55s sunk like gun emplacements just inside the Syrian border."[60]

By Saturday the war apparently caught up with the Russians.

It had always been the policy of the Soviet Government to insist that its Russian officers be kept far away from the front lines, especially when an enemy breakthrough was possible. On the Syrian front the Russians apparently thought the Golan Heights could not be scaled. At least, it was reported that some of them were cornered and captured when the Israeli troops slugged their way over the top and threw their pincer forces around the Syrian defense bastions. Alex Benson, chief political writer for the World Journal Tribune, gives this report, "Along with the gun and tank emplacements, the Israeli forces captured a valuable prize on the Qnaitra Heights—several Soviet officers who had been serving as 'advisors' to the Syrian Army."[61]

Later, Israeli officials told unbelieving newsmen that there were no Russian prisoners. Steven says this was one Israeli dispatch foreign observers doubted. They had already heard that these prisoners were being held in greatest secrecy. [62]

In the light of Premier Eshkol's long-range policy of placating the Soviets in hopes of gaining concessions for the 2½ million Jews still in Russia, one might well under-

60. *Ibid.*, p. 81.
61. Alex Benson, *48 Hour War*, p. 66.
62. William Stevenson, *Strike Zion!* p. 110.

stand his decision to avoid embarrassing the Soviet Government by exposing such positive proof of Russia's direct complicity in the war. From a politician's standpoint a group of Soviet prisoners would make excellent bargaining material.

Israel Seeks to By-Pass the United Nations

Now we come to the post-war peace.

In the beginning, Jewish leaders were among the foremost advocates of the United Nations and many of them had been in favor of the concessions which had permitted Russia to become a powerful member in spite of the charter provisions which should have excluded her. But 19 years of abusive treatment under the self-negating machinery of the UN had completely destroyed Israel's confidence in the capacity of the UN to provide any semblance of justice for little nations.

To be sure, the UN Security Council had passed a resolution calling for a cease-fire but only when Russia so desperately wanted it. The Israelis knew the UN could take no credit for the cease-fire. The lightning swift sword of Israel had forced it upon them. Only a week before the war when Israel was pleading for the UN to bring about a cease-fire which would compel Egypt to open up the Aqaba Gulf, the UN Security Council was absolutely helpless. Israel had also found the UN refusing to carry out its responsibilities during nineteen years of guerilla attacks against her borders. Now, therefore, in the hour of her fantastic victory, Israel was not about to place her fate in the hands of the dis-United Nations which had come so very close to being a contributing cause to her own total destruction.

As early as the second day of the war, Israeli officials had emphasized that any post-war negotiations must be carried out between the Arabs and Israelis without the muddling and meddling of the UN. Abba Eban had said: ". . . much could be done if the Governments of the area would embark much more on direct contacts. They must find their way to each other."[63]

When the Arabs insisted that all negotiations be conducted indirectly through UN committees, General Dayan said, "We should do better without any mediation or any third party. I don't remember a single important problem that was solved through the diplomacy of the United Nations negotiations."[64]

American reporters ask Premier Eshkol directly: "Are you interested in the United Nations playing a part in the settlement?" Eshkol replied, "We have often stated that we think the best way for the Arabs and for us to get together is without third-party-intervention. This also includes the United Nations. There are some observers who feel that the United Nations has, in the past, hindered direct talks when they were possible—as in the early 1950s. We think that face-to-face talks are the best way."[65]

This was a kind and restrained way of saying that Israel had learned through extremely bitter experience that when the UN pre-empted jurisdiction over international disputes and subsequently failed to resolve issues or take action outlined in the charter, this gigantic, cumbersome legislative monstrosity actually fed the flames of war. And Israel wanted no more of it.

Russia Tries Diplomatic Subversion in the UN

The perverted and abusive manner in which the Soviet Union had been allowed to sabotage the original design of

---

63. Quoted from Eban's talk before the United Nations. Full text in the appendix of this volume.
64. Robert J. Donovan, *Israel's Fight for Survival*, p. 147.
65. "What's Next for Israel," *U.S. News and World Report*, July 10, 1967, p. 30.

the UN was demonstrated immediately after the Arab-Israeli war. Instead of the free world peoples banding together to push through a resolution in the General Assembly branding the Arab-League as aggressors in closing the Aqaba Gulf, etc., the machinery of this world forum was turned over to the Soviets to see if they could get *Israel* branded as the aggressor. Over the protest of the U.S., Russia was allowed a special session in the General Assembly. She had two objectives: 1. to have Israel condemned as the aggressor in the war, and 2. to get a resolution passed demanding that Israel move back to her original boundaries without any matching concessions from the Arabs.

So crucial did the Soviet leaders consider this special session in the UN that they sent Premier Alexei Kosygin to New York. His assignment was to twist arms, threaten, plead and otherwise line up all of the political power possible for a show of strength against the United States and Israel. For several days the air waves of the world were used to poison the air with recrimination and wild charges. Soon, the Israeli government sent to the UN its foreign minister, Abba Eban, to meet the wild charges. Said he:

"The General Assembly witnessed an unusual spectacle this morning.

"The government of the United Arab Republic, which announced its intention to exterminate Israel, which concentrated 90,000 troops and 900 tanks for that purpose, which issued operation orders in mid-May to its commanders in the field for bombardment of Israel's airfields, which imposed a total blockade of Israel's entire southern coast, which called on other governments to join in a war of extermination against Israel, which expressed in mid-May and early June that Israel's end was near—this government comes to this tribunal to present itself as a victim of aggression."[66]

Finally a vote was taken to see if a majority would label Israel the aggressor in the war. But not even power politics and cloakroom threats could get a majority of the 122 nations to endorse such a farcical proposition. Nevertheless, when it came to the demand that Israel give up everything she had gained just as the big powers in the UN forced her to do in 1956, Russia was alarmingly successful. The resolution was approved by a majority—53 to 46. Fortunately, however, such a resolution required a two-thirds majority to attain legal status and pass, so, technically, it failed. Russia, however, hailed it as a great victory since the majority had endorsed the resolution.

But even if the resolution had passed with a two-thirds majority, Israel would have held it in total disdain. Israel had cooperated in bowing to identical demands in 1956 and as a result she had come within a few hours of being wiped off the face of the map. Russia could play propaganda games in the UN if she wished but any resolution considered by Israel to be unjust would be treated as a scrap of paper. At the close of the war Levi Eshkol had staked out Israel's position in unequivocal terms:

"Be under no illusion that the state of Israel is prepared to return to the situation that reigned up to a week ago. Alone we fought for our existence and our security. We are entitled to determine what are the true and vital interests in our country, and how they shall be secured."[67]

In a radio broadcast from Jerusalem several weeks later Eshkol announced that unless reasonable peace accords were signed by the Arabs, the Israelis would not give up one inch of Arab land conquered in the six-day war.[68] He had previously made it plain as to what Israel considered "reasonable:"

---

66. Associated Press commemorative edition, *Lightning Out of Israel*, p. 156.

67. Robert J. Donovan, *Israel's Fight for Survival*, p. 148.

68. UPI dispatch, "Israel's Premier Rules Out Early Middle East Peace Agreement," *Salt Lake Tribune*, July 31, 1967, p. 4.

1. Diplomatic recognition of Israel by the Arab states.
2. The right of unmolested passage through the Suez Canal.
3. Necessary steps to guarantee the integrity of Israel's borders.

Cloud of Despair Descends on Egypt

In Egypt, meanwhile, reports began seeping through to the outside world that an extremely serious crisis was brewing. Don Cook, reporter for the *Los Angeles Times* who had been interned in Cairo during the war, wrote an article entitled, "Nasser's Economic Plight Couldn't Be Worse."[69] He wrote:

"Here are the main points in this catalogue of economic disaster—

"Egypt is running an annual balance-of-payments deficit of approximately 500 million dollars. There is not a single country in the world where she has any trading surplus or favorable exchange balance.

"Apart from her balance-of-payments deficit, Egypt must also find 200 million dollars during 1967 . . . Egypt has virtually no industrial export trade. Her chief source of income is the Suez Canal, which produced 230 million dollars in revenue in 1966, but is now blocked for an indefinite period.

"Her cotton crop, worth 220 million dollars last year, is already committed for 1967 in trade barter deals.

"Tourism was worth an estimated 30 million dollars in overseas earnings in 1966, but the Arab-Israeli war has finished the tourist business for 1967.

"Egyptian oil consumption is approximately 190,000 barrels daily, most of which is covered by domestic production—but the Israelis have captured Egyptian wells

---

69. *Salt Lake Tribune*, June 17, 1967, p. 4.

along the Sinai coast producing 100,000 barrels daily which Egypt will now have to make up by imports. . . .

"Best estimates are that Egypt probably has a maximum of two months grain supply on hand, and no money to buy more. China's offer of 150,000 tons represents less than a month's consumption, and in any case will be a politically-diverted shipment of Canadian wheat which the Chinese are unlikely to be able to repeat. Starvation in Egypt before the summer is out looms as a distinct possibility . . . .

"Egypt is 22.5 million dollars behind on payments to the International Monetary Fund . . . Nasser also owes 70 million dollars in Commodity Credit Corp. grain bills to the United States and another 14 million dollars under the U.S. good aid program. He has received approximately 1.2 billion dollars in American aid and another 700 million dollars in help from the Soviet Union, including 200 million dollars from the Russians for the Aswan Dam."

Nevertheless, the masses of the Egyptians were so accustomed to living in such pitiful squalor and near-starvation that it was unlikely that the pending crisis would make much difference in their lives. Nasser's real threat remained political and required continuous diking lest a flood of blood sweep him out of power. He knew this would not come from the masses unless it was led by the army. Nasser's sense of survival drove him to take his first action there.

As Israel released thousands of prisoners they included many officers from Egypt's top command. These returned to Cairo in a vividly dark mood. Nasser increased his bodyguard. It had been the loss of a war with Israel almost two decades earlier which had allowed Nasser to spearhead a military coup and come to power in the first place. Now he saw a similar mood of revolutionary ambition appearing along the top fringe of Egypt's 1967 military elite. Many of these were formerly Nasser's close friends. Before they could strike out at him, he struck out at them. Within a short time 700 Egyptian officers had been demoted, transferred, or otherwise disgraced.[70]

"One night while the President [Nasser] was entertaining his old friend and former chief of staff, Marshal Abdel Hakim Amer, at dinner, armored cars and infantrymen swooped down on Amer's house in Cairo and seized a number of disaffected officers to whom Amer, himself cashiered in June, had given asylum. More than 150 other military men were also seized and all of them, Amer included, were placed under house arrest."[71]

The fact that General Amer had given asylum to suspected Army rebels was enough to place him in a very dangerous political position. A few days later Cairo announced that Amer was dead. Suicide by poison, the dispatch said. Where was the body? Buried—two days ago.

"First accounts indicated Amer died Friday morning but this was corrected officially with the announcement that death came Thursday night. The news was first broadcast to the Arab world on Cairo radio and then was announced to reporters at a news conference in Cairo.

"The official announcement, nearly 30 hours after Amer died, said he swallowed a large dose of poison—type unspecified. It said he already had been buried in his native village of Menia, 200 miles south of Cairo."[72]

Foreign observers had reason to doubt the suicide story. Why all the mystery and secrecy? Why was the body buried so quickly—in such obscurity—and why the 30-hour delay before the public was informed? After all, this man had been the vice-president of Egypt and commander-in-chief of her military forces until June 9, 1967.

Cairo was silent.

---

70. "Hail the Conquered Hero," *Newsweek*, Sept. 11, 1967, p. 34.
71. *Ibid.*, p. 35.
72. Associated Press dispatch, "Top Nasser Aide in Israel War Takes Own Life," *Salt Lake Tribune*, Sept. 16, 1967, p. 1.

Something else bothered observers. There were too many men around Nasser who were not Egyptians at all but men who had helped precipitate the bloody holocaust of World War II. Stevenson writes:

"A stream of former Nazis had been arriving in Cairo in the 1950s and they found the political climate to their liking. They sent word to old comrades in Latin America and soon Egypt was giving haven to men who could get no nearer to Europe without risking identification. They included Leopold Gleim, once Gestapo chief in Warsaw; SS General Oscar Dirlewanger and Willi Brenner, who organized the Mauthausen concentration camp; General Wilhelm Fahrmbacher, an artillery specialist who brought 34 ex-German army officers with him. Dr. Wilhelm Voss took charge of a missile production center and was joined by Professor Paul Goerke of Peenemunde.

"Some Germans still embarrassed by their Nazi backgrounds were given Arab names, among them Dr. Johann von Leers, who had been a leading anti-Jewish propagandist. Nasser employed some [former Nazis] in his propaganda agencies and others in the development of weapons."[73]

No one cared to predict what evil might come to the people of Egypt as well as others in the Mediterranean basin if Nasser continued to give asylum and prestige-appointments to this breed of fanatical National Socialists. They were also said to be working harmoniously with that other breed of socialist militants to which Nasser had attached himself—the Communist hierarchy. Recent history had demonstrated that in the brains of such men there festered the potential nightmare of terroristic destruction which the ancient prophets had associated with a great Middle Eastern war of the future—Armageddon!

---

73. William Stevenson, *Strike Zion!* pp. 102-103.

Israelis Turn Out to Be a
New Specie of Conquerors

The Arabs of Old Jerusalem, Sinai, West Jordan, Hebron, Nablus and Southwest Syria—who unexpectedly found themselves in the occupied territory of the hated Israelis— had no way of knowing what to expect from their new rulers. The conquest had been so stunning that there was never any time to adjust to the idea. The Jews were just suddenly there. It took the Arabs months to accept the fact that the Israelis really did believe in a bi-racial nation. It was a slow process. Many Arabs considered it a betrayal of their allegiance to collaborate with the Jews. Even acts of open generosity were viewed with profound suspicion.

"In the fiercely independent town of Nablus in the hills of Samaria, extremists passed the word to Arab shopkeepers not to open on Saturday, the day most Israeli tourists visited the town. Rumors spread that the Israelis would soon be gone; those who cooperated with them would be punished when an Arab government returned. As shopkeepers stood uncertainly by their shuttered stores, not sure what to do, the Israelis started a rumor of their own: shops that refused to open might never open again. Then military patrols began to paint triangular symbols on closed shop fronts. They painted only a few before the Arabs saw the writing on the wall. Shutters flew up all over town—and have stayed up. No longer does anyone doubt that the Israelis are there to stay."[74]

The thing which surprised Arabs most of all was the willingness of the Israeli occupation officials to have Arab communities continue governing themselves. In fact, the Israelis insisted upon it. Newsmen were even surprised. Here is a report written three months after the war:

"You can drive for miles on the road between Israel

---

74. "Israel Digging in to Stay," *Time*, August 11, 1967, p. 21.

and the west bank of Jordan without seeing a single Israeli soldier; they are instructed to stay out of sight. So far, Israeli administrators have managed to confine their activities to indirect rule. Israel is paying Arab civil servants' salaries, granting loans to municipalities and arranging for remittances from abroad to continue. And at night, Israeli troops conveniently look the other way as scores of Arab trucks, carrying fruit and vegetables from west-bank farms, ford the Jordan river on their way to the markets of Amman."[75]

The Israeli leaders were not noisy about what they wanted to accomplish. They were making no extravagant promises. Their policy was to be generous where possible but sharply firm where necessary. A sniper's house was likely to be torn down to its foundations. On the other hand Israel's frugally garnered finances were shared with the Arabs in occupied territory almost as though they were Jews. An American reporter stated:

"To aid the West Bank's economy some 25 Israeli bank branches have opened in the area, and last week the Israeli pound was made legal tender along with the Jordanian dinar. The Jerusalem government has virtually adopted the former Jordanian budget for the West Bank, including development plans for road building and other public works totaling $5,600,000 this year. All former local officials, including all the West Bank mayors and most city employees, have stayed on their jobs under Israeli rule. Wherever possible, Israel is keeping Jordanian law and custom intact. Thus schoolchildren will get their books free, though in Israel their parents must pay for them. Jordanian courts are back in business, with the amendment that prisoners are now sentenced not 'in the name of King Hussein' but 'in the name of law and justice.' "

---

75. "Arabs Under Israeli Rule," *Newsweek*, September 11, 1967, p. 38.

General Moshe Dayan Looms Large in Post-War Israel

Much of what had been happening reflected the thinking of General Moshe Dayan, Israel's Minister of Defense. He detested fuzzy thinking and liked humanitarian programs to be as crisp and practical as military field strategy. When he was called into the Cabinet just prior to the war he found the Labor Party (Mapai) leaders indecisive and floundering. They were spilling over with half-measures, compromises and wishful thinking. The moment they had given Dayan authority to steer them out of the crisis he swept their half-baked political cookery into the ash bin. He then set down the policies and tactics which produced one of the most brilliant military victories in history. When the war was over the professional do-gooders rushed forward to seize control of affairs lest "military men" remain dominant on the scene. To the astonishment of many foreign observers, Dayan came up with better ideas than the lot. He completely outclassed the do-gooders, both in concept and execution. Some compared his peacetime policies to those of General Douglas MacArthur in Japan following World War II.

American columnist, Joseph Alsop, went to Israel and wrote: ". . . he [Dayan] is far nearer to having a clearly thought-out policy toward Israel's main problem than anyone else can discover here."[76] Alsop noted that Dayan grasped the psyche of the Arabs and knew how to deal with them because he respected them. His method of handling the prickly political situation in Nablus was typical. Alsop quotes Dayan as saying:

"Take Hamdi K'nan, the mayor of Nablus. He doesn't like us—why should he?—but he is a good mayor. He came to me saying he must resign because he could not

---

76. Joseph Alsop, "Does Dayan Have Israel's Answer?" *Salt Lake Tribune*, September 13, 1967, p. 15.

serve under an Israeli occupation. I told him that his resignation was something for the people of Nablus to worry about, that I could not stop him and that I would not replace him. If he and the Nablus people wanted no public administration in Nablus . . . that was entirely their choice, and I would not interfere with it. So he thought for a while and did not resign."

This way Dayan's way of forcing them to govern themselves and giving them a renewed sense of dignity. It was also his subtle but highly persuasive way of teaching the Arabs that they are not captives but free residents of New Israel. Watching Dayan's ministry in operation led Alsop to comment, "Occupation without administration is the best summary one can offer of the singular formula that Dayan has adopted. All that Israel needs, he points out, is to insure that no enemy troops cross the Jordan; and for this purpose Israel only requires the use of the main roads and a few strong points on the heights above the river."

Concerning economic, refugee and humanitarian policies, Dayan is quoted as saying, " . . . if they want fuel and teachers' salaries and electricity and everything else they need, it is up to them to cooperate with us in the very small way we need." Nevertheless, Dayan insists that the Jews not become participants in anything which smacks of colonial administration. "We must not interfere, become involved, issue permits, make regulations, name administrators, become rulers."

Dayan's "grand strategy" is for a lasting peace between Arabs and Jews. He wants to make a showcase of the West Bank to demonstrate what good will can do between two semitic peoples. ". . . there are a thousand things Israel can do to make life better there." he said.

Alsop concluded his article by saying, "A more original approach to the problem of the occupiers and the occupied could hardly be imagined. But it just might work."

The Rising Anxiety of the Jews to Rebuild their Temple

Once the Jewish mind had comprehended the full implication of its fantastic victory, the Jewish spirit longed for its ancient temple. On Wednesday, June 7, 1967, when Israeli troops finally reached the famous wailing wall where there are still some of the massive stones from the earlier temple wall, Rabbi Shlomo Goren, senior chaplain for the Israeli armed forces, declared to the jubilant Jewish soldiers, "We have taken the City of God. WE ARE ENTERING THE MESSIANIC ERA FOR THE JEWISH PEOPLE!"[77]

To every Jew, orthodox or reformed, the Messianic Era means a Temple! The last ten chapters of Ezekiel tell all about it. Even the specifications are there. Jewish architects can commence their drawings with nothing more needed than the vision of Ezekiel to guide them. Nearly 600 years before the time of Christ, Ezekiel was allowed to walk in vision through the rooms and courtyards of that glorious future edifice of the latter days and record the measurement of every significant part of it. God knew the Jews would be without Urim and Thummim for over twenty-five centuries. He therefore provided the revelation for the building of the latter-day Temple before His prophets disappeared from among them.

A new book called *Strike Zion!* contains a whole section written by Leon Uris, the author of *Exodus*. He has entitled this section, "The Third Temple." Solomon's temple was the first, but it was destroyed in 587 B.C. by the Babylonians. After Cyrus, the Persian, conquered the Babylonians, he allowed the Jews to return to Jerusalem. There they built their second temple and dedicated it in 516 B.C. Five centuries later, just prior to the birth of Christ,

---

77. Robert J. Donovan, *Israel's Fight for Survival*, p. 120.

Herod the Great tried to curry favor with the Jews by reconstructing this decaying second temple. This reconstruction was referred to as "Herod's Temple," but the Jews continued to insist that it was the Second Temple which Herod had merely refurbished. In any event, it was torn down and completely demolished by General Titus of Rome when he burned and looted Jerusalem in 70 A.D. Ever since then the Jews have longed and prayed for the day when they could build their majestic Temple again. In 1967, with Jerusalem securely occupied, they knew the time must not be very far away.

The mood of the Jewish mind is caught by Leon Uris as he concludes his essay with these six paragraphs:

"And so they fought three wars for freedom in two decades [1948, 1956 and 1967]. In the end, the Jews stood alone. As in the beginning they were few but they were brave. And they crushed the enemies all around them with such swiftness that all men in all places stood in awe. It did not seem that this was an army of mortals.

"And the terrible odyssey was over. Never again would the Jews have to wail in anguish, 'Next year in Jerusalem.'

"As in the glorious times of kings and prophets, great new warriors and rabbis and scholars had risen among them.

"And when the third and final war was done they went up into their ancient capital. Many of them had dropped the names of their exile and taken ancient names. Ben Gurion and Dayan and Rabin and Meir and Eban.

"And they stood before the Western Wall of the Temple and prayed and danced and they wept for joy.

"And the Lord felt they had kept the faith well and suffered enough. And he bade them build a third Temple and dwell in their own land, forever."[78]

---

78. William Stevenson, *Strike Zion!* pp. 141-142.

Problems Which Must be Solved Before the New Temple Can be Built

The greatest single obstacle to the rebuilding of the Temple is not money, plans or lack of aspiration, but opportunity. The Jews possess Jerusalem, but they do not possess the sacred ground where their temple must be built. That spot is covered by one of the most beautiful Moslem structures in the world—the Dome of the Rock. Beneath it lies the white outcropping of rock which is supposed to have been the spot occupied by the Holy of Holies belonging to Solomon's temple. It is the spot where Abraham is believed to have offered up his son as a sacrifice. It is also the spot from which the Moslems believe their prophet Mohammed ascended into Heaven during a vision. All of this conflict of interest ties the Temple-building project into a Gordian knot.

In a special article on this subject dated June 30, 1967, the religious editors of *Time* said: "Learned Jewish opinion has long debated when and how the Temple can be rebuilt. The great medieval philosopher Maimonides, in his Code of Jewish Law, argued that every generation of Jews was obliged to rebuild the Temple if its site was ever retaken, if a leader descended from David could be found, and if the enemies of Judaism were destroyed. Since Maimonides' time, however, most rabbis have gloomily concluded that the restoration of the Temple would have to wait until the coming of the Messiah. In line with that reasoning, the chief rabbinate of Israel issued a warning after the capture of Jordanian Jerusalem that no Jew should step inside the Temple area."

The Chief rabbi apparently reasoned that there was no need to offend the Arab Moslems or give them the impression the Jews intended to commence their Temple immediately when it had been decided that the construction of the Temple could wait until the Messianic

Era had commenced. However, since the initial capture of the Old City, many leading Jewish theologians have had second thoughts about the rabbi's pronouncement. The *Time* article therefore continues:

"Nonetheless, such is Israel's euphoria [sense of confidence and well-being] today that some Jews see plausible theological grounds for discussing reconstruction. They base their argument on the contention that Israel has already entered its 'Messianic era.' In 1948, they note, Israel's chief rabbis ruled that with the establishment of the Jewish state and the 'ingathering of the exiles,' the age of redemption had begun. Today, many of Israel's religious leaders are convinced that the Jews' victory over the Arabs has taken Judaism well beyond that point. Says Historian Israel Eldad: 'We are at the stage where David was when he liberated Jerusalem. From that time until the construction of the Temple by Solomon, only one generation passed. So will it be with us.' And what about the Moslem shrine? Answers Eldad: 'It is of course an open question. Who knows? Perhaps there will be an earthquake.' "

In an earlier paragraph this article summarizes all of the problems connected with this Temple-building project and says:

"Whether or not the building of a new Temple should wait until the Messiah arrives, Jewish theology presents several obstacles to its construction. For one thing, the Law requires that the Temple be administered by Cohens (priests), who are the descendants of Moses' brother, Aaron. Yet so many nonpriestly Jews have assumed the name Cohen that rabbinical experts would face a legal nightmare in trying to trace authentic genealogies. For another, the Torah specifies that Temple ritual include daily animal sacrifices—a concept alien to the humane sensitivities of most modern Jews. An even greater obstacle is that the Temple must be constructed on its original site; this could only be done by demolishing Islam's sacred Dome of the

Rock, the spot from which Mohammed ascended into heaven [and, according to their tradition, returned again the same night]. Despite their enmity with Arab nations, devout Jews would be reluctant to destroy the shrine of another faith."

It is true that the Jews must locate among themselves those who can trace their line to Levi, the brother of Judah. It was through Levi that the Priesthood was to be administered, not Judah. Judah was to have political rule. Now that the Jews have become the rulers of Palestine they must now encourage their brother-Israelites, the Levites, who descended through Levi's grandson, Aaron, to come forth and perform the ordinances in the future Temple. They alone are authorized by God to function in that Temple before the Messiah comes.

The same problem confronted the Jews when they returned from their exile to Babylon during the sixth century before Christ. After Cyrus had issued an edict dated 538 B.C. authorizing the Jews to go back to Jerusalem and build their temple, a total of 50,000 responded. But among them were only 4,000 who could prove by unquestionable pedigree charts they were descendants of Aaron. Many others came forward claiming the right to the Priesthood but had not kept their genealogies intact and therefore they could not prove their claim. Concerning these the Bible says, "These sought their register among those that were reckoned by genealogy, but they were not found: therefore were they [considered] as polluted, PUT FROM THE PRIESTHOOD. And the Tirshatha [governor] said unto them, that they should not eat of the most holy things [as Temple priests] till there stood up a priest with Urim and with Thummim [to verify their true lineage]."[79]

Unfortunately, the Urim and Thummim, like the Ark of the Covenant, were never heard of again following the destruction of Jerusalem, so these unfortunate claimants to

79. Ezra 2:62-63.

ordination apparently had to remain outside the pale of the Priesthood service.

When the Jews rebuild their modern Temple they will undoubtedly follow this same rule in selecting worthy descendants of Levi and Aaron to administer in its sacred precincts. Only a few of the orthodox have been zealous in maintaining creditable genealogies and only these should be allowed to serve as Cohens or Priests. Actually, the number need not be large. Ezekiel assures us that this Temple somehow will be built and that prior to the coming of the Messiah the Priests of Aaron will offer up an offering unto the Lord in righteousness.[80]

So, in spite of the almost insurmountable obstacles which stand in the way of modern Temple project, it will succeed. As we shall see in the last section of this book, the ancient prophets who discussed this Temple of the last days unanimously confirmed that it would be built. When this is finally achieved it will no doubt be a "marvelous work and a wonder" just as with everything else the Lord undertakes. The main consideration at this moment is the prophetic fact that "it shall be done!"

Understanding the Jewish Self-Image

Now that the Jews have literally crashed back into the main stream of history, the self-image which these people have assigned to themselves suddenly becomes vitally important. It is their self-image which is the explanation for their survival as a people. It is the explanation for their gradual but dogged return to the land of their ancestors. It is the explanation for their successful war of independence in 1948 and their fantastic victory in the war of June, 1967. The Jews know they have a role to fill, a mission to perform, a rendezvous with destiny.

---

80. See Ezekiel, Chapter 44.

As I have talked to the Israelis in their own land, I have found them to be a compound of pride and humility. They are proud of their history and ethnological integrity but humble about the scars of ghetto life and prison camps which many of them still carry. They are proud of their new nation with its rags-to-riches Cinderella story, but humble about many inadequacies and limitations which still remain. They are proud of those Jews who reached the pinnacle of success and became big names in science, art, literature, inventions, government, economics, sociology, psychology, philosophy and a host of other fields; at the same time they were humble about those who became "lost" Jews, turned to atheism, abandoned their people and engaged in the promotion of evils which the Decalogue denounces. They are proud of their place in the Old Testament, their survival as a people during their great Diaspora or dispersion, and their prophetic destiny in modern times; nevertheless they are realistic and humble in their anxiety to measure up to and fulfill their monumental, prophetic assignment which they can neither delegate nor reject.

It all sums up in the fact that Jewish self-image emerges from the roots of Jewish history. The mentality, personality and aspirations of the Jewish people cannot be understood in any other way. It therefore becomes our task in the next section of this book to present the sweeping vista of the Children of Judah from the days of King David around 1000 B.C. to those of David Ben-Gurion, Levi Eshkol, Abba Eban and General Moshe Dayan, of June, 1967.

It is an amazing story.

PART III

THE SWEEPING VISTA OF JEWISH HISTORY

THE JEWISH HERITAGE

After the Israeli miracle war in 1967, it was said that the Jews had come smashing back into the mainstream of human history. Actually, they had never left. What really happened was that the far-flung threads of the Jewish tapestry suddenly wove themselves back into the warp and woof of modern historical consciousness. No longer were the Jews thought of as "refugees" or merely one of the "minorities." In an instant, as it were, they had come into their own as the mini-giant of the Middle East. They were a unique nation. They were a unique religion. They were a unique culture.

Down through the centuries many of the Jews have wished they were not so unique. Occasionally, in an effort to lose their singular and peculiar position among men, some would abandon the faith and fealty of their fathers. The majority, however, stuck it out. For some it was a matter of idealism. For others it was family loyalty. Sometimes it was spiritual affinity. Sometimes it was a most inhuman and atrocious form of cruel persecution which drove them together. Sometimes they didn't even know why they were clinging to the family tree. The important fact of history is that they clung.

In our own day the centripetal force which has formed a hard core unity among Jews from Siberia to Beverly Hills has been Zionism. The movement is less than a century old, but it has done more to bring this seventeen-million remnant of Israel into a congealed core of strength than anything since the Maccabean rebellion.

Suddenly a sense of ethnical pride drew Jews together from opposite poles. Back in 1946 I was assigned by the

FBI to speak at a rather important Jewish gathering in Los Angeles. My host was the leading Rabbi of Southern California. While we were eating, the Rabbi noticed that I was curiously watching some of those in attendance. He was a little embarrassed by their presence and explained, "I don't think they're fugitives from justice, but neither are they affiliates of this congregation." He hesitated a moment and then added, "Since our people became imbued with the rise of Zionism it has brought together not only our most illustrious but also some of our most notorious. I hardly know what to do with them. They are among our most liberal contributors!"

This became typical of Jewish communities all over the world. The renegades who ordinarily would have spurned with utter contempt any gathering at a Jewish synagogue or temple, now turned out as though they were part of the flock. And, as the Rabbi said, "They are among the most liberal contributors."

Not All Jews Want to Go Back to Israel

But in spite of all this effusive exuberance for Zionism by both highbrow and low, the primary motivation has been merely to provide financial support, rather than participate personally. This has been particularly characteristic of American Jews. Because so many of them are successful in their respective fields, David Ben-Gurion wanted them to migrate to Israel. This they almost universally refused to do. They would give most generously of their money, but not of themselves. Leon Uris, author of *Exodus*, explains why:

"If the Jews of Russia, Spain, or Yemen had been afforded the same freedoms we have in America, the longing for Israel would not be so acute.

"There is a great concern by the leaders of Israel over the lack of substantial immigration from America. I am asked, 'What if America turns on the Jews as has happened everywhere else? What then?'

"If such a thing were to happen in America, then Israel is not the answer for me. I would not want to go on living. There are no questions here of split loyalty. My identity as an American is total. I love my country as much as the Israeli loves his. I would no more put Israel ahead of America than John Kennedy would have put the Vatican ahead of America. I am what I am because my father was sensible enough to catch the boat and God only knows what would have happened if he hadn't.

"On the other hand, I will not turn my back on my fellow Jews whose fathers were not as sensible as mine. I do not understand that there is any conflict in supporting the right of my fellow Jews to their own nation and my being a citizen of this country."[1]

Who are the Jews? Beginning back around 1800 B.C., they were one of the Twelve Tribes who descended from the great patriarch, Jacob. One of Jacob's sons was Judah and today all those who carry in their veins the blood of Judah are entitled to be called Jews. The Jews also include all those who have been converted to Judaism down through the centuries or who have elected to intermingle with the Jews. There has been a considerable number in these last two categories and their presence in Israel today is reflected by those who have red hair, freckles, blue eyes and other characteristics not traditionally Jewish.

Nevertheless, whether blue-eyed or black, whether Swedish blond or Siberian brunette, the Jews share a common heritage and a common source of pride. It all goes back to the golden age of David, the Goliath-killer, and Solomon, his judicious, temple-building son.

---

1. William Stevenson and Leon Uris, *Strike Zion!* p. 127.

The Golden Age of the Jews

Like the Greeks under Pericles, the Jews had a golden age which lasted during the better part of two generations. The Jews were never so illustrious afterwards, and therefore they never forgot the triumph of those glorious days when Judah ruled from the Euphrates in the north and east to the river of Egypt in the south and west. The vista of Jewish history begins with the Davidic epic.

David was born around 1032 B.C. in Bethlehem. The Israelites were just emerging from four centuries of apostasy and dark ages which had extended from Joshua to Samuel. In fact, it was Samuel who was rejected by the Israelites as their political leader and who therefore had been ordered by the Lord to anoint Saul their king as the people had demanded. Then, when Saul became avaricious and was rejected by the Lord, it was Samuel who was commanded of the Lord to go to Bethlehem and ordain young David the new king. From all we are able to ascertain, David was only a teen-ager at the time. Nevertheless, Saul continued to reign over Israel for many more years, and he spent much of that time trying to capture and kill David. However, when the great Philistine war was fought around 1002 B.C., the Philistines won. Saul tried to escape, but after the pursuing Philistines had wounded him severely, he cloistered himself in a ravine or hideout and ordered his bodyguard to kill him. When the man refused, Saul took the blade of his own sword, placed it between the leaves of metal, and fell upon it.

The suicide of Saul and the subsequent restoration of peace permitted David to come out of hiding and claim the throne which God had anointed him to receive. By this time, David was thirty years of age. At first only Judah would accept him as king, but after seven years, circumstances permitted him to take over as king of all Israel. David immediately conquered the heathen Jebusite

city of Jerusalem and made it his capital. Soon, he began
expanding the landholdings of Israel by either conquest
or demanding payment of tribute. After many years of
continuous warfare he succeeded in subjugating everything
from Mesopotamia to Egypt.

David wanted to build a glorious Temple to express to
the Lord his profound appreciation for his many blessings.
The Lord, however, told David he had shed too much
blood during his lifetime and the sacred edifice would
have to be constructed by his son, Solomon. David therefore spent his last days gathering together the stone and
timbers necessary for the Lord's house, and just before his
death, he called the people together and presented Solomon to them as their new king.

Solomon's reign was peaceful, prosperous and politically stable right up to the very last part of his life. He
built a navy which sailed from Elath down the Aqaba
Gulf, and thence to Africa and the coasts of India. It
would return after three years with millions in gold,
jewels, spices, ivory, apes and peacocks.[2]

One of Solomon's most memorable achievements was
the building of the famous Temple. It was not a large
structure but it was an architectural jewel. At the front
it had two huge bronze pillars. The floor of the outer
porch was overlaid with gold as was the floor inside the
Temple. The front doors were made from thick planks of
olive wood, elaborately carved, with gold foil carefully
molded over the carving. The walls of the interior were
of carved cedar magnificently decorated with gold and
precious stones. Inside the Holy of Holies there were
two giant cherubims carved as a symbolic protection for
the Ark of the Covenant. They were each 15 feet high
with $7\frac{1}{2}$ foot wings spread out in each direction.

All parts of this great Temple were pre-fabricated and

---

2. I Kings 10:22.

brought to the Temple block for assembling. The scripture says, "there was neither hammer nor axe nor any tool of iron heard in the house, while it was in building."[3]

After a brilliant career as king, Solomon suffered from senility in his latter years which loosened his grip on surrounding kingdoms.[4] To hold them together, Solomon entered into all kinds of marriage alliances with the prominent families and royal houses of these kingdoms. This was a common procedure in those days but a mistake for Solomon. It brought a great host of heathen women to Jerusalem, and before long they had wheedled permission from Solomon to build their pagan shrines and temples all over the Mount of Olives. The record is clear that this did not occur until Solomon "was old,"[5] and apparently the victim of severe senility. These circumstances therefore mitigate against a harsh judgment of an otherwise brilliant and competent king.

The fact remains, however, that toward the end Solomon began to lose the confidence of his people and his numerous political marriages corrupted the kingdom.

The End of the Golden Age

When Solomon died, only Judah would support his son, Rehoboam, as king. The ten northern tribes split away and set up a king of their own. His name was Jeroboam, an Ephraimite. Under his administration the northern tribes turned to idolatry. They drove from their midst the Levites and Priests (the Priests being Levites who were descendants of Aaron). Practically all of these gravitated toward Judah, so Israel was split with two tribes in the south—the Jews and Levites—while the remaining ten tribes formed an alliance in the north,

3. I Kings 6:7.
4. See W. Cleon Skousen, *The Fourth Thousand Years*, pp. 270-280.
5. I Kings 11:4.

their capital being first Shechem, then Tirzah, and finally Samaria (all three are within seven miles of each other).

By 900 B.C. the great prophet of the era was Elijah who was spending practically all of his time with the northern tribes, attempting to keep King Ahab and his voluptuous, heathen wife, Jezebel, from making a moral cesspool of Israel's culture. Fertility worship, child sacrifices and sacramental degradation were the order of the day.

By 800 B.C. Elisha was making the circuit among the people and doing what he could to ameliorate the damage which had occurred during the previous century. Between Moses and Christ, Elisha was the prophet who was given the power to perform mighty miracles more extensive and spectacular than the other prophets of that period.

Around 722 B.C. history caught up with the northern ten tribes and they were swept into captivity by the Assyrians. All who survived the long series of sieges (some of which reduced the people to cannibalism and the most degraded conditions) were marched off toward the Assyrian capital of Nineveh, and before long they completely disappeared among the waves of successive migrations into Asia and Europe. They thereafter were known as "the lost tribes."

Isaiah and Jeremiah

By 700 B.C., Judah had produced a famous prophet of her own. His name was Isaiah. Isaiah was a native of Jerusalem and had as rich an endowment of the prophetic gift as any prophet in the Old Testament record. He prophesied and lived to see the fall of the northern Ten Tribes.[6] He also prophesied the fall of Judah. He knew

---

6. See details in *The Fourth Thousand Years*, p. 547.

a century before it occurred that Jerusalem and its beautiful Temple would be destroyed and he knew the nation which would do it. It would be the Babylonians.[7] Nevertheless, Isaiah knew the Jews would survive and after their exile they would return to rebuild their capital and eventually bring forth the Great Messiah from among them.

Isaiah's writings present the golden theme of the coming Messiah in such a rich tapestry that more prophetic details concerning the Savior's life and ministry can be traced to this source than any other.[8] Isaiah's entire 53rd chapter is concerning the coming Messiah.

Between 700 to 600 B.C. the great saga of the Assyrian Empire came to its bloody and tragic conclusion. For generations the Assyrians had spread a predatory plague across the civilized world. As we have already noted, one of their conquests was the northern Ten Tribes of Israel who were plundered and slaughtered, after which the ravaged remnants were hauled off to Assyria. In due time, however, Assyria's power was challenged by her tributaries. The foremost of these was Babylon. Babylon had the help of the Medes in conquering the Assyrian capital city of Nineveh in 612 B.C. and the Assyrian hosts were finally routed after several years of bloodshed and carnage which finally terminated at the famous battle of Carchemish in 605 B.C.

In this period of constant warfare, Judah was bound to get caught in the cross-fire. Although a tributary to Assyria, Judah was overrun by Nebuchadnezzar of Babylon in 606 B.C. and some of her brightest young Jews were shipped off to the Euphrates for training in the Babylonian culture. One of these was Daniel. Eight years later, Nebuchadnezzar came back to punish Judah for conspiring to ally herself with Egypt and this time the Babylonians

---

7. *Ibid.*, p. 564-565.
8. *Ibid.*, pp. 530-541.

took 10,000 of Judah's finest artisans, technicians and scholars. One of these was Ezekiel.

However, Nebuchadnezzar left the greatest prophet of the day in Jerusalem. His name was Jeremiah. God's warning to Judah through this prophet had been that they should subject themselves to the Babylonians. Under Babylonian rule they were promised a period of both peace and prosperity. It is easy to see why Nebuchadnezzar counted Jeremiah a friend. But his own people did not. The popular political strategy of Judah at the moment was to line up with Egypt and overthrow Babylon. When Jeremiah warned that this was the pathway to destruction he was imprisoned, beaten, and subjected to forced starvation.

In 589 B.C. the prophecies of both Isaiah and Jeremiah began to descend on Judah like a hive of hornets. Jerusalem was put under siege, and when her walls were finally breached in 587 B.C. the Babylonians methodically massacred the people and devastated the city. Solomon's beautiful temple, the royal palaces and the homes of the people all went down in the maelstrom of one vast, massive wave of destruction. One of those who was spared was Jeremiah. Nebuchadnezzar had issued specific instructions that the first commanders to enter the city were to see that Jeremiah was located and protected. He was allowed to stay with a few of the people in Judah, but the rest of the captives were hustled off to mighty Babylon where they remained for two generations.

The Fall of Babylon and the Return of the Jews

Over 150 years before it happened, Isaiah had predicted that Babylon, herself, would fall. He had identified by name the man who would conquer Babylon. His name was Cyrus, King of Persia. Concerning this man the Lord had said through Isaiah: "Thus saith the Lord to his anointed, to Cyrus, whose right hand I have holden, to subdue nations before him; and I will loose the loins of kings, to open before him the two leaved gates; and the gates shall not be shut. . . . For Jacob my servant's sake, and Israel mine elect, I have even called thee by my name: I have surnamed thee though thou hast not known me."[9]

It was 539 B.C. when Cyrus, the Persian, successfully entered the heavily fortified precincts of Babylon. This was achieved by digging a huge trench around the city and then diverting the river through the canal during the night. The stream bed by which the river had formerly entered the city was left dry and the hosts of Cyrus marched in. They found Belshazzar, the king, freshly murdered by his own people, so they met little resistance and order was restored almost immediately.

One year later, in 538 B.C., Cyrus authorized 50,000 Jews to return to the ruins of their beloved Jerusalem for the purpose of rebuilding it. These 50,000 "Zionists" required four months to reach their destination and were led by a man who was a direct descendant of David, named Zerubbabel. Cyrus did everything he could to encourage the Jews in this project. He gave them back all the gold and silver vessels from the former Temple which the Babylonians had captured. The total number of these expensive utensils was 5,400. Cyrus also ordered that the expenses for the restoration of the Temple should be paid out of the king's personal account. Political power shifts in the next few years prevented the Jews from enjoying the full advantage of this bequest, but it demonstrated the sincerity of Cyrus, the king of Persia, in offering it.

It was not until 516 B.C. that the reconstructed Tem-

---

9. Isaiah 45:1,4.

ple was finished and dedicated. This became known as the Second Temple. Sometimes it is called Zerubbabel's Temple. It was the same dimensions as the Temple of Solomon but not nearly so elaborate in either its structure or embellishments. Nevertheless, it became the established center of Jewish worship and remained so for many centuries.

One generation later found the kingdom of Persia under the rule of the famous Darius. Not only had he conquered all of the Middle East, but he had penetrated Europe as far as the Danube. His expanding ambitions were blunted, however, when the Greeks defeated Darius at Marathon in 490 B.C. Four years later Darius died and he was succeeded by his young son, Xerxes, who reigned for 21 years. Xerxes practically exhausted the empire trying to defeat the Greeks and avenge the disgrace at Marathon, but the Greek bastion held firm.

We mention Xerxes in our present story because he is generally believed to be identical with the king named Ashasuerus in the Bible. It is well-known that Xerxes was not his Persian name but one given this king by the Greeks.[10] His real name is believed to have been Ashasuerus who made Esther, the beautiful Jewish girl, his queen. The story of this famous young woman of the Bible is highlighted by the fact that she risked her life to save the Jews from an extermination decree. This heroic act was ever afterwards commemorated in one of the annual Jewish festivals.

Ezra and Nehemiah

Another famous Jew of this period was living in the Persian province of Babylon. His name was Ezra. He was a scholar, Priest and scribe. However, he was not a

---

10. Dr. Cunningham Geikie, *Hours with the Bible*, Vol. 6, p. 454.

prophet. He had never seen the heavens opened nor received a direct commandment from God in a personal revelation. Nevertheless, he longed to return to Jerusalem and strengthen the religious spine of the Jews which had deteriorated after the Temple-building project was completed.

The king of Persia by this time was the son of Xerxes named Artaxerxes. When he learned of Ezra's desires to lead another migration of Jews back to Jerusalem, he not only gave his consent but became an enthusiastic sponsor of the project. The Persian religion of that day was pantheistic and assumed that the universe was ruled by many gods. King Artaxerxes exhibited a great anxiety to become worthy of the blessings of the God of the Jews. He therefore took up a collection of gold and silver from his chief administrators and added substantially to it himself. He sent up additional vessels for the Temple, and not only made all of those who administered in the Temple immune from taxes and tributes, but authorized Ezra to call on the chief satrap of Syria and Palestine to furnish the money to buy the necessary animals to make the daily sacrifices.

Equally important, the king authorized Ezra to set up judges to enforce the laws of Moses. He even authorized Ezra's judges to impose the death penalty in prescribed cases—an extremely unusual concession.

When Ezra arrived in Jerusalem he found a scandalous state of apostasy, much of it due to gross ignorance on the part of the people. He thereupon determined to spend most of his time educating the people and then insisting that they carefully obey the commandments which God had given them. It is interesting that when the people heard the law of God read to them, they went into deepest mourning for the many offenses they had ignorantly committed. This convinced Ezra that what the people needed above everything else was a body of

scribes who could make copies of the scriptures and inter-
pret them for the people. He therefore made a collection
of what he considered the best authenticated scriptural
materials and these became the canon of the Old Testament very much as we have it today.

And while Ezra was busy reviving the spiritual fiber
of the people, there arrived on the scene a man who had
great talents in matters of politics, economics and the
material improvement of the people. His name was
Nehemiah.

Nehemiah was no ordinary Jew but the highly trusted
royal cupbearer of King Artaxerxes. After Ezra had been
gone fourteen years, Nehemiah became so exercised over
reports that the Jews were still living in the rubble and
ruins of their famous city and had not reconstructed anything of significance except the Temple, that he resolved
to initiate a program for the rebuilding of the whole of
Jerusalem. He went with the king's blessing. The most
delicate part of his plan was rebuilding the walls of the
city. The local satrap allowed no walls to be built lest
the people raise up a rebellion and use the walled city as
a fortress. King Artaxerxes smoothed the way for Nehemiah by specifically authorizing him to rebuild the walls
of Jerusalem. He also sent along a military guard to see
that no harm befell his faithful cupbearer while crossing
the treacherous Syrian desert enroute to Judah.

Nehemiah proceeded quietly into Jerusalem without
fanfare and stayed three days without even making himself known to the local authorities. Then he made a
secret night inspection of the entire city and mapped out
in his mind just what must be done to repair the walls.
He also figured out how it could be done in sections so he
could induce the leading princes of Judah to assume responsibility for one section apiece.

Only after all of this preparation did Nehemiah disclose
his identity. He then called upon the leaders in Jerusalem

to rally behind him and get the job done. This must have seemed like manna from heaven to Ezra who had been waiting fourteen years for this kind of community leadership to supplement what he had been doing.

The miracle of cooperation and teamwork soon made itself manifest. The High Priest set the example by gathering the Priests together and starting the reconstruction of the Sheep Gate. The wall section next to it was built by the men of Jericho. Other sections were taken on by various guilds—the goldsmiths, the apothecaries, the merchants. Some communities such as Gibeon and Mizpah each took on a section. Altogether, thirty-five volunteers are named who accepted and completed their parts of this great project. One group, however, stands out in ignoble disgrace. The Bible says the men of Tekoa "put not their necks to the work of the Lord."[11]

All of the most important landmarks around Jerusalem are described by Nehemiah in connection with the assignments he gave these volunteer labor forces. This description has been extremely important to archeologists in locating the foundations of these original walls and gates of the old city.

Malachi—Last of the Prophets

Somewhere around 400 B.C. and perhaps about the time Ezra and Nehemiah disappeared from the scene, the last prophet mentioned in the Bible appeared. He was Malachi.

During his ministry Malachi stressed three major themes. All of them echoed the pleas of Ezra and Nehemiah, so we assume that Malachi was not far behind them, perhaps even a contemporary for a short time. Malachi first accused the people of neglecting and perverting the

---

11. Nehemiah 3:5.

proper Priesthood functions. Secondly, he chastised them for offending the wives of their youth by taking heathen women in marriage. Finally, he accused the people of robbing God by failing to pay their tithes. As Malachi closed his writings to the Jews in Jerusalem he pointed down the corridors of time to "the great and dreadful day of the Lord." Speaking with the authority of God, he declared, "Behold, I will send you Elijah the prophet before the coming of the great and dreadful day of the Lord: and he shall turn the heart of the fathers to the children and the heart of the children to their fathers, lest I come and smite the earth with a curse."[12]

This is the promise of the great day of the Messiah toward which the Jews have been looking ever since. They know that in connection with that monumental event certain things must take place. One of them will be the mission which Elijah must perform preparatory to the Messianic era. A great Jewish scholar, Dr. Joseph Klausner of the Hebrew University in Israel, has written a book entitled *The Messianic Idea of Israel.* He has a whole chapter on the Elijah theme. It is called, "Elijah, the Forerunner of the Messiah."[13]

All Jewish scholars agree that with the end of Malachi's ministry the oracles of the Old Testament period were closed. For a period of four centuries the heavens were as brass. It was to be another four hundred years of dark ages similar to those which followed the ministry of Joshua a thousand years earlier.

The history of the Jews during these four centuries is best understood in the framework of world history. Malachi's ministry in the fourth century B.C. was right at the time that Persia was getting ready for her political demise and Greece was getting ready to replace her as the power structure of the Mediterranean basin.

---

12. Malachi 4:5-6.
13. Joseph Klausner, *The Messianic Idea in Israel,* New York: Macmillan Co., 1955, p. 454.

A Greek scholar named Isocrates established an academy around 390 B.C. in which he began advocating political unity for all Greece. No single Greek leader responded to the message, so in 346 B.C. Isocrates gave his famous *Philippus* oration in which he invited the new young king of Macedonia named Philip to provide the leadership which would unite Greece. Philip responded and by the time Isocrates died in 338 B.C., Philip had defeated the Athenian armies and united warring Greek states.

But in 336 B.C., Philip was assassinated by one of his own courtiers and his twenty-year-old son, Alexander, suddenly found himself in possession of a volatile but united military machine capable of carving up the Persian empire.

This Alexander had been carefully tutored for his unexpected role. He had studied under Aristotle, the famous Greek philosopher, political scientist and naturalist. He was also physically equipped for the task of empire building. He was handsome, powerfully built and possessed an affable and persuasive personality.

Alexander first started out by uniting the dissident forces of Greece, then of Asia Minor and Syria. Finally, he took Egypt in 332 B.C. and was crowned king. Then he was ready to march eastward.

In 331 B.C., Alexander's mammoth war machine captured Babylon. He then entered Persia and chased Darius III up into Media. However, Darius III was murdered by his own nobles, so Alexander pronounced himself the ruler of the whole Persian domain. Additional military action was required for a time to subdue the eastern Persian provinces, but when that was completed Alexander proceeded on to India. This became his easternmost boundary. At the height of his career Alexander suddenly died. It was June 13, 323 B.C. The ruler of the civilized world had not yet reached his thirty-third birthday.

Judah in the Cross-Fire
of Quarreling Greek Generals

As soon as Alexander had died, there was a mad scramble among his generals to seize the territories where they happened to be assigned at the time. All of them set up separate kingdoms. Greece and Macedonia went to the one-eyed general named Antigonus Cyclops, who also had the western part of Asia Minor and hoped to take Syria as well as the rest of the former Persian empire. However, the other generals stopped him and the Asiatic holdings of the empire ended up in the hands of a general named Seleucus Nicator, founder of the Seleucid dynasty of Syria.

Meanwhile, another general named Ptolemy had taken over Egypt and the African holdings of the Greek empire. Ptolemy established a dynasty of Greek Pharaohs over Egypt that lasted 300 years, Cleopatra being the last of his line.

In the partitioning of the Greek empire there were long years of war and political maneuvering. Members of Alexander's own family were caught into the fury of the struggle. His mother, half-brother, wife and son, were all murdered.

Judah also frequently found herself in the cross-fire of these military conflicts. In 320 B.C. Ptolemy I attacked Jerusalem and carried off many captives. In 314, the Greek ruler Antigonus came down and took Palestine. In 312 B.C. Ptolemy grabbed it back again. Things then took a rather stable turn. During these days many Jews migrated to Cyrene, one of the Mediterranean ports of North Africa lying about 300 miles west of Alexandria. Other colonies of Jews preferred the principal Greek city of Egypt which was Alexandria itself.

Around 275 B.C., Ptolemy II, known as Philadelphus, undertook to make the library of Alexandria the most famous in the world. He wanted to include the sacred literature of the Jews but he felt it should be translated into Greek so the local scholars could read it. Ptolemy II therefore imported a body of Jewish scholars who assembled at Pharos, an island just offshore from Alexandria, and there they completed the translation of the Torah (Hebrew version) in 72 days. This seventy-two day miracle gave the translation its name—the Septuagint version.

In 223 B.C., about fifty years after the above event, the house of Seleucus put Antiochus III on the Syrian throne. He immediately attempted to seize nearby Phoenicia and Palestine from Egypt. He thought he could get away with this because Egypt had recently come under one of the most depraved rulers since the Ptolemys took over. His name was Ptolemy IV or Philopator. He was believed to have killed his father to gain the throne, and then his first act as Pharaoh was to kill his mother and younger brother. It was thought by the Syrians that the public hostility toward this despised ruler would make him easy to defeat. But when the Seleucid armies met the Egyptian hosts at Raphia, some twenty miles below Gaza, in 217 B.C., the Egyptians beat the Syrians unmercifully and sent them streaming back toward the north.

Judah was directly involved in this conflict because the moment Ptolemy IV had won this victory he visited Jerusalem and compelled the Jews to allow him to offer pagan sacrifices at the Temple. The people launched a resistance movement and Ptolemy IV became so enraged that he went back to Egypt and started a Nazi-type liquidation of all Jews.

Ptolemy IV died in 203 B.C. and Antiochus III of Syria promptly invaded the Holy Land again. This time he was successful, and after the battle of Panias in 189 B.C. he added Palestine to the Seleucid empire. Antiochus then pressed forward to take Greece and push into Europe. But at the Thermopylae Pass he met the westward march of the Romans and after being thoroughly defeated, was pushed back. This was one of the early symptoms of a new rising power soon to be reckoned with. In fact, in the year 190 B.C., just a few years after Antiochus III returned to the mainland of Asia Minor, he was attacked by another Roman army at Magnesia (near Ephesus) where the Roman general, Scipio, beat him badly. The Romans then dictated severe terms and demanded an enormous tribute. The Syrians were forced to send hostages to Rome, including the son of Antiochus III, named Antiochus Epiphanes. The name of this infamous personality is one to be remembered. He spent fifteen years in Rome to pledge the performance of the promises made by his father and later by his brother. Not until the death of his brother would the Romans allow Antiochus Epiphanes to return home and take over the throne of Syria. Even then he ruled as a vassal of Rome.

Judah Under the Heel of Antiochus Epiphanes

It became the zealous passion of this new Syrian ruler from the house of Seleucid to unify Syria and her tributaries in every way possible. He wished to make the Greek culture universal so as to resist the threatening encroachment of the Roman culture. One of his foremost ambitions was to unite his empire along religious lines. He therefore issued edicts which not only created an impossible situation for the Jews, but was almost as revolting even to the pagan tributaries. However, in spite of all resistance, Antiochus was doggedly determined to carry out his religious reforms.

Right while massive pagan temples were being built to Zeus in Baalbeck, the military and religious zealots of Antiochus Epiphanes were desecrating the Temple in

Jerusalem by erecting an image of Zeus in the Holy of
Holies. They plundered the Temple of its wealth, burned
its sacred books, forbade circumcision or the sanctifying
of the Sabbath day on pain of death. To further mortify
the feelings of the people, the Seleucid officials sacrificed
a sow in the temple to honor Zeus. From then on the
strict observance of every heathen festival became compulsory to all Jews.

To prevent a revolt in Jerusalem, many of the Jews
were sold into slavery and the walls of the city were
demolished. What a heartbreak this would have been for
the faithful Nehemiah who built them.

The Revolt of the Maccabees

About seventeen miles northwest of Jerusalem in a
small town called Modin, there lived an aged Priest named
Mattathia. He watched what was happening in Jerusalem
with the greatest abhorrence. In fact, when the Syrian
official came to Modin and prepared to offer a heathen
sacrifice, the old man killed him. Mattathias had five sons
and they knew there would be immediate retribution by
Antiochus Epiphanes, so they took their father and fled
to the hills. The following year (166 B.C.) the courageous
old Priest passed away, but his five sons rallied behind
Judas (the third brother) to raise up a national revolt
against the Syrians and the house of Seleucid.

The family name of these brothers was Hasmonaeans,
but Judas took upon himself the name of Maccabaeus—
the Hammer—and soon the whole family was known by
this name.

Now a long series of struggles ensued which eventually
resulted in the violent death of each of these five brothers.
Nevertheless, they left their heirs in charge of a more
vigorous and united Judah than had existed at any time
since Nehemiah.

One of their heirs was John Hyrcanus who decided that since most of the Jews were not soldiers but herdsmen, farmers and domestics, he would hire professional mercenaries. He not only had in mind the defense of Jerusalem, but the expansion of Judah to the original boundaries of all Israel. This campaign led to remarkable victories. First, Samaria was defeated and the heathen temple on Mount Gerizim was destroyed. Then Idumea, the Arab kingdom to the south, was conquered. Syria tried to interfere occasionally, but her own deterioration and involvement with Roman harrassment prevented her from doing anything decisive.

With the expansion of Judah to these new dimensions, one would have thought the reign of John Hyrcanus would have been very popular. However, he had made one mistake. When he first started on his campaign the country was so poor that he could not pay the mercenaries who had been brought in to do the fighting. In desperation he burrowed into the sacred tomb of King David and expropriated the extent of his needs from the valuable jewelry and articles of gold and silver which had been preserved in its vaults for nearly 900 years. The people never forgave him for that.

But be that as it may, when John Hyrcanus died in 104 B.C., he left Judah in a more prosperous and contented state than she had been since the dark ages began.

John Hyrcanus was succeeded by his son, Judas Aristobulus, who was the first of the Maccabees to assume the title of king. However, he only survived a year and was replaced by his brother, Alexander Jannaeus. Alexander ruled for 27 years and sought to further his father's policy of recovering more of the lost territory of Israel. His campaigns resulted in the recovery of considerable territory east of the Jordan.

It was during the reign of Alexander that civil war broke out between the Sadducees and the Pharisees. The

Sadducees were the wealthy and influential Priests whose functions at the Temple kept them united in mutually agreeable doctrines and party politics. On the other hand, the Pharisees included many of the Levites and rabbis. They were much more numerous and believed that the Sadducees had apostatized by denying the resurrection, angels, spirits, and the need to follow the strict requirements of the law. However, the Sadducees were zealots in one respect. If a person were found guilty of a violation, they believed the punishment should be literally an eye for an eye and a tooth for a tooth. They did not want to allow a person to redeem his offense through the payment of money or by working out the damages as a bond servant the way Moses had taught. The Pharisees, on the other hand, although believing in the strict administration of all aspects of the law, held out for the more reasonable and tolerant policy laid down by Moses so that for all crimes except deliberate murder, the offender could redeem the offense by paying reasonable damages to the victim.

Difficulties between the Sadducees and Pharisees frequently occurred during this period. Their arguments went all the way from controversial polemics to the outright shedding of blood. This feud was still smoldering during the ministry of Jesus.

When Alexander Jannaeus died in 76 B.C., the reins of government passed to his wife, Queen Alexandra. When she died in 67 B.C., her son, Hyrcanus, held the throne for three months but was challenged by his younger brother, Aristobulus II. Now we come to the famous quarrel which ultimately took the whole kingdom of Judah into the Roman lion's den. Here is the way it happened.

How Judah Became a Tributary of Rome

For 500 years the Romans relied on a Republican form of government, but by the first century B.C., they had evolved into a series of military dictatorships. Even when they passed laws prohibiting their generals from seizing power, the very next emergency would find the Senate violating its own rules and giving almost unlimited authority to one or more of its most trusted military leaders. Thus it was that by 63 B.C., the famous generals, Julius Caesar and Gnaeus Pompey, both found themselves in virtual control of the Roman empire.

While Caesar was on a campaign in Spain, Pompey undertook the conquest of the old Seleucid empire. He came sweeping across Asia Minor and down the Orontes Valley toward Palestine, devouring provinces and kingdoms as he came. When he reached Judah he discovered the ingredients for an easy conquest as a result of the quarrel going on between the two brothers, Hyrcanus and Aristobulus II. Each of the men had eagerly pleaded with the Roman general to intervene and Pompey was happy to oblige. He intervened, but on behalf of Rome. The next thing the quarreling brothers knew, the iron-shod wheels of Roman chariots were rumbling through the cobblestone streets of Jerusalem and the Roman eagles were implanted on top of Mount Zion. Politically, it was devastating, but it was decisive. All semblance of Jewish independence under the Maccabees was wiped out and a Roman governor took over the rule of Judah.

The Rise of Antipater and His Son, Herod

Now circumstances took a turn which eventually placed Judah under the rule of an Arab. It came as the result of a quarrel between Pompey and Julius Caesar.

Caesar and Pompey joined hands with a third general, named Crassus, to form a triumverate to rule the Roman Empire. At first Caesar and Pompey were very closely allied. Pompey married a daughter of Caesar in 56 B.C., but she died in 54 B.C., and the next year Crassus was killed in the Parthian campaign. This chain of circumstances suddenly made Caesar and Pompey antagonistic competitors for power. As the split between these men became an open scandal, the Senate backed Pompey. He therefore took advantage of Caesar's absence due to a campaign in Gaul, and had the Senate order Caesar to disband his armies and return to Rome as a common citizen. Instead, Caesar cried out, "The die is cast," and marched his army across the Rubicon toward Rome. Pompey fled to Greece but Caesar followed him there and defeated him. In desperation, Pompey fled to Egypt seeking refuge.

At Alexandria, Egypt, the last of the Ptolemys was then in power—a 21-year-old girl named Cleopatra and her 15-year-old brother (Ptolemy XIV) to whom she was "married" after the custom of the Egyptian pharaohs. At the moment, however, the two were fighting over the Egyptian throne and there was serious doubt that this brother-sister marriage would ever be consummated.

When the 15-year-old Ptolemy and his advisors heard that Pompey was fleeing to Egypt, they saw an opportunity to curry the favor of Julius Caesar. They decided to assassinate Pompey. As a result, the Roman general who came to Egypt seeking refuge was stabbed to death in a small rowboat before he ever reached land. Caesar arrived soon afterwards and when Ptolemy presented Caesar with the head and signet ring of Pompey, Caesar was outraged. How dare these pompous foreigners assassinate a Roman general! He would teach them.

But the next thing Caesar knew, he was surrounded by Ptolemy's Egyptian army which threatened the extinction of the smaller Roman task force.

The thing which turned the tide for Caesar and undoubtedly saved his life was the unexpected but fortunate
arrival of several thousand troops under the leadership of
the Arab Idumean, Antipater. After fierce fighting, Julius
Caesar and his Romans were saved. Antipater was later
rewarded by being made a Roman citizen.

Now this Antipater was very much involved in the
politics of Judah. Before the arrival of the Romans, he
and his father, Antipas, had each served as governor of
Idumea, the Arab kingdom south of the Dead Sea, which
was a vassal kingdom to Judah. During the quarrel between the two Jewish princes, Hyrcanus and Aristobulus,
Antipater had thrown his weight behind the older brother,
Hyrcanus. Of course, neither of the brothers was allowed
to be king after the Romans took over in 63 B.C., but now
things were different. Antipater had become a Roman
citizen and a friend of Julius Caesar as a result of the
war in Egypt. Antipater therefore used his influence to
get Hyrcanus appointed by Rome as the hereditary High
Priest of the Jews and Roman regent or ethnark of Judah.
Then he had *himself* appointed as the administrator of
Judah! By 47 B.C., this former Arab vassal of Judah had
become its virtual ruler. This became clearly evident
during that year when he induced Rome to appoint one of
his sons, Phasael, the governor of southern Judah and
another son, the twenty-five-year-old Herod, governor of
Galilee.

But in spite of Antipater's personal ambitions, this Arab
politician proved to be a great friend of the Jewish people.
He gained more freedom for Judah than any other Roman
province. Judah was freed from tribute, Roman garrisons
were withdrawn, the people were guaranteed religious
liberty, and they were allowed to live under their own
laws administered by their own tribunals. Authority was
obtained to rebuild the walls of Jerusalem (Pompey had

leveled them) and Joppa was added to Judah so that it would have a seaport on the Mediterranean.

In 44 B.C., however, Julius Caesar was assassinated. This created chaos in Judah. Certain Jewish aristocrats who hated their Roman-appointed High Priest, Hyrcanus, decided this would be a good time to do away with his main supporter and patron, the Arab, Antipater. So in 43 B.C. Antipater was poisoned. Immediately, the son of the other contending Jewish prince, Aristobulus, tried to seize power. This son was named Antigonus. To aid his cause, Antigonus called upon the Parthians who were enemies of Rome from the Caspian Sea region. They invaded Judah, captured Hyrcanus, cut off his ears so that as a mutilated person he could no longer serve as High Priest, and shipped him off to Babylon as a prisoner. They also captured Antipater's son, Phasael, who had been governor of Judah, but Phasael committed suicide.

Herod, however, escaped. He already had an Arab wife of the Idumean aristocracy, but to further secure his position with the Jewish people, he proposed marriage to the Jewish princess, Mariamne, granddaughter of Hyrcanus. These plans were disrupted temporarily by the Parthian invasion, but Herod fled by night to the Masada fortress overlooking the Dead Sea, and took with him his first wife, also Mariamne and her mother, his own mother, his household servants and his troops. Leaving them at Masada, he made his way to Rome and was both surprised and elated to discover that he was heartily welcomed as the son of Antipater, Caesar's friend. In fact, Caesar's heir, Octavian, and Caesar's comrade in arms, Mark Antony, agreed to sponsor Herod as the new king of Judah! Herod pleaded his own case before the Roman senate and the appointment was confirmed.

Now all he had to do was to go back and capture Palestine from the Parthians.

Herod's Rise to Power

This was not easy. Herod was able to relieve the siege of Masada and rescue his family, but he had to wait until the Roman armies arrived to capture Jerusalem. It finally fell after a siege of five months. The year was 37 B.C.

Now Herod laid the foundation for his long reign of virtual tyranny over Judah. First he had Antigonus beheaded. It will be recalled that this was the son of Aristobulus who had started all the trouble by inviting the Parthians to invade. Next, Herod formalized his marriage to beautiful Princess Mariamne whom he blindly and jealously loved. To favor her, Herod appointed Mariamne's seventeen-year-old brother to be the new High Priest. However, this young man began to be so popular that Herod had him "accidentally" drowned during the water games in Jericho during 36 B.C. This was the beginning of a long series of political murders by Herod. The boy's mother (and Herod's mother-in-law), named Alexandra, learned that her son had been murdered and thereafter nurtured a heart-broken hatred against the king. She soon antagonized Herod's sister, Salome, who was married to Herod's uncle, named Joseph. Salome spitefully and, from all accounts, untruthfully, hinted to the jealous Herod that an affair was going on between Mariamne and Joseph, whereupon Herod had the hapless Joseph executed.

The next victim was Mariamne herself. No doubt Mariamne had learned from her mother about the murder of her younger brother and this affected her manifest feelings toward Herod. The madly jealous king interpreted this frigid and distant attitude as an indication that she was plotting to overthrow him. When Herod's sister, Salome, bribed Herod's cupbearer to tell Herod that Mariamne was putting "love potions" in the king's wine and that it might perhaps be poison, this was enough to stir the suspicious Herod to charge her with treason. She

was tried and in 29 B.C., the king signed her death war-
rant. The ghostly memory of his beloved Mariamne
haunted Herod the rest of his life.

Herod now engaged in a wild building spree from one
end of Judah to the other. He rebuilt the fortress near
the Temple and named it Antonia in honor of Mark
Antony. He built a marble palace for himself in Jerusalem
which could be used as a fortress if necessary. Twenty
miles south of Mount Carmel he built a marble city of
pillars and facades which became a major seaport and
was named Caesarea after Octavian, who had now become
the first emperor of Rome as Augustus Caesar. He rebuilt
the great capital of the northern Ten Tribes at Samaria
and called it Sebaste, the Greek equivalent of the name,
Augustus. The ruins of Herod's marble palace can still be
seen there. He also built himself a magnificent palace in
Jericho.

In 20 B.C. Herod sought to assuage the bitter feelings
of the Jews over the death of Mariamne by offering to
rebuild and refurbish the rapidly deteriorating Second
Temple built by Zerubbabel way back in 516 B.C. The
priestly class accepted the offer, providing he would only
replace a part of it at a time so they could be sure he
would not destroy their Temple altogether. Even though
Herod claimed he had espoused Judaism he was not
counted a genuine convert. He finished the Holy of Holies
in about two years and the adjoining section or Holy Place
required six more. However, the overall work of restoration was still going on forty years later at the time of the
Crucifixion. Before his death, Herod had actually built
the Jews a Third Temple, and one which was far more
beautiful and elaborate than Zerubbabel's. Nevertheless,
the Jews would not have a "new Temple" built by any
such person as Herod. They continued to insist, therefore,
that this was the Second Temple which Herod had merely
refurbished.

By 10 B.C., Herod's numerous expensive building projects had so depleted the resources of Judah that David's
tomb was once more opened and ransacked for treasure.
It should be mentioned that before Mariamne was
executed, she had borne two sons for Herod. They were
named Alexander and Aristobulus. Both of them had been
sent to Rome, along with Herod's other children, to be
educated at the great capital. In due time all of Herod's
children became mature and began returning home. Herod
took an immediate fancy to Alexander and Aristobulus and
decided to make them his heirs. Aristobulus was married
to his own first cousin, Bernice, the daughter of Herod's
sister, Salome. There was another son of Herod, however,
who was born of another mother and who despised these
two half-Jewish heirs to the throne. He began planting
seeds of suspicion in the mind of Herod concerning
Mariamne's sons, and before long the king thought he saw
in some of their actions the very thing of which Antipater
had been accusing them. He promptly had both of them
executed. Later, however, Herod became suspicious of
Antipater, so he had him executed, too!

As Herod came to the closing portion of his life the
long years of intrigue, murder and military maneuvering
had left deep and permanent scars. One can therefore
well imagine the fanatical and psychoneurotic rage which
took possession of him when there suddenly appeared from
the trans-Mesopotamian region to the east, a number of
"wise men" who said the long-awaited Messiah and king
of the Jews had been born. They said they had seen
the great new star which was to be the sign of his birth.
Herod carefully inquired of his own wise men concerning
the place where the Messiah was supposed to be born.
They quoted Micah 5:2, indicating that it was supposed
to occur in Bethlehem. Herod asked the men of the east
how long since they had first seen the great new star and
they told him. Herod therefore knew the age of the child.

He bade the magi to inquire in Bethlehem and if they found the child to bring him word that Herod also might go and worship. But when these men did not return, the true passions of Herod were exposed as he ordered his troops to sweep down on Bethlehem and slay every child under the age of two.

Herod did not know it, but his own measure of life had run its course. History has it that about the time he ordered the "slaying of the innocents," he became afflicted with a most loathsome, fatal disease. The stench of it was so terrible that none wished to minister to him. At the last stages his burning hatred of his enemies and his fear that his own passing might not be mourned by the people, caused him to order his sister, Salome, to gather the leaders of Judah together in the hippodrome at Jericho where Herod was dying, and, simultaneously with his own death, slaughter them. He would make the people mourn whether they wished to or not. The massacre did not come off, however, and when the news went out that Herod was dead, the people broke out in universal celebration.

Rome now placed Judah under three of Herod's sons. Archelaus was made regent or ethnarch of Judaea (southern Judah), Antipas was made governor or tetrarch of Galilee and Paraea (east of Jordan), while Herod Philip was given the region between Galilee and Damascus.

The Christian Era

By the beginning of the ministry of Jesus, many of the political forces had changed. Augustus Caesar had died in 14 A.D. and his adopted son, Tiberias, had replaced him. He was a morose, suspicious and unpopular ruler. Tiberias executed someone almost daily. Nevertheless, he kept the peace, and finally retired to Capri where he spent the last eleven years of his life in total debauchery.

One of the rulers of Judah had also changed. Archelaus, who was made governor of southern Judah, had been so tyrannical that after nine years the people had protested to Rome and, following his trial, he was banished to Vienne. For many years thereafter Judaea was ruled by Roman procurators who had their headquarters at Caesarea. In 27 A.D., Tiberias had appointed Pontius Pilate to be the procurator.

In the light of what we have already related, it can be easily understood why the presence of Jesus in Jerusalem during national religious festivals would create such a furor. The politically-appointed High Priest and his supporters were in constant fear of replacement. The Roman procurator was constantly walking a razor's edge trying to keep the peace and ameliorate the numerous opposing parties. The people themselves were full of resentment against Rome and her latest crop of tax collectors, and the more aggressive dissidents were always stirring up trouble or intrigue.

Jesus came preaching a doctrine which was bound to create a certain amount of temporary dislocation. The Sadducees resented him because he exposed the Temple clique of the day as professional holy men who had betrayed the prophets and lacerated the true spirit of the law of Moses. Many of the scribes and Pharisees deeply resented the fact that a simple Galilean could be so persuasive in dealing with the scriptures and "taught as one having authority." When he performed great miracles which were unquestionably authenticated by their own members, they could only attribute his miraculous power to the devil and divert attention from the good he did by pointing out that he performed some of his remarkable healings on the Sabbath day.

Nevertheless, there were learned men among the Jews of that day who saw in this strange but marvelous person a spirit of power which they deeply admired and pon-

dered with astonishment. Even the members of the Sanhedrin and officers of the Temple guard stood helpless when
he catalogued the people's sins and cleansed the Temple
with a swinging rope. The people as a whole were in-
clined to accept Jesus. It was their leaders, primarily,
who looked upon him as a threat. On Palm Sunday the
masses of the people were ready to accept him as the
Messiah and crown him king. In less than a week, however, the leaders had finally succeeded in getting the
Romans to nail him to a cross and execute him by crucifixion. Nevertheless, the most significant fact to remember
is that the first Christian congregations were all Jewish.
Jesus loved these people. They were his people. He took
the Gospel first to them and later he had it delivered to
the Gentiles. In the greatest of anguish he stood on the
walls of the Temple on the last day of his earthly ministry
and poured forth his lamentation:

"O Jerusalem, Jerusalem, thou that killest the prophets,
and stonest them which are sent unto thee, how often
would I have gathered thy children together, even as a
hen gathereth her chickens under her wings, and ye would
not!"

Then he commented sadly, "Behold, your house is left
unto you desolate."[14]

A short while later he sat facing the city from the
slopes of the Mount of Olives, and there he related to his
disciples what would befall Jerusalem in that very generation.[15] For over two thousand years the prophets of God
had been predicting the great dispersion of all Israel. It
had long since happened to ten of the tribes. It was now
about to happen to what was left of Judah and the Levites.

The Roman Interlude

The Roman Emperor Tiberias died in 37 A.D. and was

---

14. Matthew 23:37-38.
15. Matthew, Chapter 24.

succeeded by his grand-nephew, Caligula. At first, Caligula was very popular because he reduced taxes, expanded free public entertainment and pardoned political offenders. Soon, however, he had himself addressed as a god and proposed that his horse be elected consul. After four years Caligula drove the treasury to bankruptcy and began expropriating the estates of the wealthy to make up the deficit. By 41 A.D. his extravagant policies and harsh treatment of the people had made his administration so intolerable that the members of his own guard killed him and buried his body secretly. They then compelled the Senate to appoint fifty-year-old Claudius, an uncle of Caligula and grandson of Augustus, to be the new emperor.

Claudius took over in 41 A.D. and although a paralytic and despised by his grandfather, Augustus, he made a fairly good ruler. Claudius was killed in 54 A.D. by poison given to him by his fourth wife, Agrippina. Before the fatal meal of mushrooms she had induced Claudius to adopt Nero, her own son by a previous marriage, and give him precedence over Britannicus who was the natural heir of the emperor.

In 54 A.D. Nero therefore became the emperor of Rome at the age of sixteen. Within the year he had poisoned Britannicus, his foster-brother, and thereafter he tried three different times to kill his own mother. Failing in all three attempts he finally had her assassinated. By 65 A.D. Nero had gone through the scandal of "fiddling" while Rome burned, he had carried out a vicious persecution of the Christians, killed Paul, and finally, when the Senate tried to overthrow him, he had forced the leaders, including Seneca, to take their own lives. By 68 A.D. Nero's excesses had created such resistance that the generals in the various provinces began to take over their respective governments and the Senate felt compelled to condemn Nero to death. Nero fled from Rome and just before the soldiers were able to reach him, he took his own life with a butcher knife. There was a wild scramble for power in the provinces, and this relieved the pressure on Judah where the most important crisis in the whole empire had been boiling for two years.

The Destruction of Jerusalem

By 66 A.D. social and civic deterioration in Judah had reached a dangerously low level. Factionalism, class rivalry, brigandry and hatred of Roman rule all combined to create political unrest and spread a soggy blanket of suspicion and disunity among the Jews from Jericho to Joppa and from Tiberius to Beer-Sheba.

The Romans tried to provide procurators who could placate the people and pacify the dissidents, but to no avail. Roman officials were lucky if they lasted three or four years. Pockets of insurrection were promoted by a hard-core cadre called the Zealots, and their more extreme members, the Sicarii (because of the deadly curved knife they carried), initiated a kind of guerilla warfare from time to time. The whole situation became so explosive with insipient revolution that the Sanhedrin appealed to the Roman legate in Syria for military forces to keep the peace.

In September of 66 A.D. a force of 40,000 soldiers surrounded the walls of Jerusalem. Their commander thought such a show of force would bring an immediate capitulation, but when he attacked he found the resistance so determined that he felt compelled to withdraw toward the coast and wait for reinforcements. Jewish volunteers from the countryside then attacked him and before long this mighty host of Roman legions was in full flight. In fact, by the time the main body reached Caesarea it had lost 6,000 men. Nero was so enraged that he ordered Vespasian, his finest general, to subjugate Judah immediately. But Vespasian knew this would be no easy task. He first conquered the surrounding territory and was all ready to lay siege to Jerusalem when Nero committed suicide and Vespasian decided to suspend the siege until a new emperor was in power to reaffirm his orders to proceed.

As it turned out, however, no man in Rome was strong enough to establish himself as emperor, and after three false starts the eastern Roman legions forced the Senate to accept Vespasian, their own commander. This forced Vespasian to hurry to Rome and for nearly two years the pacification of Judah was abandoned. However, in the spring of 70 A.D. a sizable Roman army was mobilized at Caesarea and the command was entrusted to Vespasian's own son, Titus. He swept down across Samaria and then set up headquarters on Mount Scopus just northeast of the city of Jerusalem where he could look directly down into the labyrinths of the Jewish capital.

Jerusalem was surrounded by three strong rings of stone walls and there were three fortress towers at strategic points within the city. The strongest fortress was called Antonia, which looked directly down upon the Temple with its surrounding bulwark of fortified courtyards.

Titus gave the people of Jerusalem an opportunity to surrender and when they refused, the siege began. The inhabitants of the city put up a resistance of frenzied valor but Titus was able to breach the two outer walls and take the lower city after a few weeks. He then ran into such a force of opposition that he decided to put his soldiers to work building an earthen wall around the entire city and starving the people into submission. Josephus describes how the people were reduced to eating their own dead but they still would not give up. Titus finally launched a full-scale assault on the fortress of Antonia and captured it after heavy losses on July 5, 70 A.D.

Titus then commanded his aggravated and frustrated legions to attack the Temple area itself. Here was the great Temple of Herod. Jesus had predicted it would be so completely desolated that there would not be one stone left upon another. After a continuous series of fierce struggles this sector was occupied on August 10th. The loss of their sacred shrine took all the remaining heart out of the Jewish resistance. With their starved, emaciated, battle-scarred people dying faster than they could be buried, the Jewish leaders finally gave up and the upper city was overrun by the Romans September 7th. This brought the siege to an end.

It was a horrible sight which met the eyes of the conquering legions. Josephus states that over a million Jews had perished and the bedraggled remnant which survived were like cadaverous mummies.

Titus issued immediate orders that the entire city of Jerusalem should be totally leveled. His soldiers turned into demolition squads. Practically nothing escaped. Only one small segment of the massive wall that surrounded the acropolis on which the Temple stood was left intact. This became the famous Jewish wailing wall, a pitiful fragment of a shrine to which vast multitudes of devout Jews have gravitated ever since. All the rest of the city was obliterated. Today, when the tourist visits Jerusalem he does not walk on the streets where Jesus walked. Much of the surface of this city which Jesus knew lies buried beneath ten to thirty feet of solid debris.

Coincidentally with the destruction of Jerusalem, the whirlwind of Roman wrath swept down on the Jewish survivors. It is said the 100,000 of them were seized from Jerusalem and the surrounding suburbs to be worked to death as slaves in Rome's Egyptian mines. Other thousands were distributed throughout the empire to be exhibited in Roman amphitheaters and then slaughtered in their circus spectacles. Two of the most gory and inhuman of these spectacles took place at Caesarea and Berytus (modern Beirut). Titus celebrated the birthdays of his father, Vespasian, and his brother, Domitian, with spectacles in which thousands of Jewish captives died in compulsory gladiatorial exhibits and in hopeless, bare-handed combat with hunger-crazed lions and other ferocious beasts.

All the Jews who remained in Palestine were subjected to the most rigorous regimentation. Vespasian attempted to wipe out their religion. He outlawed the Sanhedrin and attempted to erase every outward token and symbol of the Jewish culture. Even the High Priesthood (order of Aaron) was abolished. Roman veterans were brought in with their families to inhabit the area around Jerusalem.

So relieved were the Romans to have the Jewish crisis settled, that an arch of triumph was built in the Forum of Rome in honor of Titus and this can still be seen today.

One final note should be added concerning the small band of Jews who held out against everything Rome could muster during a terrifying period of three years. This occurred at the Jewish Alamo—called Masada—an impregnable fortress located on a tiny plateau overlooking the Dead Sea. Dr. Nelson Beecher Keyes briefly tells the story:

"It was there [at Masada] that Eleazar, commander of the Temple and leader of the Sicarii, the Zealot extremists, now made a last desperate stand.

"Rather than suffer death at the hands of the Romans, these proud and determined people decided upon mass suicide. After tearful and touching farewells the men killed their wives and children. They then drew lots and every man in ten killed nine until all 960 were dead— the last man plunging a sword into his own breast. When the Romans entered, they found not one living soul."[16]

---

16. Nelson Beecher Keyes, *Story of the Bible World*, Pleasantville, N.Y.: The Reader's Digest Association, 1959, p. 174.

The Final Dispersion

The resilient and resurgent spirit of the Jewish people
—the tough fiber which has maintained their identity as a
people for over 3,000 years—now asserted itself. Wherever
the Jews went they formed colonies, clustered together in
all-Jewish neighborhoods of big cities or built synagogues
where peasants and farmers from surrounding villages
could join in the national religion and partake of their
Judaic culture.

Only 46 years after the destruction of Jerusalem, the
Romans found themselves confronted by festering abscesses
of Jewish revolt throughout the Mediterranean basin. It
was equally formidable as far away as Mesopotamia—that
ancient land between the Tigris and Euphrates where
Jewish exiles had established colonies as far back as 598
B.C. Basically, it was a religious war, fought with reckless
ferocity by the Jews and resisted with vengeance by the
Romans. Whole communities were exterminated by both
sides. When peace was temporarily restored, it left the
Jews seething against the Roman edicts which forbade
observance of the Sabbath, practicing circumcision, or
reading the sacred law. The Romans stopped the Jews
from making pilgrimages to their wailing wall in Jerusalem. For fifteen years there was an uneasy, volatile
armistice.

Suddenly, in 131 A.D., a Jewish leader named Bar
Cocheba appeared in Palestine with claims of a divine
commission to liberate the Jewish people. It was easy for
the Jewish people to believe that perhaps this was their
long-awaited Messiah. They rallied behind him and for
awhile there was sensational success. Then Rome brought
in an army of overwhelming proportions which smothered
the movement in a reign of terror and slaughter.

The uprising of Bar Cocheba marked the final struggle
for national independence by the Jewish people in ancient

times. Rome now scattered them to the four winds. Jews were scourged out of Palestine. The few who remained did so at the risk of their lives. It was a capital crime for a Jew to come within sight of Jerusalem or try to enter its rubble-strewn precincts. The official policy of Rome was dispersion or extinction for the Jews. In orders to survive, some Jewish migrants wandered as far away as India and China. Others were scattered down along the Arabian peninsula or into Egypt and Africa. Still others painfully made their way into the unsettled wilderness of what today is Russia and Europe. The wild terrain, hostile climate and intemperate seasons which had resisted the expanding civilization of Rome were no more congenial for the Jewish migrants. Nevertheless, through necessity they moved into these territories, discovered nothing but crude and uncouth barbarian inhabitants.

Nevertheless, Jewish communities wherever they were established, attempted to maintain some kind of communications with their spiritual center which somehow continued to survive in Palestine. With the greatest difficulty and at tremendous risk, a number of learned Jewish authorities set up rabbinical schools in old Judea and codified all the oral or explanatory commentary on the law of Moses which had accumulated during the centuries. By 200 A.D. this commentary or compilation of the oral laws was being distributed all over the Jewish world and was called the Mishnah. By 450 A.D. further explanatory notes had been required by outlying regions in order to understand the Mishnah, so this latest compilation of commentaries was called the Talmud—the Palestinian Talmud. However, when Constantine decided to make Christianity the national religion of Rome, he closed down the rabbinical schools in Palestine and forced these scholars to seek residence elsewhere. In due time—around 500 A.D.—the most authoritative version of the Talmud was emanating from the Jewish colony in Babylon where the Jews had maintained a colony ever since the days of their famous captivity under Nebuchadnezzar. The Jews of today still quote as their most authoritative commentary the Babylonian Talmud.

The Jewish Dark Ages

From the days of their first exile in 598 B.C., the Jews have always considered Palestine to be the land of their destiny as well as the land of their inheritance. That is why, no matter how gruesome the persecution, *some* Jews have always remained in Palestine.[17] However, any Jews living outside of Palestine have always considered themselves part of the so-called *Diaspora*—a collective term referring to those who have been "scattered" or "dispersed."

For nineteen hundred years, Jews around the world have been concluding their ritual prayers with the same and sometimes pitifully impossible expectations: *"Next year in Jerusalem!"* This has been a constant reminder to the believing and the orthodox that wherever they might be—from China to Amsterdam to Beverly Hills—their real home must ultimately be in Palestine, and anything else is merely a temporary interlude.

Throughout these nineteen centuries, the recurring waves of persecution continually galvanized the collective Jewish mentality to accept the fact that for some strange reason, they did not assimilate well or homogenize themselves into the host nations to which they had fled—even when they helped build those nations. Their rabbis reminded them weekly that they must watch for the great Messianic Era of salvation when they would be restored to their national home. This conviction did two things: first, it constantly regenerated the spirit of unity among

---

17. For a thorough discussion of this point, see *The Jews in Their Land*, by David Ben-Gurion, New York: Doubleday and Co., 1966, p. 168-169.

the Jews; secondly, it made them very vulnerable to any *false* Messiah who came along proclaiming that the day of salvation had come. Down through the centuries the Jews suffered severely from the false hopes built up by dozens of these phoney Messiahs who would arise among them from time to time. And there were plenty of times when they needed their Messiah.

We have already treated the Roman period when the Jews were conquered, massacred and the remnant scattered to every point of the compass. In a similar, though usually lesser degree, this same policy prevailed no matter which nation or people happened to be dominant at any given period.

For example, when the Roman politicians seized upon Christianity as the new state religion it did not improve the plight of the Jews. Proselyting was often done at the point of the sword for Jews as it was for heathens. Every kind of pressure, both legal and illegal, was exerted to achieve mass conversion. Frustrated Byzantine officials and benighted, over-zealous churchmen slopped in the blood of those who resisted.

When the Arab peoples adopted the religion of Islam under Mohammed and conquered much of the Byzantine empire, they encouraged the Jews to return to Palestine and possess the land. In fact, the early Caliphs forbade the Arabs to become landholders since they were to remain in the army of Allah to fight the holy war of liberation. Later, however, as the Islamic leaders began fighting among themselves over powers of leadership, the Jews found themselves caught in the cross-fire. Persecution and harassment soon followed.

The pressure under the Arabs, however, was mild compared to the persecution and bloodshed which descended on the Jews during the Crusades. By the 11th Century the image of Christianity had been so thoroughly debauched by the politicians who had man-handled it that it bore little resemblance to God's kingdom of peace, tolerance and forgiveness which Jesus had proclaimed. And the last people to be forgiven were the Jews. When the Crusaders took Jerusalem, the Jews and Arabs were slain *en masse* as the common enemy. Some survivors were forced into the synagogue and burned alive. Others were sold into slavery. Zealous depravity of equal proportions engulfed many of the Jewish communities in Europe. When the First Crusade was being organized, its volunteers identified the Jews as the anti-Christ and decided to launch a campaign of vengeance in Europe before proceeding to the Middle East. For two months, in 1096, the Jews located along the Rhine country and beyond, were plundered and murdered until 12,000 had perished. The Second Crusade was almost as devastating to Jews in other areas.

In 1348 the terrible plague called the Black Death spread across Europe. In England it swept away half the population. It decimated western Europe. This was blamed on the Jews. Recriminating mobs vented their sorrow and hate in the destruction of sixty large Jewish communities and fifty smaller ones.

For two or three centuries Jewish populations fortunate enough to be living in Portugal and Spain during the rule of the Arab Moors, found peace and prosperity in luxurious abundance. Jew and Arab lived, prospered, and thrived together. However, when Ferdinand and Isabella joined hands in marriage, they resolved to drive out the Moors and establish a single crown for all of Spain. The final Moorish resistance was broken in January, 1492, whereupon the Jews of that region faced a completely new era. Before long the Spanish Inquisition was sweeping thousands of Jews into exile or extinction. The same policies were followed in Portugal.

Meanwhile, in 1453, the Ottoman Turks had conquered Constantinople (renaming it Istanbul) and even earlier they had occupied Jerusalem. Under Suleiman (between 1536 and 1542) the Moslems had rebuilt the walls of Jerusalem which the visiting tourist sees today. Suleiman repaired the city's sewers and cisterns and regenerated the Pools of Solomon beyond Bethlehem so as to give the city a guaranteed source of water supply. A few Jews moved into the area near the Wailing Wall, and by 1555 A.D. there were as many as 324 Jewish householders established there.

Many wealthy and well-educated Jews who had escaped from Spain and Portugal became prominent officials in the Ottoman Empire and thereafter used their influence to protect and encourage any of the Jews who settled in Palestine. Tiberias was rebuilt as a Jewish community during this period and more Jews moved to Jerusalem. Still, the number was never large. As late as 1840 the census showed only 2,943 Jews in Jerusalem and this was 46 per cent of the total for all Palestine.[18] Nevertheless, it was a symbol.

Up in Europe the Jewish dark ages continued. England, for example, locked its ports against all Jews in the thirteenth century. Only an occasional family living insecurely and clandestinely in some city like London could escape being exiled. Not until the seventeenth century did Jews win the right of domicile in England. At that time only 34 Jewish families (of Spanish origin) were known to exist in London.[19]

On the Continent the Jews had been politically disfranchised, excluded from owning land, prohibited from joining the guilds, and herded together into ghettos where they eked out a living as hawkers and petty traders. However, this did prove a blessing in the end. The Jews were compelled by these very circumstances to establish channels of communication, trade and exchange which formed a network eventually extending around the world.

---

18. *Ibid.*, p. 266.
19. Howard M. Sachar, *The Course of Modern Jewish History*, New York: World Publishing Co., 1958, p. 44.

When the crowned heads of Europe began to compete with each other for trade, they found themselves turning more and more to Jewish entrepreneurs who knew how to make mercantilism work. Soon Jewish money was financing industry, trade, colonial expansion and national treasuries. This brought emancipation and immense power to certain Jewish houses, but it left the masses of the Jews locked up each night in their respective ghettos.

The Beginning of Jewish Emancipation

It was in Germany that a leading Jewish intellectual found the means of developing a more intimate dialogue between Jews and Christians. His name was Moses Mendelssohn. He decided that his own people had allowed themselves to become introverted, filled with inferior feelings and backward in the ways and graces of the world. Wealthy Jews in Berlin had taken him under their wing and he had succeeded in making himself one of the most popular personalities in Christian social circles. He found that he was able to present Judaism as a moral, rational and humane theology that touched the higher sensitivities of Christian intellectuals. He found no need to apologize for being a Jew.

Mendelssohn urged his own people to re-examine the scars which the centuries of persecution and isolation had inflicted upon them. He urged them to disentangle themselves from the cobwebs of Talmudic polemics and develop a speaking acquaintance with the literature and language of the countries in which they lived.

Mendelssohn was himself a living example of one who had beaten the ghetto complex. Born in 1729 of a poor family in Dessau, he left home at fourteen and walked to Berlin because he longed to be there with the Rabbi Frankel who had been his teacher. He lived in the attic of a merchant at the first, and the poverty of his life showed in his thin, delicate bones and a badly humped back caused by rickets. Nevertheless, he persisted, worked hard, studied hard, married well, and exhibited in his personal life the things he believed. In maturity, he was characterized in one of German's most popular plays by the famous German playright, Gotthold Lessing. It was called, "Nathan the Wise." In the play a Catholic friar declares, "Nathan, Nathan, you are a Christian! By God, you are a Christian! There never was a better Christian!" This was Lessing's supreme compliment to Mendelssohn. It meant that Jew and Christian had a recognized basis for treating each other with dignity and respect.

Mendelssohn died in 1786, but he had planted the seeds for a period of enlightenment that came upon the Jews far sooner than they had expected. It began with the 40,000 Jews in France. When Napoleon came to power he wanted religious equanimity as a stabilizing framework for his proposed establishment of political power. By various means he undertook to win the Catholics, then the Protestants, and finally, the Jews. He promised equality under the law, the revival of the Sanhedrin, the abolishment of the ghetto. Everywhere the Napoleonic armies planted the flag of France, similar laws were invoked. With legal barriers removed, the Jewish population commenced to circulate more freely in western Europe. Emancipation came more slowly in Austria because of the policies of the Hapsburgs, nevertheless the dam had been broken and in all Europe the Jews knew an era of unprecedented opportunity had arrived.

Even when the blaze of Napoleonic aspirations had burned itself out and passed into oblivion, the flame that had been kindled in the souls of the Jews of Europe survived. And the brighter the flame became for the emancipation of individual Jews, the stronger grew their collective anxiety over the redemption of Jerusalem and the Holy Land.

The Re-Birth of Zionism

There had been numerous attempts by Jewish leaders throughout the centuries to rehabilitate Palestine. All previous attempts had failed because of hostile political circumstances. And they were equally hostile in the early part of the nineteenth century. Nevertheless, a number of wealthy and influential Jews were anxious to do what they could to begin the gathering of the Jews to the land of their fathers. Soon after the Ottoman Empire began falling apart and Mohammed Ali secured the independence of Egypt, a prominent British philanthropist named Sir Moses Montefiore decided to initiate the first steps on behalf of his people. In 1827 he visited Palestine and in 1839 he wrote in his diary, "I shall apply to Mohammed Ali for a grant of land for fifty years. . . . This grant obtained, I shall, please Heaven, on my return to England, form a company for the cultivation of the land and the encouragement of our Brethren in Europe to return to Palestine. . . . By degrees I hope to induce the return of thousands of our brethren to the land of Israel. I am sure they would be happy in the enjoyment of the observance of our holy religion, in a manner which is impossible in Europe."[20]

Jews were not the only ones who felt the time was ripe for the return of the Jews to their traditional homeland. Any Christian scholar who studied his Bible with any degree of honesty knew that it was in the wisdom of Heaven to bring about the establishment of a Jewish kingdom in due course. In 1840, an apostle of the Mormon faith was specifically designated to make the difficult journey to Palestine and dedicate that land for the commencement of that great gathering about which the Bible spoke. His name was Orson Hyde. Traveling without

---

20. David Ben-Gurion, *The Jews in Their Land*, p. 263.

purse or script, he traveled across the Atlantic, visited the principal Jewish communities in Europe, stopped briefly at Constantinople, Cairo and Alexandria, and finally reached the Holy City. Early on the morning of October 24, 1841, he ascended the slopes of the Mount of Olives and prayed. Among other things he said,

". . . remove the barrenness and sterility of this land, and let springs of living water break forth to water its thirsty soil. Let the vine and olive produce in their strength, and the figtree bloom and flourish. Let the land become abundantly fruitful when possessed by its rightful heirs; let it again flow with plenty to feed the returning prodigals who come home with a spirit of grace and supplication; upon it let the clouds distil virtue and richness, and let the fields smile with plenty. Let the flocks and the herds greatly increase and multiply upon the mountains and the hills; and let Thy great kindness conquer and subdue the unbelief of Thy people. Do Thou take from them their stony heart, and give them a heart of flesh; and may the Sun of Thy favor dispel the cold mists of darkness which have beclouded their atmosphere. Incline them to gather in upon this land according to Thy word. Let them come like clouds and like doves to their windows. Let the large ships of the nations bring them from the distant isles; and let kings become their nursing fathers, and queens with motherly fondness wipe the tear of sorrow from their eye."[21]

Prominent Christians both in Europe and America caught the spirit of a Messianic Era for the Jews. In 1844 a British society was formed to encourage the restoration of the Jews to their homeland. Colonel Charles Churchill and Dean Stanley of England, as well as President Adams of the United States endorsed this program. Lord Byron wrote concerning the suffering of the Jews and

21. Joseph Smith, *History of The Church of Jesus Christ of Latter-day Saints*, (1948 ed.) Vol. IV, pp. 456, 459.

their need to return to their ancient national home. George Eliot wrote *Daniel Deronda*, designed specifically to create a sympathetic understanding of the plight of the Jews and the need to re-establish them in Palestine. Sir Lawrence Oliphant, encouraged by Disraeli and Lord Salisbury, labored for many years to induce the Ottoman Empire to permit Jews to settle in large numbers in Palestine. From a purely Biblical standpoint, Arthur Hollingsworth brought forward an array of prophetic writings to justify Christian support of such a program.

By 1858 a small trickle of immigration had begun. There were enough new arrivals to justify the building of a Jewish settlement just west of the Old City. Sir Moses Montefiore provided the financing so it was called Yemin Moshe in his honor. Ten years later another nearby settlement was started called Nachlat Sheva. Thus began the building of modern Jerusalem, just to the west of the old city walls.

However, the first organized migration and certainly the first agricultural colonization movement did not come until 1882. It was launched by a new-founded movement in Russia called "Lovers of Zion." When the Russian government of the Tsar began an official persecution of the Jews in 1881, it gave the necessary momentum to propel several groups toward their promised land. One pioneer group arrived under the name of the BILU— coming from the first Hebrew letters of the slogan, "House of Jacob, come ye and let us go." They founded Rishon-le-Zion (First to Zion) as an agricultural settlement. Others quickly followed. This is referred to as the First *Aliyah*— meaning the first "ascent" or migration back to the Holy City. Unfortunately, these first immigrants often knew nothing about farming, and they had no idea what the swamps which they bought from the Arabs were going to do to them. These mucky, steaming sloughs ate up the Jews. Malaria and yellow fever struck them down at an appalling rate. Nevertheless, others arrived to take their places.

In 1890 there was an upsurge of immigrants when the Jews were banished from Moscow. Rumanians, Poles and others joined them. By 1902 the First *Aliyah* had brought approximately 25,000 Jews to Palestine.

The Rise of Theodor Herzl

Meanwhile, in 1897, the first conference of the World Zionist Organization was held in Basel, Switzerland. Its founder was Dr. Theodor Herzl, a Jewish journalist and lawyer from Vienna, who had been shocked by the anti-Jewish sentiment in France during the famous Dreyfus case. He had therefore written a dissertation in 1896 called, *The Jewish State.* He felt the Jews must shortly gather together or suffer severe persecution. His idea was to create a Jewish homeland in Palestine through diplomatic negotiation with the Turkish government and by purchase of the land from Arab landholders. This first Zionist congress discussed the erection of a Hebrew University in Jerusalem, the creation of a Jewish national fund, the setting up of a Jewish world bank in London to finance colonization, the design for a blue and white flag and the adoption of a national anthem. All of this for their beloved country which did not yet exist!

In 1903, just as Herzl had feared, a terroristic and brutal persecution of the Jews broke out in Russia. In Kishinev of Bessarabia, the Jewish dead were piled in the streets like cordwood. Herzl literally worked himself to death going from one world capital to another seeking support for his new Jewish state.

He died suddenly July 3, 1904. He was only 44. Today he lies buried on a peak which is named after him overlooking Jerusalem.

By 1904 a new wave of immigration had begun called

the Second *Aliyah.* As a result, 40,000 more Jews, mostly young people, arrived in Palestine between 1904 and 1914. These young people called themselves Halutzim, meaning "Pioneers." Among them was a highly motivated young man from western Russia named David Green who came to Palestine in 1906. Later, when he began writing, he took the name of David Ben-Gurion because he thought it sounded like something out of the Bible.[22] In 1907, a young Jew named Chaim Weizmann[23] made a brief visit to Palestine. He was born in the same region of western Russia from which David Green had come, but he had struggled through years of extreme poverty to gain an education in Germany and England. Already he was on the way to becoming an outstanding scientist in the field of chemistry. One day he would become the first President of Israel and David Ben-Gurion would be its first Prime Minister.

---

22. David Ben-Gurion was born Oct. 16, 1886, in Plonsk, then Russian Poland. His father was a friend of Theodor Herzl. As a child, Ben-Gurion once boasted, "One day I will be the leader of Israel." In 1906 he went to Palestine as a farm laborer. There he helped found the first Jewish defense organization, *Hashomer* (the Watchmen). In 1910, he was made editor of a weekly Hebrew magazine and signed his first article Ben-Gurion, a name which he used from then on. He was expelled from Palestine by the Turks early in World War I for conspiring to form a Jewish state. He went to the U.S. where he married Paula Munweis, a Russian-Jewish student. He helped recruit a Jewish Legion for Canada (since the U.S. was not at war with Turkey) to fight for the liberation of Palestine. He, himself, enlisted in August, 1918 and landed in Egypt as a member of the 39th Royal Fusiliers. After the war he returned to Palestine and became one of the founders of an underground army, *Haganah,* and of the General Federation of Jewish Labor called *Histadrut.* In 1935, he was elected chairman of the Jewish Agency which made him virtual prime minister of the shadow government which was evolving into the framework for a Jewish state. During World War II he traveled widely, using his influence to ally Jewish support for a Palestinian homeland after the war was won. While spending time in London's air raid shelters he taught himself classical Greek, having previously mastered several other languages. After the U.N. Partition Plan was announced, Ben-Gurion took over as head of the provisional government and minister of defense. He directed the successful defense of Israel and was among those who insisted that Jerusalem be the capital of the nation. His Mapai Party (a Zionist-Socialist party) became Israel's dominant party and he became the first prime minister of Israel following the elections of 1949. (From the biography of David Ben-Gurion by Robert St. John.)

23. Chaim Weizmann was born in Motol, Russia, Nov. 27, 1874. He went to school

(UPI Photo)
David Ben-Gurion, architect of modern Israel and for many years
its Prime Minister.

But many difficult and desperate years lay between the
death of Theodor Herzl and the establishment of a Jewish
state.

The Balfour Declaration

The year 1917 was a crisis year for the Allies during
World War I. The United States had entered the war,
but the Bolshevik Revolution in Russia had virtually demolished the eastern front. As the tides of war swept back
and forth across Eastern Europe, hundreds of thousands
of Jews were caught in the current of conflict. Earlier,
when the Russians were advancing, they had treated the
Jews as spies and enemy aliens. When they were forced
to retreat they conducted a mass evacuation of the Jews
lest they reveal military secrets. These evacuations were
carried out so recklessly that a large percentage of these
Jews perished. Other thousands of Jews had fled from
earlier Russian purges to Rumania, Poland or Western
Europe. However, they still held Russian passports so

---

under very primitive conditions, but finally graduated from high school at Pinsk
by tutoring on the side for a living. At an early age he became interested in
Zionism. When he decided to be a chemist and study in Berlin, he also decided
to become an activist in the Zionist movement. He took his doctorate with honors
in 1898 at the University of Fribourg (Switzerland). In 1901, he was appointed
reader of chemistry at the University of Geneva, and in 1904 at the University of
Manchester. He became a British citizen in 1910. Meanwhile, in 1907, he had
made a brief trip to Palestine for the Zionists. A year earlier he had met Arthur
James Balfour for the first time and had made a great impression on that states-
man which later had much to do with the issuing of the famous Balfour Declaration.
Dr. Weizmann's most outstanding scientific contribution was the discovery of a
new process of fermentation by which acetone could be made. Acetone was
required for the manufacture of cordite, a new high explosive. Winston Churchill
was First Lord of the Admiralty and ordered Weizmann to produce 30,000 tons of
acetone. For two years Weizmann was engaged in this highly successful project
with all available government facilities at his command. This gave him extremely
favorable relations with the government when the issue of the Palestine homeland
for Jews arose. The Balfour Declaration was issued Nov. 2, 1917, providing for a
Jewish home in Palestine. Weizmann was elected president of the Zionist Organization and served for many years. In 1949, he was elected the first president of
Israel. He died in 1952.

they also were shuttled about until they were homeless and near starvation. The Zionist leaders began to feel tremendous pressures to succor these suffering people.

In response to this plea, American Jews raised millions of dollars in relief funds. However, the Zionists saw a more permanent relief in the latest victories of British troops under General Edmund Allenby who were on the verge of liberating Palestine from the Turks. They felt that if the British leaders turned out to be sympathetic to their cause, this might be the Providential opportunity to create a Jewish homeland in Palestine. The proposal which the Zionists made to the British leaders was different than one might have expected.

First of all, they did not ask for a sovereign Jewish state as Herzl had contemplated. They asked that this territory be made a part of the British Empire with a policy which allowed Jews to freely migrate and settle there. Although the Palestine Arabs were fighting on the other side, the Zionists said they would commit themselves to a policy of equal rights and privileges for all, Jewish or non-Jewish.

The British leaders contacted all available Arab delegates and found them favorable to this arrangement. Their attitude at that time is reflected in a letter from the Emir, Feisal (later king of Iraq), who wrote just after the war:

"We feel that the Arabs and Jews are cousins in race, suffering similar oppressions at the hands of powers stronger than themselves, and by a happy coincidence have been able to take the first step toward the attainment of their national ideals together.

"We Arabs, especially the educated among us, look with the deepest sympathy on the Zionist movement. Our deputation here in Paris is fully acquainted with the proposals submitted by the Zionist Organization to the Peace Conference, and we regard them as moderate and proper. We will do our best, in so far as we are concerned.

"With the chiefs of your movement, especially with Dr. Weizmann, we have had, and continue to have, the closest relations. He has been a great helper of our cause, and I hope the Arabs may soon be in a position to make the Jews some return for their kindness. We are working together for a reformed and revived Near East, and our two movements complete one another. The Jewish movement is national and not imperialistic. Our movement is national and not imperialistic; and there is room in Syria for us both. Indeed, I think that neither can be a real success without the other."[24]

With such warm and congenial sentiments apparently being expressed by all concerned, the British prepared to make an official policy statement authorizing unlimited Jewish migration to Palestine as soon as it was liberated. But opposition suddenly emerged from an amazing quarter —the leading Jewish politicians of Britain! They were then joined by the Syrian Arabs who did not want Palestine separated from Syria. The Zionists were shocked that this wave of opposition should originate from Jews who for some ideological or selfish reason had become anti-Zionists.

It is interesting that it was Christian supporters of Zionism who made the Balfour Declaration possible. They had to compromise because of the political power of such Jewish opponents as Edwin Montague, but even in its watered-down text it became the Magna Charta for a new Jewish homeland. The declaration was in the form of a letter to Lord Rothschild dated November 2, 1917:

"I have much pleasure in conveying to you, on behalf of His Majesty's Government, the following declaration of sympathy with Jewish Zionist aspirations which has been submitted to, and approved by, the Cabinet.

---

24. William L. Hull, *The Fall and Rise of Israel*, Grand Rapids, Mich., Zandervan Publishing Co., 1961, p. 139.

"His Majesty's Government view with favour the establishment in Palestine of a national home for the Jewish people, and will use their best endeavors to facilitate the achievement of this object, it being clearly understood that nothing shall be done which may prejudice the civil and religious rights of existing non-Jewish communities in Palestine, or the rights and political status enjoyed by Jews in any other country."

General Edmund Allenby took Jerusalem on December 11, 1917, and a Zionist Commission was sent to Palestine by the British Government early in 1918 to implement the Balfour Declaration. However, it was June 20, 1920, before the new League of Nations and the Allied Supreme Council had ratified this arrangement. On that date Britain was given the mandate over Palestine with the express provision that she was responsible for putting into effect the Balfour Declaration and establishing a national home for the Jews of the world who may wish to migrate there.

The Palestine Arabs Revolt

It was also in 1920, however, that Zionists came to realize that their national home was still a long way from becoming a reality. The first thing they noted was the fact the British military had unofficially circulated among officers and enlisted men a spurious document called *Protocols of the Elders of Zion.*[25] This was supposed to be the secret program of a Jewish world conspiracy to bankrupt the gentile nations, corrupt their culture, pervert their morals, and then set up a world-wide Jewish dictatorship. It was a blood-curdling document prepared by the secret police of the Tsar at the turn of the century to use as a basis for the blood purges of Jews in Russia.

---

25. The background of this spurious document is discussed in the *Appendix* of this book under the title, "The Protocols of the Elders of Zion—Fact or Fiction?"

It was obvious to the Zionists that many of the British military and also many of the British administrators had been bitterly prejudiced by this forged piece of propaganda. They were not only cool to the whole idea of the Balfour Declaration, they were hostile.

This became vividly apparent when the first Arab revolts broke out.

The Zionists had known that some of the Palestinian Arabs were extremely bitter toward the Balfour concept. Instead of looking upon the migration of the Jews as a means of introducing European culture and technology to the Arabs (as Emir Feisal had done), they considered every Jew an emissary of evil. As a result, on April 4, 1920, when thousands of Moslem villagers congregated in Jerusalem for the festival of Nebi Musa, a political demonstration developed into a full-scale riot against the Jews. The riots lasted three days. There was great damage to Jewish homes and stores, a number were killed and many were injured. The Jews were unarmed and the Arabs boasted that the British military was on the Arab side. The astonished Zionists watched the riots continue unabated while the British military stood by passively. In fact, when Vladimir Jabotinsky, leader of the Jewish Legion, attempted to enter the Old City and provide protection for the Jewish quarter, the British military not only stopped his volunteer force, but Jabotinsky and nineteen other Jews were disarmed, placed under arrest, and later sentenced to fifteen years for having arms in their possession.

This introduced the Zionists into a new era of Arab hostility and British capitulation which was to last for twenty-eight years.

They thought there might be a better balance when the British Government appointed Sir Herbert Samuel (a Jew) as the first High Commissioner to administer Palestine. However, Sir Herbert retained many of the anti-

Zionist administrators around him. The Zionists succeeded in getting him to grant an amnesty to Jabotinsky and other imprisoned Zionists, but he turned around and granted amnesty to the Arab instigators of the riots so that they could return from the areas to which they had fled. Among them was Haj Amin whom Sir Herbert Samuel not only pardoned, but very shortly appointed as the Mufti of Jerusalem. This made Haj Amin the religious leader of the Arabs, and a year later when he became president of the Supreme Moslem Council it gave him access to thousands of pounds of charitable funds, supervision of the Moslem courts, and the right to appoint the preachers of all the mosques in Palestine. Far from being a practicing Moslem, Haj Amin was a politician and a terrorist. In the coming years he would not only play havoc with the Balfour Declaration, but he would spend World War II at Nazi headquarters in Berlin feverishly fomenting plots to turn all the Arab states against the Allies.

The "Whittling" Period

The British retreat from its once firm position of a national home for the Jews, occurred in a number of stages.

The first big jump backwards occurred in 1922 as a direct result of the Arab riots of 1920 and 1921. This spirit of opposition to British policy was spreading to other Arab territories and it was therefore decided by the British to placate the Arabs by making a separate Arab state out of that part of Palestine which was east of the Jordan River. This came as a great shock to the Zionists. The Trans-Jordan area represented 35,000 square miles of arid terrain which had an extremely light Arab population. The Jews had started some of their early agriculture communes in that area and knew that, with irrigation and scientific farming, several million Jews could be settled there without risking offense to the Arabs. Now that was gone. It was illegal for any Jew to settle in Trans-Jordan. All that was left was 10,000 square miles in west Jordan which had a much heavier Arab population. As a result, the Jews restricted to the west side, found themselves paying exorbitant prices for swamps, sand dunes or anything else the Arabs would sell them.

For several years the Zionist leaders felt they were making considerable progress in developing a good working relationship with the Arabs, but in 1929 Haj Amin dispelled any illusion that there was going to be peace. On August 23, when thousands of Arabs came into Jerusalem for the Moslem sabbath, the speakers at the mosques inflamed their congregations with the rumor that the Jews were about to attack the sacred Dome of the Rock, second most sacred spot in the Moslem world. Bands of Arabs descended on Jewish quarters and an orgy of killing began. From Jerusalem the attacks spread to Tel Aviv, Hebron and other centers. Bombing, burning and looting occurred over wide sections. Once again the local police and army contingents were amazingly passive. The government provided a hundred thousand pounds to repair the damage but this was only token aid. The real relief came in the form of six hundred thousand pounds donated by Jews from all over the world.

After that the Jews had seven years of relative peace and prosperity—the greatest they had known. Visitors to Palestine were astonished at the changes that were taking place in regions which the Jews had occupied. Not only agriculture was thriving, but industry and trade were growing. Part of this was due to the fact that Hitler's persecution of the Jews had brought refugees by the tens of thousands to Palestine. The Jews looked upon human resources as their greatest form of wealth. The Arabs declared that all this immigration must immediately stop.

On Sunday, April 19, 1936, the day after Haj Amin had visited the principal Arab coastal city of Jaffa, a Jewish massacre took place in that city. It was the beginning of a four-year campaign of bloodshed and property destruction. A deeper insight into the tragedy of this period is gained from the fact that the Mufti and his ruffians killed more Arabs trying to compel them to harass the Jews than the number of Jews who were actually killed.[26] In other words, the Mufti was as vindictive against his own people as he was the Jews!

As a result of all this turmoil and upheaval, Britain severely curtailed immigration quotas and tried to restrict future land purchases. One commission in 1937 would have restricted the Jews to 2,000 square miles and the one in 1940 would have restricted them to 260 square miles. Winston Churchill denounced the Labor-Socialist coalition which had been in power for several years for having repudiated the whole spirit and intent of the Balfour Declaration.

World War II

But in spite of the shabby treatment the Jews felt they had received from their British patron, the avalanche of blitzkrieg war which threatened European civilization was enough to obscure the problems of the past and arouse a spirit of total Jewish support for the allied war effort. As a result, when World War II exploded, the Jewish Agency set up registration booths and 85,781 men and 50,262 women volunteered for war service. That was thirty percent of the entire Jewish population!

The Jewish leaders proposed that these volunteers be organized as a contingent of the British Army. To their utter astonishment, Prime Minister Chamberlain rejected the whole idea. Not until Winston Churchill had re-

26. William L. Hull, *The Fall and Rise of Israel*, p. 178.

placed Chamberlain were the Jews given an opportunity to serve in the war effort directly. A total of 33,000 were ultimately utilized and they served in all three services— the army, navy and air force. Several contingents were trained for Commando service and, as we have mentioned earlier, Moshe Dayan was one of them.

For the most part, the Arab nations assumed a position of neutrality during the war. Only Trans-Jordan declared war in 1939. Of the million or more Arabs in Palestine, only 9,000 enlisted. Egypt, Saudi Arabia, Syria and Lebanon did not join the Allies until victory was assured. In February, 1945, they joined the Allies in order to qualify for membership in the future United Nations organization.

In spite of the Zionist effort to show its good faith, the relations between Britain and the Jews was not particularly cordial during World War II. There was always Churchill's support, but the military leaders looked upon the training and arming of Jews in Palestine with the gravest suspicion. Right at the time Jews were straining every effort to demonstrate cooperation, they found their Haganah (home defense) headquarters being raided and all arms confiscated. This led to the further development of certain secret extremist groups such as the Stern Gang and the Irgun who had decided to take the offensive against British and Arabs alike. They stored arms and explosives and trained personnel in commando tactics against the day when they might be needed. The Zionist leaders cooperated with the British in discovering and arresting these terrorists, but even this did not dissolve the fog of British suspicion which hung over the Jewish leaders.

The Rising Crisis of the Post-War Period

Barely had the war terminated when the Churchill

Government was voted out and the Labour Party took over. Since the Zionist leaders also counted themselves Labor-Socialists, they might have expected a more sympathetic hearing from Britain's post-war government, but their previous encounter with Chamberlain and other Labour-Socialist politicians had taught them that mentalities of this stripe were not nearly so sensitive to the needs of the weak and the underprivileged as their party platforms pretended. And nowhere was this better demonstrated than in the person of bumbling Ernest Bevin, the new Foreign Secretary.

Because of Hitler's genocidal atrocities and the bulging refugee camps in Germany, President Truman made a special plea to the British Government to authorize the immediate admission of 100,000 Jewish refugees into Palestine. He felt there was an extreme urgency to get the liberated thousands of emaciated, displaced Jews into an environment where they would be among their own people and receive sympathetic care. The British Labour Party turned the proposal down flat.

It even went further. Immigration of any kind was shut down to a trickle. Bevin felt that it was in the best British interest to develop a friendly Arab bloc in the Mediterranean, even if it meant sacrificing past British commitments to the Jews. The British army, navy and air force were recruited to scour the coastal regions, spying out Zionist ships which came in the night loaded like cans of sardines with Jewish refugees and seeking to disgorge them into the waiting settlements which the Zionists had set up for them. All of these the Labour Party of Britain was determined to turn back—not merely to some other haven but to force them to return to the concentration camps from which they had come. Where this was impossible, new concentration camps were constructed on the island of Cyprus. Refugees who had previously reached Palestine and now anxiously awaited the arrival

of loved ones, watched in terrified disbelief as they saw
the Mandate officials forcing these ships back out to sea.
These tactics sometimes made terrorists out of Jews who
had formerly been tractable.

One of these was Nathan Friedman-Yellin, leader of the
Stern Gang. Others went into the Irgun. Even though
they were terrorists, both the Stern Gang and the Irgun
originally made it a practice to warn the British and Arabs
before they attacked. Their principal weapon was explosives and they gave the warning so the area could be
evacuated. In one tragic case the British ignored the
warning. It occurred in June, 1946, and it involved one
wing of the King David Hotel in Jerusalem where the
British had their heavily guarded Army headquarters.
Twenty minutes before the large milk cans of explosives
(planted in the basement) were timed to go off, the Irgun
called the hotel. The Government official who received the
warning reportedly replied, "We are not here to take
orders from the Jews. We give them orders."[27]

When the explosion occurred it killed 95 persons—
British, Jews and Arabs. Another hundred were maimed
or injured. Although the Zionist officials heatedly dis-
avowed any knowledge of the plot, the Palestine Administration stormed the headquarters of the Jewish Agency,
arrested the leaders and two thousand, seven hundred
other Jews. All were interned. There were widespread
searches for arms and explosives and a British Army order
forbade any soldiers to patronize Jewish establishments
thereafter.

By 1947 the situation in Palestine had become so volatile that British officers were being kidnapped and executed
in retaliation for Jews who were being arrested and
hanged. There was a virtual state of open warfare between the Mandate Government and the people for whom
it had promised to provide a National Home.

---

27. *Ibid.*, p. 243.

It was in July, 1947, that an ancient, rusted-out American coastal vessel carrying 4,300 refugees came wallowing into Palestine waters bearing the name *EXODUS* 1947. Like all the others, it was intercepted. In addition, it was rammed seven times and boarded by military personnel using a variety of weapons. Several were killed and a number injured. The people were herded onto three ships and taken to Marseilles, France. But the majority refused to disembark. For 25 days they endured the boiling heat of the Mediterranean summer sun. Finally, Bevin ordered them shipped to Hamburg. "There, in that port, in the land where they had lost all their loved ones and had themselves suffered the tortures of hell, the refugees were disembarked."[28] Thus ended the saga of the *Exodus.*

But almost simultaneously the endurance of the British Labour Party ended also. It was finally ready to capitulate. After a certain date, Bevin announced, the British government would take no further responsibility for affairs in Palestine. The Labour government declared that the United Nations would be expected to take over.

The United Nations promptly appointed a committee to investigate the Palestine problem and come up with some kind of recommendations.

In June, U.N. hearings were commenced in Jerusalem, but the Arabs boycotted the hearings and the Committee was greeted upon its arrival by a fifteen-hour protest strike. Jewish witnesses based their claim primarily on humanitarian considerations and the prior commitments of the League of Nations to create a national home for the Jews. Many Christian ministers testified in favor of some type of partitioning or compromise which would allow the Jews, without prejudice to the Arabs, to fulfill the prophetic promise that one day they would build a prosperous nation in this territory. There was one notable exception.

28. *Ibid.,* p. 263.

The Anglican bishop from Jerusalem swept all of the Old Testament prophecies aside with the declaration that these had been abrogated by the New Testament and that the Jews had no claim on Palestine whatever![29] The fact that British soldiers were hearing this interpretation of the scriptures every Sunday no doubt accounts for at least some of the antagonism which they displayed toward the Jews during this final, tragic phase of British occupation. Back in 1917, Balfour, Lloyd George and Churchill had assumed they were performing a great service which the Bible declared they should provide. A favorite scripture, often quoted, was the one by Isaiah who had referred to the gathering of Israel in the latter days and declared: "Thus saith the Lord God, Behold, I will lift up mine hand to the Gentiles, and set up my standard to the people: and they shall bring thy sons in their arms, and thy daughters shall be carried upon their shoulders. And kings shall be thy nursing fathers, and their queens thy nursing mothers. . . ."[30]

In 1917 British leaders thought they were participating in a thrilling fulfilment of prophecy. By 1947 the Anglican Church was proclaiming the whole idea to be false and misleading. It was no wonder that the average British soldier was confused.

In order to get the Arab leaders to testify, the committee had to convene in Lebanon. But the Arabs were inflexible. There would be no partition, no compromise, no more Jewish immigration. Palestine must be declared an Arab state with the Jews existing in it as a permanent minority.

In August, 1947, the committee came up with its recommendation: Palestine should be partitioned. They designated certain areas which should be given to the Jews with the provision that Jewish immigrants would have

---

29. *Ibid.*, p. 270.
30. Isaiah 49:22-23.

to be restricted to placement within these zones. They designated other areas which would be under the Palestine Arabs and Jewish refugees would be prohibited from settling there. Jerusalem was to be an open city under international supervision. All of the zones were to be closely linked economically but separated politically. When practical, British forces were to be withdrawn.

The Jews promptly accepted the recommendation. The Arabs flatly rejected it. Nevertheless, the General Assembly of the United Nations approved the plan by a two-thirds majority on November 29, 1947. Within three days the Arabs had declared an unofficial war and launched a campaign of widespread guerilla warfare against the Jews.

Initial Stages of the Arab-Jewish War

The first fighting broke out in Jerusalem. As early as November 30th, seven Jews were ambushed and killed, but on December 2, mobs stormed into the Jewish commercial center and set it on fire. Shooting into the Jewish quarter required that practically all of the area be evacuated. The British occupation officials now took the position that this was an Arab-Jewish quarrel and they should not interfere. However, the regulars in the Arab armies had been trained and were under the command of British officers. It was inevitable, therefore, that they would feel duty-bound to interfere whenever the Jews raised any substantial resistance. In fact, the British were under orders to prevent the formation of a Jewish army and confiscate any weapons which Jews attempted to import.

For six months the Jews struggled to build up some kind of organized defense and smuggle weapons in from any country which would sell them arms. As a result of the restrictions, however, only light weapons got through. These were added to the arsenal of private weapons which the Haganah (Jewish home defense) had been hiding and storing since World War II. The British were supposed to free the port of Tel Aviv by February 1, 1948, but refused to do so until they formally withdrew at midnight, May 14th. As a result, any tanks, planes, mobile artillery or heavy weapons which the Jews were able to purchase were not brought in until after the British had left.

However, as it turned out, the Jews found that during the initial stages of the conflict, they were able to hold their own with the lighter weapons available.

The greatest Jewish weapon was purely psychological. For some reason the Palestine Arabs vastly over-estimated the strength of the Jews and generated a profound fear of their capacity to retaliate. This resulted in a situation which amazed the Jews. For example, the Mufti at Jerusalem would order the Arabs to make heavy assaults against Tel Aviv or Haifa and this would be done. But the moment the Jews began resisting, the Arabs would tend to fold up and flee en masse. This created a dilemma for the Jews. The country was made up of 1,200,000 Arabs and only 600,000 Jews which meant that many resources needed to keep the economy of Palestine stabilized were in the hands of Arabs. Whenever the Arabs became frightened and fled in large numbers, especially from the larger centers, these services and resources collapsed. This accounts for the strange anomaly which developed in places like Haifa and Tel Aviv. Observers would see the Jews resist Arab assaults and then put sound trucks in the streets urging Arabs not to leave! The problem was to discourage the Arabs from shooting, but at the same time prevent them from getting frightened and running away.

Reverend William L. Hull, who was living in Palestine at the time, describes what happened at Haifa: "The Arabs fled to Acre, or by boat to Lebanon, or anywhere to escape from the city. The Jews had pleaded with them to stay. They sent out vans with loudspeakers and the Arabs were told that they would not be harmed and would be well looked after. But the Arabs had their instructions from the Arab Higher Committee, who themselves were fleeing. When the Arabs saw their leaders leaving in a hurry, they all packed what they could and joined the flight. The amazing thing is how so many succeeded in getting away so quickly."[31]

The reader will immediately recognize that we have now reached the historical setting for the origin of the much-discussed "Arab Refugee" problem. In the United States there is almost a universal misconception of what actually took place. We will therefore pause momentarily to document the facts in greater detail so that this problem can be better evaluated.

Arab Leaders Create a Stampede of Mass Migration

Between November 30, 1947, and April of 1948, the Arab opposition evolved from spontaneous or sporadic fighting to well-organized major assaults. Two weeks after the U.N. resolution ordering the partition of Palestine, the Arab League met in Cairo and decided to send troops from the neighboring Arab countries into Palestine disguised as "volunteers." This was not only tolerated by the British Mandate headquarters but the main body of the Arab Legion from Jordan moved over the Jordan River into Jericho under the command of British officers.

The main centers of attack were Jerusalem, Tel Aviv and Haifa. The large Arab city of Jaffa was immediately adjacent to Tel Aviv so open warfare was easily triggered. The Mufti (religious leader of the Moslems) took it upon himself to send in bands of guerilla raiders to all parts of the country. The situation became so explosive that the

---

31. William L. Hull, *The Fall and Rise of Israel*, p. 312.

Greek Orthodox Archbishop made a direct appeal to the Mufti to withdraw his raiders from Palestine, especially Haifa. However, the attacks increased. As a result, Jewish resistance stiffened and the local Arabs panicked. The Arab merchants fled to Lebanon. Arabs of the lower classes rushed to Acre across the bay or out into the countryside. By the end of January 20,000 had abandoned Haifa. More were preparing to leave. The same thing was happening in Arab cities to the south.

It was under these circumstances that the leaders of the Arab League initiated a cruel and deceptive propaganda campaign against their own people. They launched a drive for the mass migration of Arabs away from Palestine. It turned into a stampede eventually involving over a million men, women and children. The world has heard all about the "refugee problem" of the Arabs from Palestine. What the general public has not heard is how the problem was created. Earlier in this book I related my conversation with an Arab refugee. He volunteered the information that the official guides were not giving me the real story concerning the history of the refugees. The "official" line was that they had all been forcibly evicted from their homes by the terrorist tactics of the Jews.

Fortunately, a number of responsible Arab authorities have verified what actually took place, and these sources support the Jewish contention that the refugees were stampeded into a mass evacuation by the wild propaganda promises of over-zealous Arab leaders. A respected writer, Habib Issa, editor of the Arab newspaper *Al Huda*, made a comprehensive investigation of the whole refugee problem and published the results in the monthly issue for June, 1951. He concluded:

"The Secretary-General of the Arab League, Abdel Rahman Azzam Pasha, published numerous declarations assuring the Arab peoples that the occupation of Palestine and of Tel-Aviv would be as simple as a military parade for the Arab armies. He pointed out that the armies were already on the frontiers, and that all the millions the Jews had spent on land on economic development would be easy booty, for it would be a simple matter to throw the Jews into the Mediterranean. . . . Brotherly advice was given to the Arabs of Palestine to leave their land, homes, and property and to stay temporarily in the neighboring states, lest the guns of the invading Arab armies mow them down. The Palestine Arabs had no choice but to obey the League's advice and believed what they were told by Azzam Pasha and the other responsible League leaders: that departure from their lands and their country would be only temporary, and would come to an end in a few days, when the punitive operation against Israel was completed."[32]

The Arab Higher Committee report for 1951 has the following statement on page 23: "It was natural that those inhabitants of Palestine who found it necessary to flee took refuge in the neighboring Arab countries, and preferred to remain there and be in contact with their country so that it would be easy to return when the opportunity arose, as had been promised in the declarations of the Arab leaders. These leaders exaggerated greatly, so that many believed that this opportunity would come in a very short time. These declarations were a factor that encouraged the emigration of many residents, especially those with large families, who preferred to leave with their families, believing that the stabilization of the position in Palestine in accordance with Arab interests would take only a very short time. Most of the inhabitants in the northern area of Palestine emigrated to Syria and Lebanon; those in the southern part turned to Egypt and the Gaza Strip, while the majority of the inhabitants in the center migrated to other parts of Palestine and Trans-Jordan."[33]

32. David Ben-Gurion, *The Jews in Their Land*, p. 326.
33. *Ibid.*

Here, then, from Arab sources, is the real story behind
the famous "Arab Refugee" problem.

The Siege of Jerusalem

From the beginning of the "unofficial war" (November 30, 1947 to May 14, 1948) Jerusalem was a focal
point of continuous attack. The new or Jewish part of
Jerusalem located to the west of the Old City had at that
time only one road leading into it and that was the road
coming up from Tel Aviv. The road winds up from the
maritime plain through the famous Sorek Valley (home of
Samson) with its precipitous cliffs and steeply terraced
mountains on either side. It is ideal for ambush raiders,
man-made slides and cannonading. The Arabs had little
difficulty cutting this road which was Jerusalem's main
artery. Overnight the population of Jewish Jerusalem was
in desperate straits. Their water supply was cut off. All
sources of food were dammed off. The people were put
on 500-calorie rations.

It was the middle of April before Haganah forces could
mobilize the necessary strength to command most of the
strategic heights overlooking the Tel Aviv road and provide a relatively safe passage for a food convoy. When it
came, the convoy was seventeen miles long and carried
one thousand tons of supplies. When it reached Jerusalem,
the trucks, jeeps and busses were welcomed with tears and
cheers. Their food was gone and the regular source of
water had been shut off for seven days. This was one of the
last shipments of supplies to get into Jerusalem before
the official war broke out and Jewish Jerusalem was put
under another siege.

It is necessary to remember that the Jews were not
yet an officially organized state and therefore all action
depended primarily upon cooperation. Those who disagreed
with the provisional leaders were free to take unilateral

action without much fear of reprisal. Ben-Gurion had appealed to the Stern Gang, the Irgun and other dissident groups of the radical stripe, to follow the guidelines set down by the central committee. However, the siege of Jerusalem (which the British should have never permitted) raised the hackles of both the Stern Gang and the Irgun. They decided to make an example of an Arab village near Jerusalem called Deir Yassin. This was right at the time the Jewish forces were trying to clear the Tel Aviv road in order to bring up the food convoy.

The attack on Deir Yassin occurred April 9th. In a terrible, wanton massacre, the Stern group and the Irgun killed 200 men, women and children. Ben-Gurion was horrified. He not only denounced these Jewish fanatics, but ordered a widespread manhunt to determine who had perpetrated this outrage. It had severely damaged the image of the Jewish struggle.

Four days later the Arabs retaliated. A medical convoy of ten vehicles enroute to the Hadassah Hospital on Mount Scopus was stopped when a road mine blew up. The survivors were then fired upon for nearly six hours. British officials refused to interfere, even though a military post was only 200 yards away. Seventy-seven men and women were killed and twenty were wounded. Among those killed were two world-renowned doctors. It had tragically demonstrated what Ben-Gurion had continually preached, that "Violence breeds violence!"

The State of Israel Becomes a Reality

As the deadline drew near for the withdrawal of the British from Palestine, the Arab nations moved up their armies to the partitioned borders of Israel ready to invade at midnight, May 14, 1948. The Jewish leaders had been feverishly mobilizing the people for this terrible moment of crisis. The Arabs were coming in with tanks, planes and cannon, whereas the British had prevented the Jews from importing the heavy armaments which they had purchased and had been forced to store in foreign warehouses. The situation looked extremely bleak.

Nevertheless, at 4 P.M., May 14, 1948, David Ben-Gurion appeared before a select group of Jews at a Tel Aviv museum and presented the Declaration of Independence of the people of Israel. Several paragraphs from this document are of particular interest:

"We hereby declare that, as from the termination of the Mandate at midnight, May 14-15, 1948, and pending the setting up of the duly elected bodies of the State in accordance with a Constitution, to be drawn up by the Constituent Assembly not later than October 1, 1948, the National Council shall act as the Provisional State Council and that the National Administration shall constitute the Provisional Government of the Jewish State, which shall be known as Israel.

"The State of Israel will be open to the immigration of Jews from all countries of their dispersion; will promote the development of the country for the benefit of all inhabitants [100,000 of which were Arabs and other thousands were Christians]; will be based on the principles of liberty, justice and peace as conceived by the Prophets of Israel; will uphold the full social and political equality of all its citizens without distinction of religion, race, or sex; will guarantee freedom of religion, conscience, education and culture; will safeguard the Holy Places of all religions; and will loyally uphold the principles of the United Nations Charter."

Specific portions of the declaration were addressed to the Arabs:

"In the midst of wanton aggression, we yet call upon the Arab inhabitants of the State of Israel to preserve the ways of peace and play their part in the development of the State, on the basis of full and equal citizenship and due representation in all its bodies and institutions—provisional and permanent.

"We extend our hand in peace and neighbourliness to all the neighbouring states and their peoples, and invite them to cooperate with the independent Jewish nation for the common good of all. The State of Israel is prepared to make its contribution to the progress of the Middle East as a whole.

"Our call goes out to the Jewish people all over the world to rally to our side in the task of immigration and development and to stand by us in the great struggle for the fulfilment of the dream of generations for the redemption of Israel.

"With trust in Almighty God, we set our hand to this Declaration . . ."

So that was it. At midnight, May 14, 1948, Israel became a sovereign nation and the Arab armies prepared to march. For the Jews it was a frightening prospect, but from all appearances they possessed supreme confidence that somehow they would succeed. For the British, whose victories in history have been far more frequent than their failures, this was a sorry hour. The administration of the Labour Party both before and after World War II had been foppish. Prior to the war, the sellout to Hitler at Munich in violation of all previous British commitments was typical of the cynicism, capriciousness and vacillation which characterized the quality of leadership during those troubled years. Nevertheless, the British people made a brilliant comeback under Churchill's leadership and fought World War II through to a triumphant conclusion. Regrettably, as soon as the crisis had passed, the Labour Party returned to power and leaders of a lesser caliber took over.

Both the Arabs and the Jews were caught in the web of doubletalk, false patrimony and abandonment of both morals and principles which pervaded Labour Party policies during the post-war period. When the resolution to partition Palestine had come up in the United Nations, the British would not take a position. They abstained from voting. When the resolution was passed by a two-thirds majority the Labour Government refused to support it. They allowed May 14, 1948, to approach with absolutely no effort to provide for an orderly transfer of administration to the partitioned area. In fact, strenuous efforts were made to prevent the Jews from even developing any adequate defenses. They allowed anarchy and chaos to plague the whole territory even while claiming exclusive authority for the maintaining of order. Nor did the bias and generosity exhibited toward the Arabs buy any friendship for Britain. To their amazement, Mandate officials found the Arabs zealously anxious to have the British get out. The image of the great British people had been sadly tarnished by this whole affair.

The Arab-Israeli War

The United States was the first to grant official recognition of the new nation of Israel and this came shortly after midnight. Fifteen other nations, including the Soviet Union, soon did the same. This was encouraging, but the cold facts were that Israel was going to have to fight for her existence absolutely alone. Some rabbinical scholars saw this to be a literal fulfillment of Isaiah's vision of Jerusalem's redemption in the last days when he wrote: "And I looked, and there was none to help; and I wondered that there was none to uphold: therefore mine own arm brought salvation unto me; and my fury it upheld me."[34]

In the beginning, however, Israel had little "fury" available. She had only light weapons—no artillery, no

---

34. Isaiah 63:5.

tanks, no fighting planes, no ships of war. Only gradually could these be brought in during the first month of the war following the removal of the British blockade. The Jews did develop a six-inch mortar which they dubbed *Davidka*. It was short-ranged and its directional control was scarcely predictable, but it had the advantage of making a loud noise. A rumor spread among the Arabs that this was an atom bomb device. This devastated Arab morale for several days.

Had the Arabs hit the Israeli with their full potential early in the war, perhaps the outcome would have been different. For some reason, however, the Arab buildup was slow. They knew the Jews only had about 6,000 trained soldiers, and therefore they thought about 20,000 Arabs with the latest British equipment would be sufficient.[35] But the Jews mobilized large volunteer forces with a zeal in them which always seems to emerge when men and women are fighting for their homes and families. As a result, for the most part the Jews were able to hold the line.

The Arab Legion planned two main drives—one for the port of Haifa and the other for Jerusalem. Fighting became so bitter in Old Jerusalem, however, that the drive for Haifa had to be abandoned and all Arab forces redeployed to Jerusalem. The fighting was house to house and garden to garden. Nevertheless, the heavy shelling with British guns finally took its toll among the Jews and the Old City was reluctantly—even bitterly—surrendered to the Arabs May 27th. The entire Jewish sector was then blown up, including the ancient Hurvah Synagogue, so it could not be reoccupied. The Arab Legion thereupon concentrated its attack on the new or Jewish Jerusalem which lies west of the Old City.

However, in spite of heavy shelling every day, the

35. William Hull, *The Fall and Rise of Israel*, p. 333.

Jews were able to maintain most of the strategic heights in this area and hold back several attempted frontal assaults. Meanwhile, fierce fighting was going on in other parts of Israel. On three occasions the U.N. Security Council attempted to get a cease fire but the Arabs refused. They said they were winning. Finally, the U.N. mediator, Count Bernadotte of Sweden, arranged a truce for June 11 with the understanding that it was to be a cooling off period of four weeks. Both sides used it to entrench their positions and acquire an increased supply of arms even though this was contrary to the truce agreement.

By this time, the first Israeli shipments of tanks and artillery were beginning to arrive and also some planes. Consequently, when the four-week truce was over the Israelis found themselves in a much stronger position. They therefore launched a hard offensive. Ben-Gurion initiated a policy which every afterwards characterized Israeli strategy: "When surrounded by an enemy, Attack! Attack! Attack!" William Hull describes some of the results during this phase of the war:

"Sarafand, the big military camp which had held thirty thousand British troops and had been turned over to the [Arab] Legion, was captured. The camp was surrounded by an extensive mine field, but Jewish commandos lassoed the high trees bordering the camp, swung themselves over the mines and the barbed wire defenses and with only a small force quickly captured the whole camp. Later Lydda Airport was captured; then the Legion was driven out of the towns of Lydda and Ramleh. Nazareth in the north was captured and ultimately all Galilee was in Jewish hands. The Arabs were on the run and only the quick intervention of the British delegates in the Security Council, which brought about a second truce, saved the Arabs. A very few more days and not only would the Old City of Jerusalem have been captured, but the Legion would almost certainly have been driven right back across the Jordan."[36]

The second truce began July 18. It was to continue indefinitely. In September, however, a tragedy occurred which seriously hurt the Israeli cause. The Stern Group, or a branch of it, successfuly carried out an assassination plot against popular Count Bernadotte, the U.N. mediator, and his adjutant, Colonel Saraut. The murders took place in Jerusalem. Once again Ben-Gurion was outraged by the ferocity of these fanatics and outlaws who had implanted themselves in the Israeli ranks. Three days later all Israeli separatist groups were anathematized. The Irgun surrendered and handed over its arms to the army under a 24-hour ultimatum. Ben-Gurion announced that any dissident groups would not be tolerated and, if necessary, the whole strength of the army would be deployed against them.

Under the second truce, the Egyptian Army in the Negev was supposed to allow supplies to get through to Israeli bases to the south. On October 15 the Egyptians attacked a food convoy and fighting began again. By October 21, the Jews had captured Beer Sheba and all of the northern Negev. On November 16, the U.N. Security Council instructed Israel and Egypt to open peace negotiations. Israel agreed to comply but Egypt demurred. Israel then launched a new campaign and her forces eventually occupied all of the Negev including Elath on the Aqaba Gulf of the Red Sea.

By the spring of 1949, the Arab nations perceived nothing in the future but gains for Israel if this war continued. They therefore made overtures for an armistice. The Jews agreed. Egypt and Israel signed an armistice agreement February 24, 1949, and the other Arab states soon followed. Israel now occupied 8,050 square miles of

---

36. *Ibid.*, pp. 341-342.

Palestine—the whole of which is only 10,400 square miles. The remainder, consisting of 2,350 square miles, was attached to the kingdom of Trans-Jordan so the Palestinian Arabs had gambled and lost everything. This part of Palestine had a population of 750,000 Palestinian Arabs, but half of these were refugees. Another 350,000 refugees were located in the Gaza strip which Egypt continued to occupy after the war.

As we have already noted, the Arab leaders looked upon these displaced Arabs as a threat to the employment and standard of living among their own people. The refugees were therefore confined to camps and villages under strict curfew. They were prohibited from becoming citizens of the host countries, competing for jobs, or buying land. To keep them from starving to death, United Nations Relief and Works Agency was authorized to provide approximately $40,000,000 per year in various kinds of aid. Over 60% of it comes from the United States. The tragedy of the Arab refugees is summed up by the editors of *Life* in the following:

"The early Zionists, looking toward a binational state, never thought they would, could or should replace the Arabs in Palestine. When terrorism and fighting mounted in 1947-48, Arab leaders urged Palestinian Arabs to flee, promising that the country would soon be liberated. Israelis tried to induce the Arabs to stay. For this reason, the Israelis do not now accept responsibility for the Arab exodus. Often quoted is the statement of a Palestinian Arab writer that the Arab leaders "told us: 'Get out so that we can get in.' We got out but they did not get in."[37]

Historically, it was tragically ironical that while the Arab countries were putting over a million Arab refugees into quarantine, the Israelis were seeking a million Jewish refugees to come in and help build up the land:

---

37. *LIFE*, Special Edition, *Israel's Swift Sword*, p. 89.

"During the first seven and a half months of the state, 101,819 immigrants arrived; in 1949, 239,076 followed. First came the internees from Cyprus—illegal immigrants expelled from Palestine by the Mandatory government and housed on the island; then came refugees from the concentration camps in Germany. In the following two years, 343,306 more immigrants came in, and the Jewish population also rose by 88,338 as a result of natural increase during these four years. These were years of flood tide in immigration, in which the number of Jews in the country (650,000 at the founding of the state) was doubled."[38]

It was all a matter of how one looked at refugees. To the Jews they were a symbol of strength and the key to prosperity. To the Arabs they were a threat to prosperity and the symbol of a sub-culture plague.

Crisis after the Armistice

In the fall of 1949 the Communist and Arab countries combined to push through a resolution on December 10th that all of Jewish Jerusalem be taken away from Israel and combined with the Old City as an international sector. Once this had possibilities, but now both the United States and Britain voted against this provocative and unrealistic maneuver. Ben-Gurion answered this threat by immediately moving the capital of Israel from Tel Aviv to Jewish Jerusalem. "In the tempest of war," he declared, "when Jerusalem was beleaguered, we were compelled to establish the seat of government for the time being in the official quarter near Tel Aviv. But the State of Israel has had, and will have, one capital alone: Jerusalem the Eternal. . . ."[39] Ben-Gurion had thrown down the gaunt-

---

38. David Ben-Gurion, *The Jews in Their Land*, pp. 342-343.
39. *Ibid.*, p. 342.

let. If the U.N. tried to occupy the sacred city there would be another war.

Under the armistice the Jews were supposed to have access to the Wailing Wall in the Old City. The Arabs served notice that no Israeli would be allowed in the Old City, let alone at the Wailing Wall.

On January 25, 1949, about three weeks after most of the fighting was over but even before any armistice was signed, the people of Israel had their first election. Ben-Gurion became prime minister and the newly-elected parliament (Knesset) elected Dr. Chaim Weizmann president of Israel. The principles of government submitted to the Knesset as guide lines for the development of Israel are worth noting:

1. Collective cabinet responsibility (similar to Britain).

2. Liberty, equality, and democracy as the foundation of the republican regime.

3. A foreign policy of loyalty to the principles of the U.N. Charter, friendship with all peace-loving states, and a constant effort to achieve a Jewish-Arab alliance.

4. Defense based on compulsory service by all men and women, as would be laid down by law.

5. A policy of ingathering of the exiles.

6. A development policy designed to double the population of the state within four years; rapid and balanced settlement of the sparsely inhabited areas of the country and the prevention of over-concentration in the cities; encouragement of private capital and private and cooperative initiative, with efforts to develop labor enterprises in town and country.

7. General education for all the nation's children; teaching of Hebrew to the new immigrants; fostering of pure and applied research in all the natural sciences; education in Arabic, with the study of Hebrew, for all the

country's Arab citizens; expansion of agricultural and vocational education.

8. Rehabilitation of ex-soldiers.

9. Labor laws to ensure freedom of organization for the workers, the fostering of trade unions, and the fixing of minimum wages; encouragement for collective bargaining; the establishment of a network of social insurance institutions; laws for the defense of the workers.

10. Appointments to the Civil Service on the basis of examinations.

The financial crisis in Israel was resolved by a bond drive among the Jews of the world, but primarily among those in the United States. By the end of 1963, $651,325,000 had been raised and a prospering Israel had already paid over $200,000,000 back.

The real boost to Israel's finances, however, came from outright donations through the United Jewish Appeal. The generosity of world Jewry might well have been a suggested pattern for wealthy Arabs in their own countries. The Jews donated over a billion dollars by the end of 1963.

The next crisis in Israel was over religious schools. The government allowed free choice as to whether children attended religious or non-religious schools. The Religious Front voted against the government and Ben-Gurion resigned. He finally took over again after no other party could form a new government. Freedom of choice remained the rule.

In 1952 the Government demanded reparations of one-and-a-half billion from Germany. Chancellor Adenauer of West Germany looked with favor on the request. But in Israel the whole idea fomented the worst political crisis in the history of the new state. Mobs formed around the Knesset and the leader of the Herut Party had to be suspended for three months for conduct unbecoming a member of the Knesset. The protestors felt that a price had been put upon the lives of their dead relatives. Ben-

Gurion said it was nothing of the sort. He said it was simply a reparation for the property which the Nazis had taken from the Jews and which the German people were still holding and using. With Adenauer's surprising acquiescence, Ben-Gurion was able to successfully establish his point.

In 1953, Ben-Gurion resigned in order to retire to the Negev and prove that under a good system of government no one is indispensible. President Chaim Weizmann had died November 9, 1953, so Ben-Gurion felt it was time for him to step down, too. However, by early 1954 the security of Israel was considered so weak that Ben-Gurion was asked to take over as Minister of Defense. He consented and later, when elections were held in 1955, he moved back up to prime minister.

While all of these various political crises were being solved, the nation of Israel was also feeling its way along a rocky precipice of social and economic development. Many stories are told of those early days. In the beginning when Israel was virtually bankrupt, Ben-Gurion was pestered by a persistent constituent who wanted a position. Finally, after months of petitioning, B.G. told him, "All right, I shall make you Minister of Colonies." "But we have no colonies," the applicant protested. "So what?" said Ben-Gurion. "Did it bother Eliezer Kaplan when I made him Minister of Finance?"

This rather typified the nonchalant good humor of the leaders of Israel as they bull-doggedly solved one "impossible" problem after another.

As thousands of refugees poured in, they first filled up the communal settlements (the *kibbutzim*). After these were filled they settled them in tents or temporary structures next to where they expected to build permanent quarters. In this manner the work camps became the permanent locale for its residents so that they would not have to be uprooted when permanent dwellings were available.

During the first five years the Israeli government sponsored the construction of more than 200,000 permanent housing units for its refugees. In the same period of time these refugees grubbed out rocks, built terraces and pioneered irrigation projects. By the end of the five years the amount of cultivated ground in Israel had doubled!

Refugees were provided housing and food free of charge when they first arrived. After processing they were assigned where their abilities seemed most needed. During their first two years they were expected to learn Hebrew, learn a skill, and learn how to use various weapons so as to defend their country if necessary. The *kibbutz* or communal settlement adapts itself rather well to these needs without excessive cost to the government. Everybody works without pay but receives his necessities. The *kibbutz* is basically a "survival" level of existence and therefore people are free to leave them when they wish in order to earn or enjoy a higher standard of living. No matter how long they have worked in the *kibbutz* the workers take nothing with them when they leave.

Israel Under Siege

From the time of the armistice in 1949, the Arab nations had boasted that they would smother Israel with a permanent economic blockade. They also said that when the time was ripe their armies would be back to avenge the Israeli victories of 1948 and 1949. As we have noted earlier in this book, Nasser decided that 1956 should be the year. As early as January 2, 1956, Ben-Gurion began calling attention to the growing crisis. There had been a continuous violation of Article VIII by Jordan which had guaranteed free movement of traffic on vital roads, including the Bethlehem and Latrun-Jerusalem roads. Jordan was supposed to restore free access to the hospital and university on Mount Scopus but had refused

to do so. It had also violated its guarantee of providing
free access to the Holy Places and use of the Jewish ceme-
tary on the Mount of Olives. It had refused to permit the
resumption of operation of the Latrun pumping station
after the Arabs had blown it up. Ben-Gurion also had a
controversy with Egypt. She had violated the armistice
agreement by refusing to let Israel use the Suez Canal.
In 1951, when the U.N. Security Council confirmed the
right of Israel to use the Canal, Egypt defied the Security
Council. Ben-Gurion described what had been happening:

"All our four neighbors—in breach of the principles
of the U.N. Charter—have organized a boycott and a
blockade against Israel, which has continued since the end
of the fighting. In defiance of international law and in
violation of the terms of the armistice agreement, Egypt
blocked the way to Israel's shipping through the Suez
Canal, and later also in the Red Sea strait. . . . But our
neighbors were not content with violating the U.N. Charter
and defying the provisions of the armistice agreements;
they also organized a guerilla war against the citizens of
Israel. . . . Bands of saboteurs and murderers would cross
Israel's border and ambush any Israelis as they came across.

"These incidents . . . increased in number, particularly
from 1951 onward. In 1951, 137 Israeli citizens were
wounded or killed by these bands of murderers. . . . In
1952, the number of casualties rose to 147, including 114
victims of gangs from Jordan. In 1953, the number rose to
162, gangs from Jordan being responsible for 124. In 1954,
Egypt began to compete with Jordan in this sphere, and
the casualties rose to 180, Jordanians responsible for 117
and Egyptians for 50. In 1955, the Egyptians gained the
lead. Out of 258 casualties inflicted on Israel by gangs of
murderers from across the border, only 37 were due to
attacks from Jordan; 192 were the work of the *fedayun*,
especially organized Egyptian gangs whose function at
first had been to fight against the British during the Suez

Canal dispute, but who had been transferred to the Gaza Strip when the dispute ended. . . .

"The Egyptians also became expert in minelaying on Israel's roads, and in 1955 alone, 49 of their mines took a toll of life and limb in Israel.

"During the past five years we have suffered 884 casualties from the operations of regular and irregular military bands, including 258 last year alone. . . ."[40]

As the year went on, open warfare broke out along the various borders. The armies of Egypt, Jordan and Syria were placed under the Egyptian chief of staff, Abdel Hakim Amer. Israeli forces were placed under Moshe Dayan. On October 29, 1956, the Israeli forces reacted to the penetration of Egyptian bands into Egypt. They launched a lightning, seven-day-war. This is what historians now call the 1956 Arab-Israeli war. When it was over the entire Sinai peninsula had been swept clean of Egyptian military forces.

So now our story has come full circle. The familiar names with which this book began have now appeared on the scene again and the stage has been set for the evolution of events which eventually led to the fantastic victory in 1967 which we have already described.

Let us close this section with a final note from David Ben-Gurion. He described the major problems now facing the state of Israel to be five-fold:

"First, to bring home the congregations of Jewry that remain in lands of Islam and communism, at the mercy of discriminatory policies; and, as well, to encourage and accelerate . . . [the migrations] from countries of comfort. To do this would mean doubling the present population of Israel in the next 15 years. . . .

"Second, we must people and settle the untilled spaces, north and south. . . .

"Third, a way must be found of closing the cultural

40. *Ibid.*, p. 352.

and educational gap that divides children of European
immigrants, with their background of general enlightenment from the children of immigrants from Asian or African environments, who came bare and beggared, victims
of century-old stagnation and privation. . . .

"The fourth problem is paramount. We must dispel the
hostility of the encircling Arab peoples and make a covenant of peace between them and Israel that will culminate
in economic, cultural, and political cooperation, and
advance the well-being of the whole Middle East. . . .
That peace is bound to come if democratic governments
come into being in the Arab states, for then the leaders
would be forced to pay greater heed to the domestic
needs of their people in the fields of education, hygiene,
and economic development, and would be restrained from
dissipating their energies in an arms race.

"Lastly, we must play our part in ensuring social
progress and in shaping a new society wherein there is
neither exploitation nor discrimination, a society built
upon mutual aid and love of mankind. . . . Our Prophets
in ancient days demanded that the Jews be a dedicated
people, a light unto others. No Jew forgets the lesson,
every Jew is guided in his course, wittingly or unwittingly,
by that aspiration, by a conviction that the source of
Israel's rebirth and strengthening, is trust in the purpose
its Prophets preached."[41]

What, then, did its Prophets preach?

They etched in remarkable, prophetic detail what we
may expect now that the Jews are becoming firmly established in their ancient homeland.

It portends potential good, not only for Jews, but also
for Arabs. It is to this final phase of the future that we
now turn our attention.

---

41. *Ibid.*, pp. 376-377.

PART IV

PROPHECIES CONCERNING THE FUTURE

PROPHECY AND MODERN TIMES

The most dramatic and significant thing about events which are transpiring in the Middle East today is the fact that they were anticipated by practically every Prophet in the Old Testament. In an age of cynicism and scholarly sophistication, mankind is confronted with the miracle of historical events unfolding in an orderly pattern just exactly the way they were predicted by inspired men of God living nearly 3,000 years ago!

This clearly demonstrates that in the millions of seemingly independent events which provide the tapestry of human history during each passing day, the divine wisdom of Providence knows that some are far more significant than others. These jewels of historical importance are detected in the prophetic prism as they cast their first glimmer of light on the horizon of unfolding reality. It is the role of the Prophet to transmit these fragmentary rays of the anticipated future with sufficient clarity to guide the discerning and give confidence to the faithful. God knows that there is danger in revealing too much, therefore, the profession of the Prophet is a delicate, high-precision calling.

Prophecy Based on a Scientific Principle

Someone has described prophecy as "history in reverse," and to a certain extent this is true. Prophecy, however, is anticipation, not predestination. This is why the Prophets of God are constantly emphasizing the theme: "CHOOSE ye this day whom ye will serve." From a divine source Prophets learn that if choice is made in one direction, the results can be specified and if choice is exercised in another direction, the opposite results can be expected. Thus, there is nothing magic or mystical about prophecy. It is based on the scientific principle of cause and effect. As modern man is becoming better acquainted with the possibilities of computerized information, he is better able to appreciate in a limited way the magnificence of the omniscient mind of God. The capacity of God's superior intelligence to maintain a conscious awareness of the multitude of factors contributing to any given situation is sufficient for him to anticipate with the most accurate precision exactly what is going to happen. Men are gradually learning how to do this on a finite scale themselves. Once these contributing factors are locked into the computer the results are inevitable. This is why God is constantly warning of trends which lead man toward catastrophe. He knows that some new elements must be introduced into the milieu or the results will be destructive and evil.

Some people have acquired the impression that the God of Abraham, Isaac and Jacob is some kind of capricious, wand-waving potentate who facetiously maneuvers His powers around about through the universe to merely satisfy some casual or passing whim. This is a false concept of God which partakes of the Dark Ages. Erasmus boldly struck this doctrine down in his treatise on Free Will. God is a personality who operates within the framework of law, reason, love and justice. Every scientist in the field of research, every doctor who ministers to ills of mankind, every engineer, chemist or physicist knows that we live in an orderly universe. God was a scientist, doctor, engineer, chemist and physicist before them all. His program for human salvation—both temporal and spiritual—is worked out according to scientific, pragmatic principles and prophecy is part of that program.

Nevertheless, prophecy must be administered with

extreme care. We are in this life to be tested and to learn how to exercise our free agency according to correct principles and in accordance with divinely revealed moral laws. Every Bible scholar knows that this is the basic message of both the Old and New Testaments. Therefore that Superior Intelligence who is seeking to teach us and guide us must refrain from revealing too much of the future or men would be robbed of their power to choose. He reveals just enough to warn us but not enough to overwhelm us.

In this connection, two characteristics of prophecy are worth noting. First, God rarely if ever reveals dates when things will occur. His Prophets are only allowed to describe the signs of the times or the general period when it will occur. It is a characteristic of false prophets to constantly emphasize dates. Secondly, when prophecy is given, it may be subtle, even metaphorical, but when it comes to pass the fulfillment is *literal*. The Great Flood was literal. The dispersion of Israel was literal. The destruction of the Temple was literal. As we shall see, things which are happening in the Middle East today are literal.

The Problem of False Prophets

God has constantly warned against false prophets. These are they who come among us as fakers and pretenders. They don't know the future, but for a price they are happy to stake their reputation on a guess. When time wipes them out, others take their places and the faker moves on to fresh territory. Until they are actually exposed, false prophets are pleasant fellows to have around. They possess an uncanny capacity to tell a man, especially a king, just about anything he wants to hear. True Prophets, on the other hand, are extremely controversial. They meddle in politics and upset the euphoria of people's private lives. That's what outraged King Ahab and Queen Jezebel. They had spent a fortune surrounding themselves with hundreds of phony prophets. These fakers would just get the king and queen settled down into a pleasant state of mind where they could enjoy living in their sins, when along would come Elijah with prophecies that would scare the living daylights out of them. For people who need repentance, Prophets are a nuisance.

True prophets are also a morbid liability to politicians with unholy ambitions. This applies to the current situation in the Middle East. As we shall see shortly, the words of the ancient Prophets offer solace to both Arabs and Jews if these people provide themselves with the right leaders. God has decreed that Israel is going to be redeemed in this age, and only those leaders who can accommodate their ambitions to this frame of reference are going to survive. The Arab leaders owe it to themselves to get past the fragments of scripture found in the Koran and dig into the original Biblical sources to which Mohammed was always referring. There they will find that the ancient Prophets knew about our day and they prophetically computerized exactly what is going to happen. God wanted all who were willing to be a part of it. And there is a pretty ugly ending for those who decline. God honors man's right to have the freedom to choose, but there is no such thing as freedom from consequences once the choice is made. The purpose of prophecy is to help both Jews and Arabs make the right choices.

How Much Territory Will Israel Ultimately Occupy?

Here is a good provocative question to ask the ancient prophets. And both Jews and Arabs should be interested in their reply. To fully appreciate how literally their

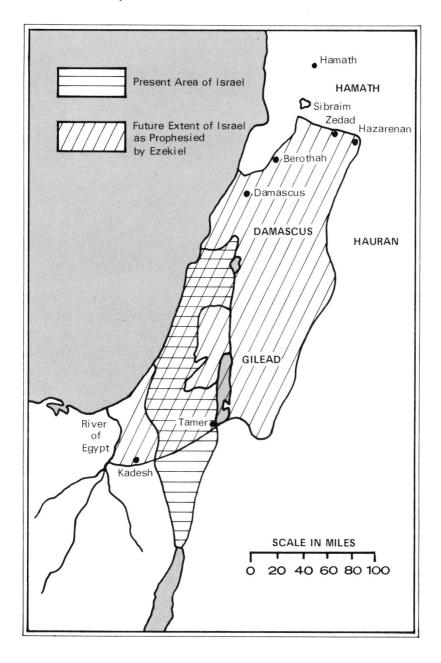

THE ULTIMATE DIMENSION OF ISRAEL ACCORDING TO SCRIPTURE

declarations are coming to pass, let me briefly describe
something I ran across approximately two years before
the recent Israeli-Arab war. On one of my visits to the
Middle East I was told that the Israelis were pushing for
a permanent peace treaty and making all kinds of overtures to the Arabs which, if they had accepted, would
have frozen the existing boundaries of Israel. At the time,
the Jewish leaders simply declared that what they wanted
was peace, not territory.

But whether the leaders of Israel wanted more territory or not, the fact remained that the scripture said they
were going to require a minimal amount of space before
they could perform certain services and obligations which
are essential to the future welfare of mankind. Of course,
it should be appreciated that many Jews are not scrip-
torians. Only a few are like David Ben-Gurion with a
rock-of-Gibraltar conviction that every prophecy in the
Old Testament will be literally fulfilled. So the Jewish
leaders were offering commitments which would have
made it extremely difficult for them to do all the things
the canon of scripture says they ultimately must do.

Nevertheless, it was rather amazing how it all worked
out. Instead of accepting the offer, Egypt provoked a
war, intimidated Jordan and Syria into joining her, and
even though Israel pleaded with Jordan and Syria to keep
out of the conflict, they insisted on coming in. As a
result, Israel had to fight all three of them and ended up
with vast quantities of new territory, most of which she
is now compelled to hold in order to protect herself from
similar attacks in the future. Whether the Jewish leaders
wanted it or not, circumstances catapulted them into
territories they were not even seeking.

And the end is not yet.

It was the Prophet Ezekiel who described what the
boundaries of Israel ultimately must be. Interestingly
enough, it does not include Sinai, but it does include

most of Jordan and most of Syria.

In the 1967 Arab-Israeli war, General Dayan of Israel deliberately avoided taking any more of either Syria or Jordan than he felt was necessary to protect Israel's natural borders. The troops were ready and able to take the Suez Canal, perhaps even crash on in to Cairo. They were ready to take Damascus and conquer Amman. But the Jewish central command said no. Instead, the Israeli made direct overtures to the Arabs for face-to-face negotiations designed to eliminate existing tensions and develop their mutual economic interests without interference from the U.N. or the big powers. The Arab leaders spurned this invitation and took off for Moscow for new tactical advice. The Soviet Union responded with promises to rebuild the shattered military resources of the Arab countries and get ready for "a second round." For the Arabs, this was tragic. The prophets have already anticipated the results—more territory for Israel.

The key to Arab prosperity and peace is not to be found in the devious devices concocted by the conspirators of the Kremlin. The ingredients they seek are actually in Israel. While Arab leaders have been wringing their hands in vengeful polemics, Jewish leaders have been paying the salaries of Arab officials in occupied territories and trying to figure out a way to get the Arab refugees out of their wretched slum camps and down on the Negev or some other undeveloped territory where they can go to work and win a place for themselves in a prosperous, expanding economy. This is what the Arab leaders should have been doing for them during the past nineteen years. Instead, they imprisoned their fellow Arabs and spent billions in armaments hoping to wipe out Israel. Now both their hopes and their resources are bankrupt. Only the ashes of hate seem to remain, and the Soviet Union will do everything possible to fan the dying coals into a new flame. But for the Arabs a "second round" can bring nothing but another dose of self-cremation. Some day they must realize that the diabolical stratagem of the Soviet is to fight Israel down to the last Arab.

If a holy Prophet rose up among the Arabs today, he would very likely say, "Good people, go back and read the words of King Feisal. Therein lies your formula for peace and your promise for prosperity." King Feisal's words are worth repeating. In the days before irrational passions and over-zealous terrorists from both sides had left their bitter scars, he said:

"We feel that the Arabs and Jews are cousins in race, suffering similar oppressions at the hands of powers stronger than themselves, and by a happy coincidence have been able to take the first step toward the attainment of their national ideals together. . . .

"With the chiefs of your movement, especially with Dr. Weizmann, we have had, and continue to have, the closest relations. He has been a great helper of our cause, and I hope the Arabs may soon be in a position to make the Jews some return for their kindness. We are working together for a reformed and revived Near East, and our two movements complete one another. The Jewish movement is national and not imperialistic. Our movement is national and not imperialistic; and there is room in Syria for us both. Indeed, I think that neither can be a real success without the other."[1]

There is actually no sound reason why King Feisal's expressed aspirations for these two great peoples could not some day become a magnificent reality.

The ancient Prophets knew that the Arabs would always have vastly larger domains than Israel. But for Israel to build her Temple and set up a spiritual center for the Millennial Era, it is essential that a cloistered district be created from which Israel can function and render the service which will be required of her.

---

1. William L. Hull, *The Fall and Rise of Israel*, p. 139.

The Prophet Ezekiel described the territorial dimensions which Israel will finally occupy when conditions in the Middle East have been fully stabilized. The accompanying map gives the approximate boundaries for this sequestered district which Ezekiel describes in Chapter 47, verses 15 to 21. It should be of some comfort to the Arabs to know that Israel is not destined to become a colonial empire. The full extent of her mission as outlined in Holy Writ can be accomplished within the modest boundaries shown.

The Rise of a Great New Leader in Israel

Five different prophets of the Old Testament speak of the day when the Jews will be gathered to their ancient homeland and then make reference to a great political, military and spiritual leader who will arise. Jeremiah, Ezekiel, Isaiah, and Hosea all refer to him as "David" and "the prince," but Isaiah and Zechariah also refer to him as "the BRANCH." All agree, however, as to the time when he shall rise up to become a great leader among the Jewish people and all agree as to the nature of the service he will render. Let us begin with the writings of Zechariah.

Zechariah speaks of the latter days when "the Lord shall yet comfort Zion, and shall yet choose Jerusalem."[2] He says, "And the Lord shall inherit Judah, his portion in the holy land, and shall choose Jerusalem again."[3] It will be a time when "Jerusalem shall be inhabited as towns without walls for the multitude of men and cattle therein."[4] The Jewish people will have a High Priest once

---

2. Zechariah 1:11.
3. Zechariah 2:12.
4. Zechariah 2:4.

again whose name will be Joshua and the Lord promises
that if this Priest and his associates are faithful, "I will
bring forth my servant, the BRANCH."[5] Then the scripture says, "Behold, the man whose name is The BRANCH:
and he shall grow up out of his place, and HE SHALL
BUILD THE TEMPLE OF THE LORD . . . and he shall
bear the glory and shall sit and rule upon his throne;
and he shall be a priest upon his throne; and the counsel
of peace shall be between them both [between Joshua
and this righteous ruler called the BRANCH]."[6]

As we shall see in a moment, this is not only the man
who will build the new Jewish temple in Jerusalem, but
he will be the one who welcomes the Messiah when He
comes to that temple.

Isaiah also speaks of this Branch and says he will grow
out of the roots of Jesse (meaning he will be of the royal
lineage, even as David of old). Isaiah attributes these
qualities to the Branch:

"And the spirit of the Lord shall rest upon him, the
spirit of wisdom and understanding, the spirit of counsel
and might, the spirit of knowledge and of the fear of the
Lord.

"And shall make him of quick understanding in the
fear of the Lord: and he shall not judge after the sight
of his eyes, neither reprove after the hearing of his ears:

"But with righteousness shall he judge the poor, and
reprove with equity for the meek of the earth: and he
shall smite the earth with the rod of his mouth, and with
the breath of his lips shall he slay the wicked.

"And righteousness shall be the girdle of his loins, and
faithfulness the girdle of his reins."[7]

Later in his writings, Isaiah refers to this leader as
"David" and says the Lord will raise him up to be "a

---

5. Zechariah 3:8.
6. Zechariah 6:12-13.
7. Isaiah 11:2-5.

witness to the people, a leader and commander to the people."[8]

Ezekiel also talks about our modern day when the Jews will begin to gather home. The Lord said to Ezekiel, "And I will set up one shepherd over them, and he shall feed them, EVEN MY SERVANT DAVID: he shall feed them, and he shall be their shepherd. And I the Lord will be their God, AND MY SERVANT DAVID A PRINCE AMONG THEM; I the Lord have spoken it. . . . And they shall no more be a prey to the heathen, neither shall the beast of the land devour them; but they shall dwell safely, and none shall make them afraid."[9]

The attributes of this leader who is called David, the Prince, or The Branch, are so exceptional that some Biblical scholars thought perhaps this might be the Messiah, Himself. However, a careful analysis of all the details furnished by the Prophets clearly shows that he is a gifted leader who has "fear [respect] of the Lord,"[10] who is the Lord's "servant,"[11] who will build the Lord's Temple,[12] who will make sacrifices unto the Lord,[13] and is specifically called David the prince,[14] not David the Messiah.

Just as Zechariah specifically describes David, the Prince, as a temporal ruler, so does Ezekiel. To Ezekiel the Lord declared:

"And I will make them one nation in the land upon the mountains of Israel; and one king shall be king to them all: and they shall be no more two nations, neither shall they be divided into two kingdoms any more at all. . . .

"And David my servant shall be king over them. . . .

---

8. Isaiah 55:3-4.
9. Ezekiel 34:23-24,28.
10. Isaiah 11:3.
11. Ezekiel 34:24.
12. Zechariah 6:12.
13. Ezekiel 45:17; 46:12.
14. Ezekiel 34:24.

and my servant David shall be their prince for ever.

"Moreover I will make a covenant of peace with them; it shall be an everlasting covenant with them: and I will place them, and multiply them, and will set my sanctuary in the midst of them forever.

"My tabernacle also shall be with them: yea, I will be their God, and they shall be my people."[15]

After Prince David has built the great new Temple, he will be given an inheritance near it,[16] and the entire 46th chapter of Ezekiel describes the important part he will play in administering its various ordinances.

To appreciate the well-nigh universal interest which so many of the prophets had in this David of the "latter days" let us conclude our discussion of him by quoting Jeremiah and Hosea. Jeremiah said:

"For, lo, the days come, saith the Lord, that I will bring again the captivity [this time by the Lord] of my people Israel and Judah, saith the Lord: and I will cause them to return to the land that I gave to their fathers, and they shall possess it. . . .

"For it shall come to pass in that day, saith the Lord of hosts, that I will break his yoke from off thy neck, and will burst thy bonds, and strangers shall no more serve themselves of him.

"But they shall serve the Lord their God, AND DAVID THEIR KING, whom I will raise up unto them."[17]

Hosea refers to these identical circumstances with these words:

"For the children of Israel shall abide many days without a king, and without a prince, and without a sacrifice, and without an image, and without an ephod, and without teraphim:

"Afterward shall the children of Israel return, and seek

---

15. Ezekiel 37:15-27.
16. Ezekiel 45:7.
17. Jeremiah 30:3-9.

the Lord their God, and DAVID THEIR KING; and shall
fear the Lord and his goodness IN THE LATTER DAYS."[18]

The Building of the Third Temple in Jerusalem

As we have pointed out earlier in this book, almost
the moment the Jews regained possession of Old Jerusalem in 1967, they began talking about the possibilities
of building their third Temple. It will be recalled that
the first temple was that of Solomon which was constructed
nearly 1,000 B.C. and completely destroyed by the Babylonians around 587 B.C. A descendant of David, named
Zerubbabel was then allowed to return from the Babylonian captivity and rebuild the temple. This was called
the Second Temple and it was dedicated in 516 B.C. Just
before the Christian Era, King Herod offered to replace
this Second Temple with a much more beautiful edifice
but the people did not trust him and so they insisted that
he simply refurbish the Second Temple. All authorities
agree, however, that Herod actually replaced the older
Temple a section at a time so that Herod's elaborate
structure really became a completely new building.
Nevertheless, it was never acknowledged as a new Temple
by the Jewish people, but merely an embellishment of the
old. They therefore refer to the great new Temple they
now wish to build in Jerusalem as the THIRD Temple.
Historically, it is the fourth.

One of the rather exciting things about the study of
prophecy is that seemingly "impossible" predictions miraculously maneuver their way through to fulfillment. That
is precisely the situation confronting the Jewish leaders
today as they contemplate the practical possibilities for
the rebuilding of their Temple. Earlier, we quoted from

18. Hosea 3:4-5.

some of the news magazines which have itemized all the reasons why this proposed Temple cannot be erected. The very fact that the site for the Temple is presently occupied by one of Islam's most sacred mosques is sufficient to wipe out any smattering of optimism that this project is practical or possible. And just in case there might be any doubt as to how the Arabs feel about all of this, we have the typical Arab reaction in the remarks of Mr. Jamali, Arab representative from Iraq, who told the U.N. Trusteeship Council, "If we want to follow prophecies, I am afraid Jerusalem is going to be destroyed because, IF THE TEMPLE OF SOLOMON IS TO BE ERECTED ON THE SITE OF OUR MOSQUE, THERE IS NO DOUBT THERE IS GOING TO BE DESTRUC- TION. . ."[19]

So here is an official Arab challenge in direct defiance of Biblical prophecy—a pronouncement that Jerusalem itself will be destroyed before the building of the Temple will be permitted. Under existing circumstances I know of no historian, politician or scriptorian who would dare to suggest just how this Gordian knot might be cut. All we know is that it will be cut. The fact that the whole thing looks so utterly impossible to us now is something we should remember after it finally comes to pass. If it follows the pattern of other prophecies it will be worked out over a considerable period of time and in such gradual phases that its final accomplishment will seem nothing more than a natural evolution of events. So just to drama- tize the fulfillment of this prediction when it does finally come to pass, let us spread upon the record this current conviction: "That as of 1967 the practical possibility of the Jews building a Temple in Jerusalem appears to be a fantastic and impossible dream."

---

19. Excerpts from the verbatim record of the Twenty-Eighth Meeting of the U.N. Trusteeship Council, Geneva, Switzerland, February 20, 1950, in the files of the author.

A major lesson of life, of course, is that all things are possible with God. That's why it should be exciting to see just how He is going to work this one out.

That He will work it out the Prophets are quick to assure us. Zechariah even identifies the coming Prince David as being the Jewish leader who will supervise the work.[20] Zechariah even had a special message specifically addressed to the modern Jews who are assembling in Israel. He wrote:

"Thus saith the Lord of Hosts; Behold, I will save my people from the east country, and from the west country;

"And I will bring them, and they shall dwell in the midst of Jerusalem: and they shall be my people, and I will be their God, in truth and righteousness.

"Thus saith the Lord of hosts; LET YOUR HANDS BE STRONG, YE THAT HEAR IN THESE DAYS THESE WORDS BY THE MOUTH OF THE PROPHETS . . . THAT THE TEMPLE MIGHT BE BUILT."[21]

And it must be built with clean hands. The message continues:

"These are the things that ye shall do; Speak ye every man the truth to his neighbour; execute the judgment of truth and peace in your gates.

"And let none of you imagine evil in your heart against his neighbor; and love no false oath: for all these are things that I hate, saith the Lord."[22]

The question might arise, "How will the Jews know how to build their Temple? Where are the plans?"

The answer to that question is rather amazing. God apparently anticipated that when it came time to build the Temple of the last days, the Jews would have neither prophets nor Urim and Thummim. Therefore God revealed to Ezekiel nearly 600 years before Christ exactly

---

what this temple would be like. He was given the measurements and architectural arrangement of not only the Temple itself but the entire area surrounding it. All of these details are in the last ten chapters of Ezekiel. The Jews, therefore, have everything they need to proceed with the schematic design of this prophetic structure. Ezekiel even provided a detailed description of the ritual and sacrifices which will be required.

So the stage is set and the opening scenes have commenced which will finally bring about the literal fulfillment of all these things. There is no doubt but what this generation will live to see a beautiful Temple of Israel arise on the Temple plaza in Old Jerusalem.* (See p. 282.)

Israel's Coming Era of Prickly Prosperity

According to the Prophets, the period through which Judah must pass between now and the coming of the Messiah is one of anguish and trouble mixed with unprecedented prosperity. On the one hand the land will become fruitful. There will be numerous cities and vast multitudes will gather within the borders of Israel until the people will say, "The place is too strait for me: give place to me that I may dwell."[23]

At the same time there will be periods of savage warfare and political unrest. In this connection the Prophet Joel has an ominous prophecy which is aimed directly at the Arab nations. He describes conditions as they will exist when the Messiah comes and says: "And it shall come to pass in that day, that the mountains shall drop down new wine, and the hills shall flow with milk, and all the rivers of Judah shall flow with waters, and a fountain shall come forth of the house of the Lord, and shall water the valley of Shittim.

---

23. Isaiah 49:20.

"EGYPT SHALL BE A DESOLATION, AND EDOM SHALL BE A DESOLATE WILDERNESS, for the violence against the children of Judah, because they have shed innocent blood in their land."[24]

This would clearly indicate that prior to the coming of the Messiah, Egypt and Edom (the name for the Arab peoples in ancient times) will have indulged themselves in further genocidal attacks against Judah. The consequences, according to this prophecy, will not be the annihilation of Israel, but the desolation of Egypt and Edom.

This prophecy implies, however, that Judah will feel the devastating force of these attacks and the circumstances will be such that innocent blood will be shed in their land. In 1967, Dayan restrained the Israeli armies from pursuing the Arab armies to their respective capitals. The Arab leaders learned nothing from this gesture, however, and were champing at the bit for a "second round" almost before they had buried their 35,000 dead. Obviously, future attacks on Israel would make restraint less and less likely. If the current trend of attacks continues in the same spirit of hate-intoxicated fury, the prophets are loud and clear as to what the Arab leaders may ultimately expect: *oblivion*. The Prophet Zechariah was as emphatic as the Prophet Joel. He said that not only "the sceptre of Egypt shall depart away," but "the pride of Assyria [Iraq of today] shall be brought down."[25]

Centuries ago, another great nation had a similar prophecy hanging over its head. Its capital was Nineveh. When Jonah delivered his prediction of total destruction and indicated that their fate was already in the prophetic computer, the king of Nineveh threw the whole city into mourning and sack cloth to supplicate the heavens for

---

24. Joel 3:18-19.
25. Zechariah 10:11.

another chance. This is all that was necessary, the scripture says, to avoid the Sodom and Gomorrah fate which otherwise awaited them.

Now, who is the Jonah who will take the message to the Arabs today? Their fate is also in the prophetic computer unless one or many can reach them in time to persuade their leaders that the planned massacre which they are still trying to impose on the Jews is actually planned suicide for themselves. Anyone who has lived among the Arabs and learned to love them cannot help but deplore the stupidity of their leaders who seem to learn nothing from three successive defeats and are therefore unlikely to respond to the more gentle warnings from the ancient Prophets of God.

Armageddon!

Somewhere up the trail of the not too distant future, Israel will finally have her famous Battle of Armageddon. Many of the prophets as well as John the Beloved saw it in vision and left some extremely interesting and remarkable details concerning that tragic, oncoming event. There are many things which must take place in the Holy Land before the time will be ripe for that event, so its moment of fulfillment is not in immediate prospect. Nevertheless, many factors mentioned by the Prophets are already in gestation, so it could erupt within the foreseeable future.

It is not our purpose here to make an in-depth examination of the many ramifications of this much-discussed item in Old Testament and New Testament prophecy. We shall merely touch the highlights so the reader may visualize the circumstances which the Prophets describe as the setting for Armageddon and the coming of the Messiah. In fact, the reason Armageddon has always fascinated scripture students is because it terminated in

the miraculous manifestation of God to man. It is therefore of equal interest to both Christians and Jews.

We have already seen that the prophetic Prince David
will have appeared on the scene and completed the
Temple before Armageddon. The people of Israel by that
time will have become a powerful and wealthy nation. Its
gathering hosts will be splitting the territory at its seams.
Ezekiel makes it clear at the close of his writings that the
territory of Israel is never going to be very large. The
destiny of Jerusalem during the Millennium is to be a
spiritual center. Therefore, the territory supporting it
need not be large.

Prior to Armageddon the Jews are to pass through
an extensive period of preparation and sublimation. Here
are excerpts from Chapter 36:

"Ye mountains of Israel, hear the word of the Lord.
. . . I will take you from among the heathen, and gather
you out of all countries, and will bring you into your own
land. . . . And I will put my spirit within you: and
cause you to walk in my statutes, and ye shall keep my
judgments, and do them. . . . In the day that I shall have
cleansed you from all your iniquities I will also cause you
to dwell in the cities, and the wastes shall be builded."

In this chapter Ezekiel lays great stress on the need
for the Jews to cleanse themselves. As with any other
nation which might be called to take upon itself such an
elevated assignment, the Jews are going to be required to
do a great deal of soul-searching, repenting and refining in
order to qualify for this task. In his writings the Jewish
Prophet, Ezekiel, made no bones about the fact that during their dispersion these descendants of Jacob had con-
taminated themselves and strayed far from the faith of
their fathers. But he also saw the modern Jews struggling
to rise to the great challenge. He wrote:

"Then shall ye remember your own evil ways, and
your doings that were not good, and shall lothe your-

selves in your own sight for your iniquities and for your abominations. . . ."[26]

In due time the scripture says they will become a "holy flock" acceptable to the Lord.[27] In Chapter 37 Ezekiel describes how the Israelites will gather in from all over the world and the Lord will give them a righteous leader, Prince David, who will build the beautiful Temple which the Prophet had seen in vision.

But the bounteous wealth, the flourishing cities, the garden-of-Eden abundance will be more than the envious gentile nations to the north can stand. Ezekiel takes their names from the tenth chapter of Genesis which is called the Table of Nations. He wants the reader to understand that it is a vast coalition of gentile peoples—Magog, Meshech and Tubal. All three of these were sons of Japheth, father of the gentiles. And their ruler and leader will be a powerful dictator (also described by Daniel) whom Ezekiel calls Gog, chief prince of Meshech and Tubal. Ezekiel addresses a whole chapter of his writings to this confederacy of evil might which will come sweeping down on Jerusalem from the north. Here are excerpts from Chapter 38.

"Thus saith the Lord God; Behold, I am against thee, O Gog, the chief prince of Mesheck and Tubal. . . . Thou shalt ascend and come like a storm, thou shalt be like a cloud to cover the land, thou, and all thy bands, and many people with thee . . . and thou shalt think an evil thought:

"And thou shalt say, I will go up to the land of un-walled villages; I will go to them that are at rest, that dwell safely, all of them dwelling without walls, and having neither bars nor gates,

"To take a spoil, and to take a prey; to turn thine hand upon the desolate places that are now inhabited, and

26. Ezekiel 36:31.
27. Ezekiel 36:38.

upon the people that are gathered out of the nations, which have gotten cattle and goods, that dwell in the midst of the land. . . .

". . . it shall be in the latter days."

Apparently the outlying districts will fall rather easily before Gog's massive military onslaught because the Prophets all speak of the major Armageddon conflict as though it will be centered around the siege at Jerusalem. This siege will last $3\frac{1}{2}$ years.[28]

Several of the Prophets tried desperately to describe the terrible forces of God as they saw it in vision. Imagine a Prophet living several centuries before Christ attempting to describe modern, mechanized warfare. Among all of them none was more vivid than Joel. He came the closest to communicating the actual terror of modern war machinery. He wrote in his second chapter:

"A day of darkness and of gloominess, a day of clouds and of thick darkness, as the morning spread upon the mountains: a great people and a strong; there hath not been ever the like, neither shall be any more after it, even to the years of many generations.

"A fire devoureth before them; and behind them a flame burneth: the land is as the garden of Eden before them, and behind them a desolate wilderness; yea, and nothing shall escape them.

"The appearance of them is as the appearance of horses; and as horsemen, so shall they run.

"Like the noise of chariots on the tops of mountains shall they leap, like the noise of a flame of fire that devoureth the stubble, as a strong people set in battle array.

"Before their face the people shall be much pained: all faces shall gather blackness.

"They shall run like mighty men: they shall climb the wall like men of war; and they shall march every one on his ways, and they shall not break their ranks:

---

28. Daniel 7:25; Revelations 11:2.

"Neither shall one thrust another: they shall walk every one in his path: and when they fall upon the sword, they shall not be wounded.

"They shall run to and fro in the city; they shall run upon the wall, they shall climb up upon the houses; they shall enter in at the windows like a thief. The earth shall quake before them."

John the Revelator says that it will be during the siege of the Jewish capital that God will first begin to make bare his arm on behalf of this people. He will raise up among the Jews two mighty prophets. Then, as the hosts of Gog sweep down against the city, these two prophets will stand forth to resist them. No military power available in Jerusalem will be sufficient to stop Gog and the scripture therefore promises that God will do it through these two Prophets. They will be endowed with powers comparable to those of Enoch, Elijah and Moses. Concerning them, John wrote:

"If any man will hurt them, fire proceedeth out of their mouth, and devoureth their enemies; and if any man will hurt them, he must in this manner be killed. These have power to shut heaven, that it rain not in the days of their prophecy; and have power over waters to turn them to blood, and to smite the earth with all plagues, as often as they will."[29]

Ezekiel says this is to be a period of great earthquakes and extremely frightening physical disturbances,[30] nevertheless, Gog in his stubborn fury will continue the siege. In fact, the scripture says that after the $3\frac{1}{2}$ years have been completed, Gog will make one final, gigantic effort which will result in a breakthrough. "The city shall be taken, and the houses rifled and the women ravished; and half of the city shall go into captivity. . . ."[31] John says

---

29. Revelations 11:5-6.
30. Ezekiel 38:19-23.
31. Zechariah 14:2.

the two Prophets will be allowed by the Lord to become
martyrs and will be killed. This will be considered such
an achievement that the warlords of the gentiles will
celebrate it with great rejoicing. The bodies of the two
Prophets will lie in the streets for $3\frac{1}{2}$ days because Gog
will not allow them to be buried. Instead, he and his
armies "shall rejoice over them, and make merry, and
shall send gifts one to another because these two prophets
tormented them that dwelt on the earth."[32]

But at the end of the $3\frac{1}{2}$ days, even as Gog is about
to make his final, overwhelming assault to subjugate Jerusalem, a miracle will occur. John, looking upon the scene
in vision, said:

"After three days and a half the Spirit of life from God
entered into them, and they stood upon their feet; and
great fear fell upon them which saw them. And they
heard a great voice from heaven saying unto them, Come
up hither. And they ascended up to heaven in a cloud;
and their enemies beheld them."[33]

For Gog and his legions this is the end of the war.
Something is about to happen to him which will wipe out
five-sixths of his hosts. Without his realizing it the moment in history has arrived for the appearance of the
Great Messiah.

The Coming of the Messiah

When the Messiah makes Himself manifest he will
come exactly the way the Jews always expected him. He
will come as a King of Glory, smashing the vicious enemies
of Israel, and manifesting the most magnificent though
frightening display of power since the days of Sinai.
Zechariah describes the appearance of the Messiah as he
comes in glory with his hosts:

32. Revelations 11:10.
33. Revelations 11:11-12.

"Then shall the Lord go forth, and fight against those nations, as when he fought in the day of battle.

"And his feet shall stand in that day upon the mount of Olives, which is before Jerusalem on the east, and the mount of Olives shall cleave in the midst thereof toward the east and toward the west, and there shall be a very great valley; and half of the mountain shall remove toward the north, and half of it toward the south.

"And ye shall flee to the valley of the mountains . . . and the Lord my God shall come, and all the saints with thee."[34]

As the survivors from Jerusalem race from the stricken city into the cavernous valley which will open before them to the East, they will no doubt rejoice. They will rejoice not only because they have been rescued but because of their inner satisfaction that they faithfully waited for their true Messiah through all the centuries. And now He has come. For all of them it will be a thrilling moment as they look upon Him in adoration and amazement. Then Zechariah describes an astonishing thing that will happen. This Jewish Prophet says, "And one shall say unto him [the Messiah], What are these wounds in thine hands? Then he shall answer, THOSE WITH WHICH I WAS WOUNDED IN THE HOUSE OF MY FRIENDS."[35]

Nothing could strike the Jewish mind with a greater shock than this. Yet a forewarning of it has been in the Jewish scripture all these years. In an earlier chapter it is even plainer. Speaking in the first person the Lord declares:

"And it shall come to pass in that day, that I will seek to destroy all the nations that come against Jerusalem. And I will pour upon the house of David, and upon the inhabitants of Jerusalem, the spirit of grace and of supplications: AND THEY SHALL LOOK UPON ME

---

34. Zechariah 14:3-5.
35. Zechariah 13:6.

WHOM THEY HAVE PIERCED, AND THEY SHALL MOURN FOR HIM, AS ONE MOURNETH FOR HIS ONLY SON, AND SHALL BE IN BITTERNESS FOR HIM, AS ONE THAT IS IN BITTERNESS FOR HIS FIRSTBORN."[36]

It is in this hour that Jew and Christian will finally be able to see eye to eye. From then on, both will be worshipping the same Messiah. Both will have come to know the reality of his power, his greatness, his goodness and mercy. And most important of all, they will both have come to know his true *identity*. When the Jews suddenly realize that this marvelous being who stands in their midst is none other than the glorified personage of that same humble Jew who walked among their fathers twenty centuries earlier—that Galilean who was inadvertently mistaken for a false Messiah and slain—there will ascend unto heaven a smoke of lamentation the like of which the land of Israel has never known. Zechariah describes it:

"In that day shall there be a great mourning in Jerusalem, as the mourning of Hadadrimmon in the valley of Megiddon. And the land shall mourn every family apart; the family of the house of David apart, and their wives apart . . . all the families that remain, every family apart, and their wives apart."[37]

And when they have purged themselves of their sorrow, they will rise up to perform the great task which will now confront them.

After Armageddon

Meanwhile, a tremendous avalanche of chain-reaction events will be taking place across the world. For one thing, a devastating cataclysm will have engulfed Gog and

36. Zechariah 12:9-10.
37. Zechariah 12:11-14.

his multitude of warriors. They will have fallen victim to a sudden plague which almost sounds like a consuming burning from nuclear fall-out. The scripture says:

"And this shall be the plague wherewith the Lord will smite all the people that have fought against Jerusalem; Their flesh shall consume away while they stand upon their feet, and their eyes shall consume away in their holes, and their tongue shall consume away in their mouth.

"And it shall come to pass in that day, that a great tumult from the Lord shall be among them; and they shall lay hold every one on the hand of his neighbour, and his hand shall rise up against the hand of his neighbour."[38]

To add to the tumult, the same terrible earthquake which split the Mount of Olives in two will have rocked and cracked the crust of the earth across whole continents. Ezekiel describes how it will change the terrain of Israel,[39] and John saw how the cities of the various nations would crumble into rubble.[40] Many other cataclysmic events also will occur during this period but these examples are sufficient to illustrate why the hearts of men will "fail them for fear" when the Messiah comes.

Ezekiel says only one sixth of Gog's hosts will survive,[41] and Joel was told that this remnant would flee into a barren and desolate land facing the sea.[42]

The Prophet Ezekiel tells us that it will take the Jews seven months to cleanse the land of its dead.[43] The fallen hosts of Gog will all be buried together in a great valley which will be called Hammon-gog, meaning "the multitude of Gog."[44] And Israel will be made rich with the treasures and spoils which will be left by those multitudes who

---

38. Zechariah 14:12-13.
39. Ezekiel 38:18-20.
40. Revelations 11:13.
41. Ezekiel 39:2.
42. Joel 2:20.
43. Ezekiel 39:12.
44. Ezekiel 39:11.

had intended to despoil Judah.[45] The accumulated weapons, supplies and equipment left by the army of Gog will supply Israel with sufficient fuel to last seven years.[46]

The period following Armageddon will be one of mammoth cleansing and reconstruction for Israel. The carnage of war, earthquake and widespread devastation will gradually give way to make room for beautiful new buildings, re-populated cities and a broad vista of luxurious, cultivated fields and orchards.

At the great Temple which will have somehow survived Armageddon, the sons of Levi will begin making offerings in righteousness which will be acceptable to God. The Temple will then be honored with the presence of the Messiah. Ezekiel describes it:

"And the glory of the Lord came into the house by way of the gate whose prospect is toward the east . . . and, behold, the glory of the Lord filled the house."[47] As Ezekiel beheld the vision of it, he wrote, "Then said the Lord unto me; This gate shall be shut, it shall not be opened, and no man shall enter in by it; because the Lord, the God of Israel, hath entered in by it, therefore it shall be shut."[48]

Immediately the name for the city of Jerusalem will be changed. Instead of "Jerusalem" it will be called by a new name which means, "The Lord is there."[49] The words in Hebrew are, "Jehovah-Shammah."

From then on great changes will take place throughout the entire earth and Jerusalem or Jehovah-Shammah will be honored as a great spiritual center for all mankind. It will not be a Jewish center, a Moslem center or a sectarian Christian center. It will be the headquarters for the worship of Jehovah-Christ by all men.

45. Ezekiel 39:10.
46. Ezekiel 39:9.
47. Ezekiel 43:4-5.
48. Ezekiel 44:2.
49. Ezekiel 48:35.

In that day the genius of the Tribe of Judah will fully flourish. Their qualities of leadership and penetrating intellectualism will be yoked to the spiritual aspirations of the Messianic Era. They will play a prominent part in implementing the vast undertaking which will usher in God's long-awaited Millennium of universal peace and unprecedented prosperity.

After 3,000 years of travail the Jews will have their reward. It was the Jewish Prophet Zechariah who saw the end of the matter. He wrote:

"Yea, many people and strong nations shall come to seek the Lord of hosts in Jerusalem, and to pray before the Lord.

"Thus saith the Lord of hosts; In those days it shall come to pass, that ten men shall take hold out of all languages of the nations, even shall take hold of the skirt of him that is a Jew, saying, We will go with you: for we have heard that God is with you."[50]

---

50. Zechariah 8:22-23.

° As this book was about to go to press the following remarkable development came to our attention. According to an article in *The Christian and Christianity Today* (Aug. 4, 1967) "five hundred railcar loads of stone from Bedford, Ind., considered to be among the finest building stone in the works, is being freighted pre-cut to exact specifications, and one consignment has already been dispatched to Israel.

"This report, received from authoritative sources in Sellersburg, Indiana, said cornerstones for the third Jerusalem Temple are already in Israel. Materials for this Temple have been secretly in preparation for seven years, the report went on, and it is believed American Jews are mainly responsible for financially undergirding the whole project."

APPENDIX

THE PROTOCOLS OF THE LEARNED ELDERS OF ZION— FACT OR FICTION?

When Adolf Hitler wrote *Mein Kampf* (My Battle) he included a vitriolic attack against the Jewish race, and blamed most of Germany's problems on the German Jews. He said the Jews were out to take over the world and offered as his proof a publication called, "The Protocols [minutes of proceedings] of the Learned Elders of Zion." This was supposed to have been the plans drawn up at a secret meeting by Jewish leaders for the complete domination of all nations and the building of a Jewish world-dictatorship.

The document Hitler was talking about was first published in Russia in 1903 and was subsequently published in a more extended form in Russia and later in Western Europe and America. It described all the techniques that could be used to destroy representative governments and western, Christian culture, thereby permitting the seizure of political power throughout the world. Being a highly inflammatory document, the *Protocols* made excellent propaganda for Hitler, but equally serious was the fact that it seemed to be accepted evidence of Jewish duplicity even by many well-meaning people.[1]

---

1. Henry Ford was one of these. He became extremely exercised after reading this document. *The New York World* of February 17, 1921, quotes him as saying, "The only statement I care to make about the *Protocols* is that they fit in with what is going on. They are sixteen years old, and they have fitted the world situation up to this time. They fit now." A series of articles in Mr. Ford's *Dearborn Independent* were published weekly between May 22 and October 2, 1920, on the "international Jewish conspiracy." These were subsequently published by Mr. Ford in a pamphlet called *The International Jew*. According to the Universal Jewish Encyclopedia, under "Elders of Zion," the following appears: ". . . in a letter to

Those who published the *Protocols* often wrote horrendous introductions so that the reader could not possibly miss the pointed implications which the publisher felt it contained. The copy in my own files is undated but appears to be of the early 1920 vintage and says "It [Protocol XI] proves that the desire for a 'National Home' in Palestine is only camouflage and an infinitesimal part of the Jew's real object. It proves that the Jews of the world have no intention of settling in Palestine or any separate country, and that their annual prayer that they may all meet 'next year in Jerusalem' is merely a piece of their characteristic make-believe. It also demonstrates that the Jews are now a world menace, and that the Aryan races will have to domicile them permanently out of Europe."[2]

Imagine reading such an introduction and then finding lurid passages in the *Protocols* such as the following (which are supposed to be secret Jewish plans): "We are interested . . . in the diminution, the killing out of the GOYIM [non-Jews]. Our power is in the chronic shortness of food and physical weakness of the worker because by all that this implies he is made the slave of our will, and he will not find in his own authorities either strength or energy to set against our will. . . . By want and the envy and hatred which it engenders we shall move the mobs and with their hands we shall wipe out all those who hinder us on our way."[3]

It can be readily seen why such a document would serve the purposes of someone like Hitler. As hate literature against the Jews, it could not have been written any better if he had composed it himself.

For many years it seemed that only the Jews were

Louis Marshall, dated June 30, 1927, Ford retracted and apologized for the publication, claiming that he had been duped by his assistants."

2. *Protocols of the Learned Elders of Zion*, p. 7.

3. *Ibid.*, p. 21.

anxious to run down the facts and discover where this so-called *Protocols of the Learned Elders of Zion* actually came from. However, the matter eventually ended up in the courts. In 1934, several Jewish societies in Switzerland brought suit against two Swiss Nazis for distributing the *Protocols*. Based on the evidence Jewish scholars had collected, they charged that the *Protocols* were a complete forgery concocted by one of the Tsar's agents while in France and that it had nothing to do with the Jews. At the trial in Bern, which attracted wide attention, it was shown that most of the material was lifted or adapted from a French publication by Maurice Joly, who had written it as a satire against Napoleon III. It was designed to show how a clever fellow could organize a secret force to destroy democratic nations and set up a tyrannical world empire. The book was called *A Dialogue Between Machiavelli and Montesquieu*. In this book it was not the learned Elders of Zion who were doing the plotting but Machiavelli. The author of the *Protocols* had obviously lifted words, phrases and ideas from this source.

The trial also brought out the origin of the publication of the *Protocols* and how it had been used by the Russian officials to influence Tsar Nicholas II even before it was published. The author of the forgery was identified as a writer named Golovinskii who had done this work for a Tsarist agent in Paris named Rachkovskii. The date of its origin was put at around 1899-1901.

The trial at Bern accomplished much good by bringing before the scrutiny of a court the true origin and purpose of this spurious document. As a result, various reference works began warning students of the fraudulent nature of the *Protocols*. It is noted that the latest edition of *Webster's College Dictionary* has this to say: "PROTOCOLS OF THE ELDERS OF ZION: A set of forged writings created by the Russian reactionaries in 1903 and circulated by anti-Semitic propagandists, purporting to be a record of a series of meetings in Basel in 1897 for plotting the overthrow of Christian civilization by Jews and Free-masons."

After hearing this evidence, the court at Bern reached a verdict that the *Protocols* were a forgery and therefore could not be distributed. Subsequently, a higher court held that under the broad and permissive laws of Switzer-land, the fact that the *Protocols* were a forgery could not be the basis for banning them. Therefore this material continued to be circulated even in Switzerland.

It was brought out that in the very beginning the *Protocols* were circulated as something that "could" have been passed at some secret Jewish meeting. Only later was it specifically attributed to the World Zionist Congress in 1897. It was also discovered that at its inception the document was not presented as merely a Jewish docu-ment but as a conspiracy between Jews and Masons!

Adolf Hitler continued using the *Protocols* to justify the mass arrests of Jews on the ground that they were part of a racial conspiracy against Germany and the rest of the world. Once arrested, extermination soon followed for vast numbers of them while the remainder virtually starved to death in labor corps or concentration camps.

The Nazi terror against the Jews resulted in two mi-grations: one to Palestine where the Jewish population soon reached over a million, and one to the United States where the immigrants joined with the Jewish population which was already here and eventually rose to a total of over five million. The Jews in the United States then became the principle source of outside financial support for the Jews in Palestine. It was this combination of dedicated Jewish nation-builders in Palestine and the liberal financial support of the Jews in America that made much of Israel's success possible.

Index